A Shorter History of Australia

Professor Geoffrey Blainey's first book was completed when he

A Shorter History of Australia

Further revised & updated

Geoffrey Blainey

VINTAGE BOOKS
Australia

A Vintage book
Published by Random House Australia Pty Ltd
Level 3, 100 Pacific Highway, North Sydney NSW 2060
www.randomhouse.com.au

First edition published 1994
Vintage edition published 2000
Updated and revised editions published by Vintage in 2009, 2014

Addresses for companies within the Random House Group can be found at
www.randomhouse.com.au/offices.

National Library of Australia
Cataloguing-in-Publication Entry

Blainey, Geoffrey, 1930–
A shorter history of Australia/Geoffrey Blainey.
Rev. and updated ed.

ISBN: 97808 579 84388.

Aboriginal Australians – History.
Australia – History.

994

Cover image by David Rose, *Magpie and Orange Branch*
Cover design by Jenny Grigg
Typeset by Midland Typesetters, Australia
Printed and bound by Griffin Press, South Australia

Random House Australia uses papers that are natural, renewable and
recyclable products and made from wood grown in sustainable forests.
The logging and manufacturing processes are expected to conform to the
environmental regulations of the country of origin.

10 9 8 7 6 5 4 3 2 1

Contents

Preface   vii
Map of Australia   x

Part One
The Rise and Fall of Black Australia
1   When sea was land   3
2   The coming clash   17
3   A poor paradise   25
4   Arabs of the grasslands   39
5   The fading of the yellow flannel   53

Part Two
'The Land I Love'
6   The first gold rushes   71
7   The age of the marvellous   88
8   Eyes   111
9   The rise of the sporting hero   122
10 Riding the disaster   133
11 The flush of violet   143

Part Three
From Gallipoli to Uluru
12	The war to end war	169
13	What an 'unlimited future'!	183
14	A tidal wave from Japan	203
15	A car and a mountain	217
16	Black and green resurrection	243
17	A nation on walkabout	258
18	Symbols in the wind: the Queen and Mr Mabo	271
19	The vast open spaces	284
20	Sails and anchors	298

A short chronicle of Australian history	309
Further reading	315
Index	319

Preface

This book sets out in a fairly simple way my view of Australia's history. For many years I have been intermittently writing a very long and many-sided book about Australia's history, a book which I might never finish. This book is a condensed version, written at the suggestion of Sue Hines of Reed Books who asked for no more than 80,000 words.

One defect of a short book is that much of importance has to be omitted. Towards the end of the writing I found myself adding an episode or observation that somehow had to be fitted in, and searching for a part that could be deleted. In a short book the explanations of why events take place have to be slimmed, with some factors omitted and others just hinted at. I express thanks to the skilled editor, Sally Nicholls, for many suggestions.

The book tries to explain how the present Australia arose. I think economic events, especially technology, were more influential than political events but the book says much about politics. The social history is skimmed, to my regret, except for a few themes. Sport is included because it is a curious mirror of Australian attitudes.

The book rests partly on research in original sources – old books, diaries, newspapers, parliamentary reports, biographies. A well-read historian will discern where a lot of it can be found. The book also rests on the work of many historians, some dead and some not yet in their prime. Often we can be deeply influenced by people we do not agree with.

One difficulty was how to balance and blend the contrasting Aboriginal and European histories of this land. I do not share the desire of many historians and commentators to denounce sweepingly the white history of Australia in order to enthrone the black history and the present-day Aboriginal demands. Nor is there merit in the opposite extreme of denouncing black history as barbaric. Both phases of history have their distinctive merits. My own attitudes and preferences of course are present but on some important topics I have tried to give space to alternative viewpoints, though I don't necessarily accept them.

The role of people suffers in a short book. Rarely do I give a sketch of an influential person: space does not allow it. When a celebrated Australian's style, background and influence are touched on in some detail, as in the oil man D'Arcy or the prime ministers Chifley, Menzies and Whitlam, it is because they are influential and also because they are bodies on which clothes can be hung, thus depicting part of an era.

My views partly came, no doubt, from my early teachers. I owe a debt to many who taught me at school: I think of A. L. Moore at Ballarat High, and A. A. Phillips, A. E. Gwillim and R. R. Belshaw at Wesley College, and such historians as Kathleen Fitzpatrick, John O'Brien, Manning Clark and R. M. Crawford who helped me as a student at Melbourne University or later on. Historians I admired when fairly young included E. O. G. Shann and Brian Fitzpatrick in Australia and T. B. Macaulay and Thomas Carlyle, J. M. Keynes and Arnold Toynbee in England.

We all learn from people of our own age, and I learned much from people who were my contemporaries, give or take seven years on either side: they are too many to name. I also learned, without knowing it,

• • • • • • • • •

history from the towns I lived in when young and a bit about Australian life when working in such mining towns as Queenstown, Tasmania, and Mount Isa, Queensland, in the 1950s, and when travelling later to many places in Australia, or sitting on various federal boards and committees between 1967 and 1984. So my debts are many, to people, ideas, books and, not least, to students I taught. When I am sensible I am conscious of what I don't know.

I also give special thanks to my wife, Ann.

Melbourne, May 1994   Geoffrey Blainey

For these enlarged editions of 2009 and 2014, I have rewritten or expanded on various episodes and themes, making changes to almost every page. I have also described significant events and trends of the early twenty-first century. A final chapter summarises key factors that shaped and still shape this country's history. In all there are now 20 chapters instead of 17. For this fourth edition, most of the changes were made from chapters 18 to 20. Likewise the chronology and reading list have been updated and enlarged. In making these revisions I am indebted to many people and books. I especially thank John Day of Wangaratta and Peter Yule of Melbourne, and Random House editor Brandon VanOver.

January 2014   Geoffrey Blainey

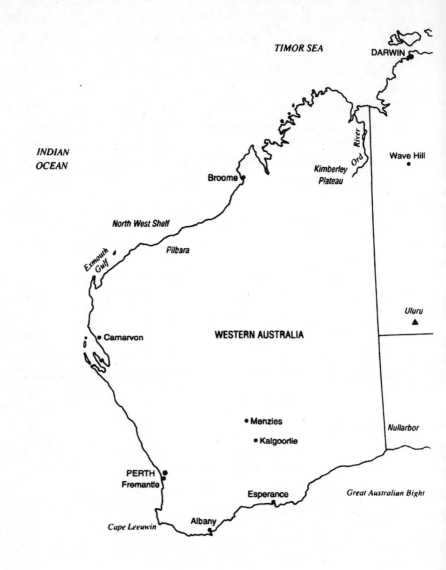

TIMOR SEA

DARWIN

INDIAN
OCEAN

Wave Hill

Broome

*Kimberley
Plateau*

North West Shelf

Pilbara

*Exmouth
Gulf*

Uluru ▲

Carnarvon

WESTERN AUSTRALIA

Nullarbor

Menzies

Kalgoorlie

PERTH
Fremantle

Esperance

Great Australian Bight

Cape Leeuwin

Albany

0   500

kilometres

part one

The Rise and Fall of Black Australia

When sea was land

About 60,000 years ago the whole world was cooler. Snow sometimes fell on lands that now boast sunny beaches and mild winters. Of the world's surface about one-quarter was covered with ice: today the ice covers a mere tenth. The oceans were lower, and dry hills and plains extended across vast areas criss-crossed today by shipping routes. The 'North Sea' of today could be walked over with dry feet. Dry land and a few large freshwater lakes occupied what is now the Baltic Sea. The sixty kilometres now separating Asia from North America were not yet covered by the Bering Sea.

The first Aborigines came to Australia when the level of the sea was possibly 120 metres lower than it is today. In that epoch, the gap of sea between Asia and Australia was not so wide. Sumatra and Java were joined to Asia by land. Even the island of Bali was part of Asia's landmass though it lay on the very edge of deep water. The island of Timor was closer to the Australian continent than Tasmania now is.

The first Aborigines, so far as is known, came from Asia. They possibly came in a series of short voyages and land treks spread over many generations. Slowly they leap-frogged their way across the narrow seas and islands, some people presumably settling in Indonesian islands and others finally reaching Australia. There must have been more than one wave of immigrants. The first group probably arrived more than 50,000 years ago and the last groups came less than 5,000 years ago, each group consisting of small numbers of people who stepped into shallow coastal water from a small raft or canoe. Those first arrivals deserve to be famous in world history but their names and year of landing are forgotten. Forerunners of Christopher Columbus and James Cook, they had discovered a distinct, habitable continent. There had not been such a discovery in the previous history of mankind, for all members of the human race had hitherto lived on the linked landmass of Asia and Africa and Europe. Even America was uninhabited when these first adventurers reached Australia.

New Guinea and Australia formed a continuous land, and indeed the discoverers were more likely to have come ashore near the western side of the present New Guinea than in present-day Australia. A map of that big continuous land, when it was first occupied by Aborigines, would not be recognisable to our eyes. For much of the human history of Australia the coastline lay far from the present beaches and capes. The rivers, the Swan and Yarra, Brisbane and Burdekin, ran through their present valleys but were longer, flowing far beyond the points where they now enter the sea. At that distant time, nearly all of the islands that lie within sixty kilometres of today's coast were joined to land. No boat was needed to reach Tasmania.

The ports we know stood far from the ocean. Aborigines who went to the headland where the Sydney Opera House now stands saw a river winding its way along a valley in the direction of the gap between the sandstone 'heads' – higher than the ones we now see – and so out towards the distant sea. The sites of Perth, Adelaide and Brisbane were some days' walk from the nearest beach. From Darwin to the sea would have called for more than a week of walking. The people of hundreds of later generations who spent their life not far from the present Darwin might not even have known that the sea existed. From the site of the present port of Melbourne a man who set out for the sea had to travel in his wooden canoe down the winding Yarra River, which drained the area now covered by Port Phillip Bay. When his canoe reached the present heads, some eighty kilometres by river from Melbourne, there was still no sea. As he paddled to the south-west, the river was enlarged by the Barwon and then by the mighty Tamar with its chilly waters flowing from the high ice-lands of Tasmania. Eventually the combined Yarra-Barwon-Tamar reached the ocean somewhere to the west of what became King Island, maybe three weeks of travelling from the place where the journey began. An Aboriginal adventurer could walk from the present continent of Australia to Tasmania, though a few wide rivers had to be crossed. He could even walk north to the present island of New Guinea. No Torres Strait barred his path.

When the first people moved to the far south-east and the highest ranges in a continent which lacks high mountains, they saw snow on the loftiest slopes even in summer. The rivers flowing inland from the Great Dividing Range carried the melted snow in summertime, and the water in inland lakes and rivers was slow to evaporate, for the summer was cooler. In central Australia the nights were intensely cold in winter, and the summers lacked the searing heat we have come to expect. The lakes of central Australia were more attractive then, for they contained fresh water, and their fish, mussels, waterbirds and foodplants must have supported many people.

There were glaciers in Tasmania some 30,000 years ago, when the first Aborigines arrived by land. Their Tasmanian peninsula was the dead end of the whole habitable globe. Its people were the world's most southerly, for the colder parts of South America, perhaps even the warmer parts, were not yet settled. New Zealand, too, was uninhabited, the Maoris only arriving in their long canoes centuries after the birth of Christ.

2

The whole continent must have been surprising to these first explorers. It was drier than the Indonesian islands they had left behind. Many of the grains, yams and fruits had to be cautiously tasted, for they were unfamiliar. Many of the native creatures had not previously been seen by human beings: some are no longer to be seen. The Aborigines saw giant kangaroos, about three metres tall. They saw the diprotodon, a vegetarian animal about the size of a rhinoceros but related more to the wombat. They found a python five metres long and a goanna bigger than any we will see. Some of the birds they saw and some of the smaller marsupials have also disappeared. The entry of the human race into new regions is usually accompanied by the extinction of species. Changes of climate also helped to extinguish creatures seen in abundance by the first Aborigines.

In recent years, archaeologists have investigated caves which reveal the bones of some of these vanished species. Mammoth Cave, lying south of Margaret River in the south-west corner of the continent, contains the bones of the long-beaked echidna, great kangaroos, and the striped Tasmanian tiger, variously known as thylacine or marsupial wolf. The recent discovery of tools nearby and the observation that the charred bones carried butchering marks suggests that most of the animals were killed by Aborigines and carried there to be cut up, cooked and eaten. The Tasmanian tiger and the Tasmanian devil flourished on mainland Australia, becoming extinct relatively late in the long Aboriginal era. While the devil still flourishes in Tasmania, probably the tiger is extinct. A few Tasmanian tigers were alive in the

1930s, one in captivity and several in the wild, but all the reported sightings of them in recent years are open to grave doubt.

Aborigines are sometimes depicted as an unchanging people in an unchanging world, but their way of life changed. There are fascinating survivals of a mysterious culture in the tropics of Western Australia. The yellow sandstone caves and escarpments of the North Kimberley display thousands of ingenious rock paintings, of a sophistication and grace perhaps unrivalled in any other part of the world at the time of their creation. The people depicted have hooked noses and wear headcloth tassles. Some of the tall, decorated people convey an air of the Mardi Gras. An Egyptian influence is detected by a few critics. The art, practised at least 20,000 years ago, seems not to be related to that of the long-present Aboriginal inhabitants. The focus of belated research, the thousands of art galleries may well reveal much about the history of this coastal region which was settled so early.

The physical world of the Aborigines was not static. Earlier Aborigines saw molten lava trickling over ground where they hunted and camped. In north Queensland, volcanoes were active on the Atherton Tableland. In western Victoria, not far from the sea, volcanoes erupted. Near South Australia's Mt Gambier is a recent volcano, active only 5,000 years ago. To the east, an Aboriginal stone axe was once found beneath the volcanic ash deposited by the eruption at Tower Hill.

The present predictions that the world's climate will become warmer, and that the oceans will rise, are fears of mighty change. But it is a change of a far smaller magnitude than the Aborigines experienced. In the space of fifty lifetimes, as we shall see, they endured a period of profound warming and an astonishing rising of the seas. But they survived with admirable tenacity.

Their way of life of 200 years ago is better known than their life of 20,000 years ago, though many habits and activities must have persisted. In essence the people were nomadic, the extent and frequency of their movements varying from district to district. In the entire continent there was probably no group of people who spent more than six months in the one place. Generally they did not hoard food except in small quantities; they herded no livestock; they planted no crops. They travelled lightly, carrying few possessions. They could weave impressive nets and carrying bags but generally they carried little with them, except fire, when they moved camp. The young children they sometimes carried on their back in holders made of kangaroo skins. In cold districts a fur coat was skilfully tailored from dozens of possum skins.

While their technology was simple, they possessed one powerful instrument: fire. When they moved camp they usually carried a burning or smouldering firestick rather than go to the trouble of making a new flame with friction on wood or stone. They used fire for almost every task. For warmth during winter they slept between tiny fires, and in summer they used the smoke of a fire to keep away the mosquitoes. On the plains they skilfully used smoke to signal their exact movements to distant friends, and they lit fires to drive animals towards the waiting hunters. They cooked meat and fish and some vegetable foods in the hot ashes of fires. They set alight scrub and dry grass at certain times of the year in order to facilitate their own movement across the country or to encourage the growth of new grass after the rain fell. In some regions their persistent burning changed the flora. Many of the grasslands were probably the creation of Aborigines.

Their grandest houses were simple shelters. At Lake Condah on the undulating plains of western Victoria stood clusters of one-room stone houses, the walls rising perhaps a metre, the roofs made of rushes or brushwood, with doorways but no doors. In these dwellings the people had to crouch. Some tropical areas also held substantial houses though they were not occupied permanently. In the dry inland the families normally slept under the sky, with a low pile of brushwood and leafy branches to fend off the winter wind.

• • • • • • • • •

In most parts of the country Aborigines were virtually naked. They wore no hats and no shoes, but sandals were sometimes worn on the hot sand of inland deserts. In cold Tasmania they would smear their bodies with animal fat to keep out the winter cold. To paint the naked body for ceremonies was one of their fine arts. Some used red and white clays and the ochre collected from the top of an iron-ore deposit, with the additional ornaments of bird's feathers and perhaps a necklace of animal's teeth. Their rockcarving, woodcarving and painting were to be admired more by critics in the twentieth than in the nineteenth century. If impressive symbolic art is one test of a civilisation, then many Australian tribes scored highly.

Moving systematically through their own lands in search of food, they were not strictly searchers. They knew the land so well that they usually collected food with ease. They knew the seeding and fruiting times of scores of edible plants and the nesting and breeding times of hundreds of birds and animals, and so they specifically sought their food according to the time of year. They ate a much wider variety of foods than a typical European ate in the year 1800, and probably they were less likely to face famine. In poor terrain, Aborigines might eat a hundred different greens, nuts, seeds, yams and bulbs in the course of a year. Their way of life, while it seemed so elementary, was based on daily ingenuity and alertness and an impressive array of knowledge.

It was the women who gathered the edible plants. As vegetable foods were dominant in the diet of most inland peoples, women were really the main breadwinners. On the coast they were the ones who gathered shellfish, a vital part of diet. Thus in the winter of 1829, Tasmanian women were observed by George Robinson diving for shellfish, with a hand-made basket of rushes slung over the shoulder, and a sharpened stick with which they pried the shellfish from the rocks: 'They are excellent divers, keeping under water for a considerable time; they ascend to the surface for a second or so and then dive and continue down until they have filled their baskets'.

On the coast and inland rivers, fish were a vital food. The evidence can be seen in the occasional mounds of sea shells that stand, almost like pyramids, along the tropical coast. Consisting of hard litter from millions of meals, the numerous mounds near Weipa on Cape York are estimated to contain a total of nine billion shells. In Tasmania these ancient rubbish heaps reveal that – perhaps because a taboo was imposed – Aborigines ceased to eat the normal finned fish about 3,000 years ago. When Europeans arrived, the Tasmanians were still shunning the flesh of boned fish.

Most Aborigines lived and travelled in small groups, consisting perhaps of a couple of families. It was not uncommon for a man to have more than two wives. Marriage was arranged when a girl was young, sometimes before puberty, and girls entered their first marriage at a much earlier age than did men. Usually the older men had priority in choosing women.

While the rules and rituals of life were intricate the technology was simple. For the cutting edge of a weapon there was no iron. Indeed a stone axe depended on its weight as much as on the sharpness of its blade. On the other hand, clever weapons were invented in Australia. The returning boomerang was devised here, maybe as long as 10,000 years ago. Even more impressive was the spear-thrower, a simple wooden instrument which in effect extended the reach of the hunter's arm, enabling him to throw a wooden spear a long distance. The bow and arrow were not Aboriginal weapons except in the region nearest Papua.

Amongst the regional oddities was the curved wooden sword used in north Queensland's rainforests. Made of hardwood and fitted with a handle, the sword could be as high as a full-grown man. The defence against the sword was a large painted shield, shaped from the buttress roots of the native fig tree.

• • • • • • • • •

Courage and fear were strong strands in daily life. It is now said that violence was not common, but the evidence points to violence. Death through fighting probably occurred often enough to curb the growth of population. The avenging of deaths was frequent: even a death through natural causes could be attributed to the evil spirits working on behalf of an enemy, and so in due course that enemy would be the target of a surprise attack. Women and sometimes children fell in episodes that were more like massacres than fights. In 1875 in central Australia, perhaps as many as eighty to a hundred Aborigines were killed in an Aranda fight; and the limbs of the infants were deliberately broken. Revenge was bound to follow. In small populations the deaths through warfare could statistically be more devastating than those suffered by whole nations in a century of European wars. The avenging missions were one reason why Aborigines had trouble, after Britons arrived, in uniting with neighbours in order to fight the 'common foe'. Often the common foe remained black.

Those wounded in battle did not necessarily die. For wounds and illnesses, trusted remedies were passed from old to young. Most remedies called for the use of leaves, roots, grasses or herbs. Many were hit-or-miss but many were sound and some were brilliant. Narcotics, including a native chewing tobacco, were picked from the trees and traded over a wide outback region. The leaves of one plant were dried and chewed, and the nicotine inside was liberated with the aid of an alkali ash derived from the burning of an *acacia* wood. Made into a wad, it was carried behind the ear. The placing of the wad in that sensitive spot helped the skin to absorb the drug, which the capillary system then forwarded to the brain. The modern antidotes to seasickness, placed behind the ear, affect the brain in a similar way.

Deep was the delight when oldish men chewed the wad and then passed it to those next to them. With the aid of this minor pain-killer, Aborigines could endure fatigue. One is said to have walked 200 kilometres in two days with nothing to sustain him but 'a chew of *pituri*'. In 1861, when the British explorers Burke and Wills were slowly dying in central Australia, their solace was *pituri*.

3

Aborigines were religious, believing that the world was the work of mythic creators who retained power long after they had created every valley, rocky outcrop and species of animal and bird. The performing of age-old rituals ensured that these divine ancestors continued to give benefits. The world the Aborigines knew was rigid but they believed it had once been incredibly malleable. Thus the Murray River, in the eyes of one group living near its mouth, was once a narrow straight river. Then the powerful Nguruderi in his canoe chased the great fish, the Murray Cod, down the stream, and the cod swished its tail and so created wide bends in the river. When Nguruderi finally caught the fish in Lake Alexandrina, he sliced it into pieces with his stone knife, and as he tossed the pieces back into the lake he turned them into bream and perch, mudfish and sprats, so creating new species.

Aborigines probably did not inhabit a secure world. The forces of evil could never be defeated permanently, but those people who commanded magic had enormous powers for evil and good. It was believed that a mere mortal was capable of jogging on air, three or four feet above the ground. Miracles often occurred. Many Aborigines believed they could stop the rain, start the rain, cool the hot day or heat the cool day.

In languages their skills were impressive. European newcomers were often captivated when they heard them speak for the first time. Bishop Salvado, a Benedictine who conducted a mission to the Aborigines in Western Australia, thought their voices were more attractive than those of Asia and Oceania. Many of the sweet sounds reminded him of Italian, while the 'heavy sonorous sounds' called to mind phrases from his own Spanish tongue. He found, as he learned the local language, that Aborigines said much in few words. The simple repetitions of their songs delighted him as he sat by a campfire at night, sharing the merriment or sadness of their poems and songs: 'They go on repeating these for an hour or two, getting more and more pleasure from them at each repetition – what Europeans would find infinitely boring sends them into ecstasies of delight'.

More languages were alive in Australia than in Europe in the year 1800. Maybe 250 different languages, most of them now silent, were spoken. A typical adult probably knew two or three languages and several dialects. It is easy to minimise this proficiency by imagining that the languages were quick to be learned, but they were complex in grammar, being more like Latin and Sanskrit than modern English. Thus the Dyirbal language, once spoken in the sweeping rainforests of north Queensland, made a clear distinction between he, she and it, and also had a fourth gender which a speaker was careful to use when mentioning the name of each of several hundred edible plants. Most Aboriginal languages were further complicated because, when real or potential in-laws and cousins were spoken to, a roundabout style of speaking was deliberately chosen. Then the nouns, adjectives and verbs could be different to those used in normal speech. One grammar book describing one of the few Aboriginal languages that has survived runs to 500 pages.

In the few Aboriginal languages that were later studied closely by linguists, the vocabulary was much smaller than that of a modern European language. A typical Aboriginal language held perhaps 10,000 words – as many words as are employed by the average speaker, though not by a fluent speaker of European languages. Somehow the idea became popular that there was just one Aboriginal language;

and so a boomerang was described as the Aboriginal word for the wooden throwing stick. In fact a boomerang was known by different names in different parts of the land, and in Tasmania the weapon and so the word were unknown. Many Aboriginal words that are part of the English language came from the languages spoken around Sydney where native animals and Aboriginal weapons were first seen by newcomers. Words like koala, wombat, wallaby and boomerang came from Dharuk, a language spoken around Sydney. Dingo is probably another such word. In contrast the native dog was called mirigang on the Shoalhaven, not far south of Sydney, and in some regions it was called the warrigal, a name used widely by early British settlers.

Kangaroo passed into English from the language spoken around Cooktown in north Queensland, where the first British explorer, Captain Cook, was to spend weeks ashore in 1770 after his ship struck a coral reef. There he heard the Aboriginal name kangaroo, which probably signified the large black kangaroo rather than the species as a whole. How to spell it was not an easy decision, and Cook and his scientist Joseph Banks wrote it down as kanguru or kangooroo. Curiously the Dutch did not report the existence of kangaroos during all their earlier visits to the west Australian coast, and so it was left to Cook's men to make this remarkable discovery, news of which astonished the zoological world.

A few Aboriginal words entered the English language only in the twentieth century. Thus the word didgeridoo was unknown to the average soldier who went away to fight in World War I. Indeed in far-north Australia, where that long wooden musical instrument probably originated, the word was not used. There was intense regionalism and therefore diversity not only in languages but also in customs, rituals, food preferences and religion.

Even the time was measured in different ways. A young Aranda girl living in central Australia soon learned that a particular word was used for the sunset, but there was another word to describe the instant just after the setting of the sun. The brief colouring of the evening sky with red and yellow was known as alknara, and then came the twilight which was literally described as the time when a tuft of grass could no longer be distinguished from a neighbouring tuft. There was a word for the middle of the night, and a phrase which pinpointed the time when the Milky Way glittered in the sky. So the words specifically describing each stage of night formed their long procession, going well beyond that time when, at the approach of morning, the bandicoots scurried back to the shelter of their burrows. In essence, the time between sunrise and sunset was divided by the Aranda into about eighteen named phases.

4

There is scope for wide disagreement on the relative well-being of the Aborigines. Their way of life, like every way of life the world has known, possessed defects and weaknesses, but they themselves could be proud of their achievements in colonising a difficult terrain, in making use of an astonishing range of foods and medicines, in showing ingenuity in many facets of daily life, and in managing to survive in arid areas which today are virtually uninhabited. Some scholars recently came to the conclusion that perhaps the Aborigines once numbered as many as one million, but they made that estimate with an inadequate knowledge of the duration and intensity and wide extent of droughts in this land. If their estimate is true, then occasionally the large population must have been rapidly cut down by a disastrous famine, the disaster being compounded by the fact that the people did not hoard food on any scale. An alternative and older view is that the maximum population in Aboriginal times was less than 500,000 and perhaps as low as 250,000 and that the available foods were more than ample for those smaller

• • • • • • • • • •

numbers, except in a prolonged drought. My inclination, on present evidence, is to conclude that in most centuries the Aborigines were fewer than 500,000 and that for them the food was usually plentiful. We still do not know but have to contemplate the possibility that in long droughts, prevailing over much of the continent, the population might have been halved.

Population even in a period of lush seasons was probably kept down by cultural pressures. Thus children until about the age of three were usually fed with mother's milk and that limited the chance of pregnancy. Moreover, in some regions the men did not have sex with women who were breast-feeding their babies. Under those conditions a woman did not give birth to children in quick succession. Population was also curbed by the likelihood that few people reached the age of fifty. Life was also cut short by fighting.

Only a fraction of the knowledge of that remarkable way of life has survived. Much has been recaptured in the last fifty years; more will be retrieved in the next fifty. Only in the last half-century were many of the vital fragments of knowledge assembled about the most remarkable event in the human history of Australia: the rising of the seas.

The coming clash

For most of the human history of Australia, the islands of New Guinea and Australia were joined. It was about 18,000 years ago that people began to notice a change that is more astonishing in retrospect than it would have seemed in any one lifetime. The world's climate became warmer and, as masses of ice were melted, the seas began to rise. Aborigines who lived on wide plains sloping gently to the sea were the first to see the waves encroaching, especially at high tides. For century after century the seas continued to rise. The reefs where countless generations of Aborigines had collected shellfish now became inaccessible, so deep and wide became the sea. Salty marshes, where in season they had hunted birds, became part of the sea. Sacred sites, perhaps a rocky knoll or cave which was the annual goal for long journeys on foot, were submerged. The waves broke over expanses of grassland where kangaroos had grazed. New islands were formed as the seas rose and then were submerged as the seas rose higher. Groups of Aborigines were driven back by the sea into the tribal territories of neighbours, perhaps leading to bloodshed.

Over a period of at least 12,000 years the seas came higher, rising at a slow pace and in some centuries even retreating a little. Some places that once were 300 kilometres inland were now in sight of the sea. Tasmania became separated from the continent of Australia maybe 10,000 years ago, but the crossing of the sea gap was still possible on a calm day for several centuries to come. Far to the north was formed a vast bay which eventually became the Gulf of Carpentaria. It covered the land where hundreds of generations of Aborigines had slept and hunted, danced and argued, and watched the stars at night. About 8,000 years ago Australia was cut off from New Guinea. The infant Torres Strait, at first so narrow that a spear could be thrown from shore to shore, became wider.

In sum total about one-seventh of the land of the combined continent of Australia and New Guinea had been lost to the sea. An area eight times the size of the present Italy had been swallowed. Probably no other inhabited continent lost such a high proportion of its land as Australia lost during this besieged phase.

For a startlingly long time there must have lingered, here and there, a tribal memory of this puzzling flooding. We know that in Melbourne in 1857 the editor of a pamphlet called *Facts and Figures* was given a fascinating snippet of news by a white settler: 'I was told about three years ago by one of the Aborigines of the Mount Macedon Tribe, that his grandfather could recollect tracing the Yarra down to the Heads where it entered the sea.' A century later, novel techniques of investigation established that thousands of years earlier the Yarra River did flow down to the Port Phillip Heads, some forty kilometres to the south as the crow flies, and that the ocean eventually crept past the Heads and far inland, covering the old bed of the Yarra. It was not that Aborigine's grandfather who remembered the old river but a grandfather perhaps a hundred times removed. So the story of that remote flooding had been handed down and down.

The warmer climate transformed the interior. On Tasmania's higher mountains the Aborigines saw glaciers slowly melt and vanish. On its west coast they saw, generation after generation, the vegetation slowly turn from dismal tundra to rainforest. On the mainland they saw rivers which had been filled by melting snow throughout the summer begin to dry up in December or earlier. Grains, nuts and greens which had long flourished on the plains of one region were imperilled by the new climate and replaced by others. Grasslands in central Australia slowly became half-desert. In compensation, some regions which had been too cold now had a longer growing season. What we now call a tropical climate began to occupy vast areas. All along, in each region, the slight or profound changes in the habitat of edible animals, fish and insects affected the way of life and the seasonal movements and the diet of the inhabitants.

Higher seas pushed back the coastline of south-east Asia. The present western Indonesia, which was traditionally an integral part of the continent of Asia, became a chain of islands that included Java and Sumatra. The slow rising of the seas distanced Australia from the outside world. It became more and more isolated from the once-near island of Timor as well as from western New Guinea.

When at last the seas ceased to rise and ceased to swallow coastlines and islands, the Aborigines were largely living in isolation. But they were not entirely isolated from the Indonesian archipelago and from New Guinea. Communication was now difficult and even hazardous but not impossible.

One sign of that contact was the coming of the half-tamed dingo. A large and dignified dog, it was to be seen around Aboriginal camps when the first British arrived. Indeed, Aboriginal women were known to mother a dingo pup and feed it with the milk of their breasts. The dingo had probably arrived in Australia some 4,000 years previously, coming in a small raft or boat in the company of people. It spread around the continent. Maybe only two or four dingoes ever reached Australia but they multiplied until they numbered hundreds of thousands.

The dingo came from an outside world where a host of animals and plants had recently been domesticated or regimented so that they could serve human beings. The astonishing fact is that no other domesticated animal or plant arrived. Australia for long evaded the most dramatic revolution the world's peoples had so far experienced.

2

Towards the end of this global rising of the seas the most important chain of events in all economic history was beginning. This revolution, which began in various parts of the northern hemisphere over 10,000 years ago, was more important than the beginning of the industrial revolution in England more than 200 years ago. The ancient or neolithic revolution witnessed the planting of seeds, the harvesting of crops, the herding of goats and sheep and other animals, and the hoarding of food. It gave rise to a settled rather than a moving population – to villages and towns, to the working of metals, to the making of pottery, to the digging of irrigation channels. It led to the collecting of taxes, the rise of powerful rulers and priests, and to the creation of armies larger than any previously known. In effect the new way of life required a smaller proportion of people to be involved in producing foods, thus releasing many people for other activities. It was a vital step towards the specialisation on which the world now depends.

Versions of this novel way of life, based on the domestication of chosen plants and livestock, could initially be seen on the south coast of Turkey, on the flood plains of the great rivers of the Middle East, and perhaps in other scattered places. The new way of producing and hoarding food enabled the world's population to multiply. The new way of life used land with more efficiency. It spread across the landmasses, jumping to the islands. It was really the first Green Revolution. The valleys where Paris and London now stand were relatively slow to adopt the first farming revolution. They were many centuries behind the Valleys of the Nile and the Tigris in economic development. They slumbered as part of a Third World for three or four thousand years while the hinterland of the eastern Mediterranean and Persian Gulf blossomed and boomed. Eventually Europe adopted a version of the new way of life. The Americas adopted it; perhaps they invented their own version of it. Parts of east Asia took up gardening and gathered herds even before Europe took to the new way of living and working.

These far-reaching changes penetrated the highlands of New Guinea more than 6,000 years ago. They reached and captured the islands of Torres Strait, changing the way of life of everyone living there. On those islands, some of them within a day's canoeing of the Australian coast, arose gardens tilled by the Melanesian. As far as we know, the concept of gardening did not extend to the Australian continent until the British brought it.

Only a few large and isolated parts of the world were able to resist or escape the change. By 1788 the dry parts of southern Africa, a large expanse in the interior of South America, the whole of the Arctic and all of Australia formed the only remaining regions where the ancient, skilled but sparsely peopled economy of hunting and gathering could still be seen. Australia was far and away the largest zone on the globe where the doomed way of life survived. Why the new economy based on gardening and herd-keeping did not reach Australia is not easily fathomed. Certainly the soils near the coast of northern Australia were not attractive and even today carry few settlers. There is another explanation: the new way of life was probably partly spread by military conquest, and the rising of the seas made Australia less vulnerable to an invader with small forces.

Australia was not completely isolated. Its tropical coast had regular visitors from the outside world for at least two centuries before the

British arrived. These visitors came annually from the Indonesian archipelago, sailing in small craft with matting sails. Macassans, they came from the south end of the island of Sulawesi. They made use of the seasonal winds, sailing to Australia with the north-west monsoon and usually making the voyage of 2,000 kilometres in a couple of weeks. On stretches of coast often settled closely by Aborigines, these fishermen caught the trepang or sea-slug in shallow water, boiled it ashore and then smoked it in the hot sun. When the dry south-east monsoon began to blow, they hoisted their sails and, with heavy twin rudders, steered a course to their home port of Macassar. The trepang found its way to Canton and other parts of southern China where it was an aphrodisiac and, above all, a delicacy on the tables of the wealthy: indeed, many of the ships were owned by Chinese middlemen.

In busy years at least 1,200 Indonesians arrived with the trepang fleet and busied themselves in the catching and curing of the sea-slug. Relations with Aborigines were usually smooth, though there were occasional episodes of bloodshed. Aborigines even went to Indonesia with the fleet and then returned to their homeland. In the Philippines in 1676 an Italian priest, Father Riccio, met visitors who were possibly Aborigines. 'One can walk through the interior of their country', he recorded, 'for more than two years without ever seeing the sea'.

In Arnhem Land and on other stretches of the long low-lying coast, the annual visitors made little impact. The Aboriginal way of working, thinking and of seeing the world had its own tight logic, and it did not easily budge or crumble when competing ideas and new objects arrived. Aborigines, however, did marvel at the cutting materials which the newcomers could occasionally provide: iron and broken glass were far sharper than the Aborigines' bone and stone tools, and were eagerly seized and used. But there was far from enough iron and glass to alter the way of life of more than a few thousand of the Aborigines then living in the continent. Some Aborigines did learn to make dugout canoes using iron axes. For entertainment some learned to smoke a pipe of tobacco and drink alcohol, but such 'luxuries' were scarce.

If the Indonesians had settled on the land in northern Australia, they might have begun the slow revolution. But there is no evidence that they tried to settle. The soil rarely was as fertile as their own soil. Presumably on their own islands they did not yet suffer from overcrowding. Perhaps in most months the climate of northern Australia was too dry for their liking. Moreover the trepang they wanted could be won with only a temporary residence. With annual visits they blended the best of both worlds.

3

Europeans were about to enter Australia. The contrast between the ways of life of the British Isles and of the Aborigines was almost the most dramatic contrast in the world. The British brought so many ideas and goods which Aborigines could not begin to imagine. They brought all the results of the 10,000-year-old neolithic revolution and they also brought the first results of the new industrial and scientific revolutions. They brought sheep and sheep shears, horses and harnesses, cattle and pigs, and a variety of dogs and cats. They brought fruit trees, and tropical and temperate vegetables unknown to Aborigines. They brought fences and carts and large permanent houses and ocean-going ships. They brought an ability to distil spirits, brew beer and make wine – hazardous liquids for a continent where alcohol was virtually unknown. They brought skills in weaving wool, in making linen and leather. They brought the art of writing and printing, of keeping accounts, of hoarding information in books and hoarding food and drink in barrels, kegs and sacks. They brought thousands of laws, all devised to meet needs and solve problems on their side of the globe.

They brought firearms, not of high accuracy, but demoralising when first seen and felt.

Britain showed, more than any other people in the previous history of the world, its most advanced skills in the actual objects it manufactured: an infinite variety of new articles and machines could be seen in their homes, streets, factories, mines and wharves. In contrast, Aborigines were at their best in showing skills, often ingenious, rather than in manufacturing articles. That widened the gulf of understanding between the two peoples. Judged by boats and houses and other items, the Aborigines did not initially impress foreigners who could build ships capable of crossing the oceans.

The fact that the British rather than the Indonesians were the intruders meant that the confrontation was even more bewildering, because the British led the world's latest economic advance – the industrial revolution and the age of steam. In Australia they faced Aborigines who had not yet experienced the first economic revolution. Here were inhabitants of the land that had just invented the steam engine meeting people who, making no pottery and working no metals, did not know how to boil water. Here was an utter contrast in peoples, for they spoke very different languages, had very different histories, followed their own distinct customs, rituals and religions, and held contrasting attitudes to property, plants and livestock. In their use of the land and their technology they were ages apart. At first, even with goodwill on both sides, they were incompatible.

· · · · · · · · · ·

A poor paradise

A small ship riding wild seas off South Africa heralded the beginning of the end of the Aborigines' secure world. When that first Portuguese ship rounded the Cape of Good Hope in 1486 and followed a new route to India, which was the commercial mecca of that era, she heralded the Europeans' arrival in every harbour and valley in this part of the world unfamiliar to them. More ships – Portuguese, Dutch, then British and French – sailed past South Africa to India, Japan, China, Java, Sumatra and Timor and loaded cargoes of pepper, calico, tea, china, sandalwood and other commodities. A few of these ships eventually sailed close to the Australian coast where they were undoubtedly seen by Aborigines walking near the beaches.

2

Perhaps the Portuguese were the first Europeans to see Australia. Portugal created a small fortified post in Timor in 1516, and the occasional ship sailing to and from Timor must have been driven by the north-west monsoons to within sight of islands or coastline in north-west Australia. Probably they found nothing worth finding. About a century later, from lookouts high up the masts, many Dutch sailors saw parts of the same coast and nervously watched the white of the waves beating on half-submerged rocks. Pioneering a sea route that used the prevailing winds between Holland and Java, they sailed due east from Cape Town until they reached the vicinity of the western Australian coast and then steered north. On that sea route numerous Dutch and a few British ships struck the Australian coast itself. Deepwater divers have found the remains of their cargoes.

The map of Australia holds names given by these brave voyagers travelling in tiny sailing ships. The strait at the north-easterly point of the Australian continent thus has a Spanish name, Torres. The north-west coast is guarded by the Bonaparte Archipelago, one of a necklace of French names. The wind-blown cape at the south-western corner of the continent carries a Dutch name, Cape Leeuwin. These Europeans had the chance to colonise Australia but thought it sensible to sail away. The coast they passed was sandy and dry. The naked Aborigines were not really traders and compared with other exotic peoples they had no attractive goods for sale.

Buried minerals lay near that long coastline seen by early Portuguese, Spanish and Dutch sailors. But nearly all that gold, iron ore, uranium, bauxite, copper, petroleum and silver-lead-zinc lying often within walking distance of the sea was worthless in 1700. There were also diamonds – enough to delight the gem merchants of Amsterdam – but the first pipe of payable diamonds was not unearthed in Western Australia until 1979. The European navigators came too early. The massive deposits of minerals were of no use until new technology liberated them. In the last century and a half, Australians have depended as much on the rise of new technology as on their own soil, grasslands, minerals and other resources.

The east coast of Australia, facing the Pacific Ocean, is friendlier than the west coast. The British navigator, Captain James Cook, was probably the first to sail along that entire east coast. He had begun his voyage from England in 1768 with orders that, in aim, were almost the equivalent of landing men on the moon two centuries later. His mission was to be on the tropical island of Tahiti on the morning of Saturday 3 June 1769 and observe with the most precise surveying instruments the swift transit of the planet Venus across the sun, a rare event from which it was hoped to calculate for the first time a crucial fact of astronomy, the distance of the sun from the earth. From Tahiti he sailed to New Zealand, already found but not landed on by the Dutch, and explored its entire coast before he discovered the adjacent coast of Australia in April 1770. The granite headland he first saw was close to the present border of Victoria and New South Wales. Sailing along the coast in clear weather he saw smoke rising from large fires and knew that the country beyond the sandy white beaches was inhabited.

Sailing into Botany Bay, close to where Sydney's airport now stands, he was pleased with what he saw: the climate was 'wholesome', the harbour seemed safe, the fish and especially the stingrays were edible, several pockets of the soil were fertile, or so he imagined, and the few Aborigines were given more to 'hostile gesturing' than armed attack. The people were so few that the idea arose that perhaps the interior of this big land was uninhabited. The expanse of grass astounded Cook, prompting him to write that 'here are Provender for more cattle at all seasons of the year than ever can be brought into this Country'. At all seasons of the year? He was only there for one week and understandably made a costly mistake of judgment. He thought it was the dry season when in fact it was the rainier season. On this particular week, several streams were running fast through the 'meadows', but when the next British expedition arrived, at another time of year, the same land seemed hungry and mean. The meadows had shrivelled and vanished.

Botany Bay became a place of promise to Britain only after the North American colonies rebelled to form the United States. Britain previously had sent many criminals to serve out their sentences in the plantations and towns of North America. Now, unwanted in the United States, where else could they go? In 1786 the arguments for sending convicts from the overcrowded British prisons to Botany Bay came to the fore. They would found a British strategic base in a promising part of the world at a time of intense naval rivalry between England and France. The convicts could also develop two strategic commodities, masts cut from the tall straight Norfolk Island pine and canvas and rope made from the unusual flax also growing on Norfolk Island. Strong masts and strong sails were vital to naval supremacy, as England had again learned in recent naval battles and blockades during the American War of Independence.

Botany Bay, so far from England, would be a costly destination for ships hired to carry out convicts, guards and initial supplies; but one advantage was that the ships could then sail north to China to take on boxes of tea as cargo for the return voyage to England. In such a rich soil, blessed by such a fine climate, the convicts would surely grow more than enough to feed themselves. In short, Botany Bay, the focus of the convict plan, was believed to be a kind of paradise.

Later, the name Botany Bay came to serve as a symbol in the English language for desolation, loneliness and cruelty, but originally the name stood for the wonder and bounty of nature. It was initially believed that the Botany Bay settlement would grow sugar, coffee, cotton and other tropical plants, as well as so much food that the convicts – once their day's farming was done – would have too much spare time on their hands. Elizabeth Macarthur, writing in England in October 1789 to console her mother before she set out with her officer husband for this faraway land, expressed the contemporary faith that nature was even kinder in Australia: 'The sun that shines on you will also afford me the benefit of his cheery rays, and that too in a country where nature hath been so lavish of her bounties'. She added that in Botany Bay the 'flowers luxuriantly abound', and fruits will flourish after seeds are planted and tended.

The First Fleet, with soldiers, convicts and supplies, sailed from England on 13 May 1787. A straggling convoy of eleven ships, it called at the Canary Islands for a week and anchored at Rio de Janeiro for a month and Cape Town for another month. All were foreign ports, the British Empire being weakly represented in the south Atlantic, Indian and Pacific oceans. When finally the fleet sailed from Cape Town with about 1,000 men, women and children and 500 head of livestock and poultry aboard, it reminded its commander, Captain Arthur Phillip, of Noah's Ark. As for his own cabin it was so full of plants for the colony that it was 'like a Small Green house'.

Reaching Botany Bay eight months after leaving the Isle of Wight, Phillip hurriedly searched for Cook's green meadows. Not finding them, and deciding that even the harbour was not safe in the face of certain winds, Phillip moved the colony a few miles north to the magnificent Sydney Harbour. Guarded by two sandstone capes, it seemed to him to be the finest harbour on the globe with space for 1,000 large warships to shelter from storms. More important, the deep water came right to the rocky shore so that ships could be roped to the trees and then the cargo could be safely carried the short distance to the shore. At Sydney Cove he raised Britain's flag on 26 January 1788. Unfortunately that was to become Australia's national day, Australia Day, instead of the more dramatic 18 January, when one of the most remarkable voyages of colonisation in human history had ended with Phillip sailing into Botany Bay.

3

There was not much to celebrate in the huts and tents of early Sydney. Trees and bushes had to be cleared, the soil was not fertile, and most of the early harvests were pitiful. Every person had to eat an early version of a tin-opener diet, for the weekly rations of flour, rice and cured beef were dished out from barrels. Dozens of convicts and marines, lacking fresh food, became 'pale tawney' in the face: their breathing became heavy, their gums bled or itched, and dark or yellow bruises appeared on their legs. They were suffering from the seaman's curse, the disease of scurvy. Relief came at last when the greens, berries and creepers eaten by Aborigines were added to the diet. For many of those convicts who laboured hard with hoes and axes and saws, the weekly food ration was not enough. A convict named Black Caesar ate his whole ration in a day. The 188 women were each entitled to only two-thirds of the male ration of food, and some must have felt acute pangs of hunger.

Most of the convicts knew how to steal: it was the story of their life. To those who tried to thieve food from the government's store, Phillip replied with formal trial and punishment. Five people were hanged in the first year and others were flogged repeatedly on the bare back. Convicts tried to escape. As most ships which had conveyed them to Sydney were making ready to sail away to the Chinese port of Canton, some convicts decided that China must be just over the hills. They set out on the hopeless task of walking there, and vanished in gorge and plateau. Soon there were incentives for those who stayed. Convicts who served their sentence were often granted a small farm. Few knew how to farm though some were willing to learn.

A ship had to be sent all the way to Cape Town, the nearest port, for emergency supplies. More and more convicts had to be sent to Norfolk Island where the richer soil grew pleasing crops. By 1793 more people lived on this small island than in Sydney town. Meanwhile the hope was high that an English fleet would arrive with supplies – a hope that was frustrated for another two and a half years.

In its first years the convict settlement failed dismally to fulfil its promise. It might well have been abandoned if that had been a simple task. But a retreat would first require the despatch of a major and costly naval expedition from England. Such an expedition, if decided upon, could not easily be organised, partly because the French Revolutionary wars broke out during the fourth year of the convict colony. British vessels could not be spared. It would have been even costlier to retreat from Sydney than it had been to settle it in the first place.

Relations with the Aborigines were one consolation. They could have been disastrous but were not. On many days Governor Phillip and the marines and the convicts came across Aborigines who were fishing, hunting, gathering plant foods, and painting themselves with clay and ochre for ceremonies. On many days the new settlers were probably peered at by Aborigines from the security of bushes and rocks. Neither the black nor the white people could understand the other. The role of leaders, the social organisation, the language, the attitudes to the land, and the religious beliefs were unintelligible to each side. For the Aborigines the arrival of the British in 1788 and the fact that they stayed must have been the strangest of events. The local Aborigines had never seen a deep-sea sailing ship; their own bark canoes were tiny. They had never heard the sound of a flute and a deep booming drum, never seen a cow or a pig or a cat, never seen a hat or a pair of boots or anyone fully clothed. They had never seen tobacco burning in a pipe, or anything so sharp and durable as an iron knife. The iron pot and kettle of England were unfamiliar to these people, who traditionally cooked on an open fire or in hot ashes; the planting of seeds in the ground was a mystery to people who were not farmers; and the tying up and flogging of an English convict was a sight to make them wonder or wail.

Governor Phillip, hoping that his people would live in peace, promised to 'punish any person who wantonly harmed Aborigines'. Except when British lives were endangered, he fired no guns at Aborigines. A party of French explorers who had briefly landed at Botany Bay were probably the first to fire shots at Aborigines. Even good intentions on both sides – and they were not always present – resulted in fear and confusion. Convicts cutting rushes for the thatching of huts were clubbed or speared. Aborigines were shot or maltreated by convicts. These numerous isolated incidents pointed to what one naval officer called 'endless uncertainty'.

In trying to converse with Aborigines, Governor Phillip had one unusual advantage. Like nearly all the black men, he could point to a missing tooth on the right side of his upper jaw. Possibly in their eyes he almost seemed to be one of them. He himself tried to treat them with patience, goodwill and dignity. Probably there were Aborigines who treated him in the same spirit. Phillip, however, could not escape misunderstandings or hostility. In September 1790 he was wounded by a spear that was about three metres long. It hung from his right shoulder, jutting towards the ground, as he ran away. He was lucky to live; the wound was not infected and the surgeon was capable. To his credit Phillip did not seek revenge, preferring to think that he had been speared by people who themselves had been injured or had good reason to be afraid.

Phillip hoped to entice a few Aborigines to settle in Sydney and virtually become Europeans. Eventually he captured Abaroo, who dined at his table and received many kindnesses. When the disease of smallpox broke out amongst the Aborigines, Abaroo was a victim. We are told that he received everything 'which medical skill and unremitting attention could perform'. Whereas some Aborigines tended to abandon their kinsfolk who fell down with smallpox, Phillip tried to save some of the sick. Abaroo died and was given the honour of a burial place in Phillip's own household garden, where one of Sydney's skyscrapers now stands.

In the following ten years more convicts left the British Isles in crowded ships which sometimes stank, for bedding could not always be aired. In rough seas the sleeping dormitories took in water. Certain prisoners, after living for years in hulks or old ships moored in English rivers or harbours, were unfit when they boarded their deep-sea ship. Others, dressed in rags or threadbare clothes, suffered from cold except when the ship was slowly sailing in warm equatorial seas. Towards the end of the voyage the flour – their main food – might contain a colony of weevils. Meanwhile the drinking water tasted strange, and the salted meat, when cooked, smelt like a steaming vat of offal. In several of the early convict ships the death-rate was high. Between 1801 and 1815, one in every twenty-four convicts died during the voyage to Australia. Deaths were also frequent in those ships which carried British soldiers to India or Spanish settlers to Chile, for their diet was deficient and any infection spread quickly in the crowded quarters.

The typical convict sent to Australia was a youngish English thief. Many were once-only thieves and others were persistent but petty thieves. Of each party of twenty convicts reaching Australia during the entire history of the system, thirteen came from England, six from Ireland and one from Scotland. The Irish convicts were very numerous when compared to the total population of their homeland.

A minority of convicts had been sentenced to exile for life. More than half had been sentenced, in the courts, to exile for a total of seven years, but the typical convict had already served part of that sentence before being escorted aboard the convict ship. By the law they were free to return home once their sentence was over, but few could afford to pay for a berth in a returning ship. A few worked their passage as sailors, or even went home in triumph as relatively rich settlers. A few of those who managed to find their way home were convicted of a new crime and sent back to Australia.

What did they steal? Folklore used to insist that they were judged harshly for stealing goods of no consequence, say a few loaves of bread, a roll of cloth, or a pair of rabbits. Mostly they stole items well worth stealing. Thus, of the convicts who sailed from Portsmouth in the *Calcutta* in 1803, most had stolen items which they had hoped to resell. James Coward – described as a Kentish labourer with brown hair, dark complexion, grey eyes and a height of five feet three inches – stole two black oxen. Daniel Crawley, a tallish tailor with brown hair and dark hazel eyes, had been acquitted of an earlier charge of forgery but was found guilty of a charge of stealing a yard of red woollen cloth, part of which was concealed under his waistcoat. The cloth was worth ten shillings, maybe equal to one week's wages. Michael Crener, alias McGuire, was convicted in Canterbury court by seventeen justices of the peace on a charge of assaulting a man and robbing him of his knife, a pair of gloves, a handkerchief and six halfpennies. Robert Cooper, probably a Dorset gypsy, was charged with stealing nine he-asses and four halters. He was 57, old for a convict. His wife, unlike the wives of many of the married convicts, did not come with him in the convict ship *Calcutta*. Cooper lived out the remainder of his life in southern Tasmania, running cattle on his own small farm, and died in his early nineties. The founders of several of Australia's richest families, whose fortunes were to come from wool, humbly arrived in that same convict ship.

A convict setting foot on Australian soil was rarely more than 50 years of age. Occasionally a boy thief arrived, spending his tenth or eleventh birthday in the new land. Amongst the thieves might be small parties of political prisoners, usually from Ireland: no more than two of every hundred Irish convicts could truly be called political prisoners. Later convicts would include young Englishmen who, as a protest against unemployment, had broken the costly machines in northern textile factories or the steam-driven threshing machines on

• • • • • • • • • •

southern farmlands. They were rebels against a new technology that threatened their jobs. A few who came were pioneer trade unionists, their crime being to 'conspire' to form a trade union and so harm their employers' business.

A typical female convict was a domestic servant who had been caught committing a petty larceny. In Australia she was usually taken up by a man, and often she had no say in the matter. The evidence suggests that most female convicts were capable parents and that their children were at least as successful, economically, as their cousins who remained in the British Isles. Many of the sons of convicts entered the skilled trades or acquired sixty-acre farms. Most of the daughters of convicts married young, and had no hesitation in marrying an ex-convict if he had money.

4

By 1813, the twenty-fifth anniversary of New South Wales, one-quarter of the white population was under twelve. Mostly the children of convict parents, they thrived because the climate was healthy, their diet was sound, and the population was not crowded. They were surprisingly free of the whooping cough, scarlet fever and measles that killed so many British infants, but this meant that they lacked immunity and so were susceptible if by chance an epidemic later broke out. When many soldiers finished their term of duty in the New South Wales Corps and returned to England with their Australian-born children, a similar tragedy awaited them. Reaching a strange land, these children had to face for the first time the common infections of childhood. In the harsh English winter of 1811 'the measles acted like a plague', and within a fortnight sixty of these colonial children and many of their mothers died.

• • • • • • • • •

In time the native-born children were called 'currency lads and lasses'. Currency meant local money rather than the sterling coins and banknotes issued in England. As ten shillings in local currency was worth less than the same sum in sterling, the phrase currency lass suggested that she was just a little inferior. She herself did not think so. Like many terms of distaste it became a term of pride. In 1827 the surgeon and pastoral settler, Peter Cunningham, writing his book *Two Years in New South Wales*, praised the currency lads and lasses, noting their fair hair and blue eyes, their reddish or sallow complexion when young, and a tendency to be taller and slenderer than English immigrants of the same age.

The native-born could be recognised at a glance, or at least Cunningham thought so. They did not drink heavily, were honest, and the poor reputation sometimes fixed on them stemmed unjustly from the wild behaviour of the children of 'three roguishly prolific families'. He observed that the lasses liked to display their curly hair with a dash of exuberance, fastening it with combs of tortoise shell. Generally they were modest and mild-tempered, and were capable servants in a house. Unfortunately they lost their teeth at an early age.

The shape of Australia was known by the 1820s because every stretch of coast and nearly every bay and inlet had been explored by British or French ships. One momentous discovery was the strait proving that the most southerly corner of the continent was actually a large island. Officially called Van Diemen's Land but later known as Tasmania, it was first settled by the British in 1803. The site selected was Hobart, on the charming and wide estuary of the Derwent. Above the little town stood the hump of Mount Wellington, and those who climbed the lower slopes could see, less than two decades later, the results of the convicts' hard work: the small farms occupying clearings in the forest, and the roads, wharves, warehouses and barracks. The yellow sandstone of the bigger buildings was mellow in the sunlight. In 1825 Tasmania became independent of New South Wales but it was still heavily dependent on the convicts, whether landed directly from the British Isles or shipped from Sydney for further punishment.

Already Tasmania was a haven for seafarers. Ships and boats small and large were built of local wood. On the rugged offshore islands, tens of thousands of seals were clubbed to death and their skins sent away to provide warmth to wealthy northern Chinese enduring their cold winters. Whales were caught in sheltered bays or in the open ocean and their oil extracted to burn the lamps in European offices and to grease the new steam engines of the industrial era. Whaling – pursued in Tasmanian waters and on a long stretch of Australian coastline – was the country's first important source of exports.

New South Wales was the official name of the huge British territory in eastern Australia. To describe the whole continent, the names New Holland and Terra Australis were often used. To describe the white inhabitants a new word was creeping into conversation. A few were beginning to call themselves 'Australians'. Matthew Flinders, a naval officer who was the first person to sail around the continent, publicly favoured the name Australia from about 1814, though he was conscious that Europe's geographers or high officials in London and Sydney still used the old name of New Holland or the Latin phrase Terra Australis, meaning land of the south. He thought Australia was 'more agreeable to the ear' than the longer Latin name. Lachlan Macquarie, the longest serving of the early governors, occupying the post from 1810 to 1821, first used the word Australia in his official correspondence in 1817.

It is likely that local people were already using 'Australia' in daily conversation before it became official, and soon the word was on almost every tongue. Many of the native-born people especially liked it, as E. S. Hall of Sydney observed in an official letter in 1829:

> I, Sir, speak as father of eight Australian-born sons and daughters; and
> though I myself glory, and shall die glorying, in the name of *English*man,

yet my children glory in *another* name. To be *Australian* is their signal word, as opposed to Emigrants.

Hall described how the Australian-born youngsters sitting around the dinner table or engaged in the annual reaping of the harvest – he owned a little farm at Surry Hills – loved to give cheek to British immigrants. At least six of his children were daughters, and they seemed as fervent as the lads towards Australia, the only land they knew.

Their Australia was not yet a country: it was simply a coastline. Little was known of what lay in the interior. Much of it was believed to be dry but could everywhere be so dry? The feeling was widespread that somewhere in the centre lay green pastures and a vast sea or lake whose overflow perhaps found its way along an Australian Nile to some unmapped estuary in the north-west. Some Australians were now seeing in the remote interior the future of their land.

Arabs of the grasslands

In the history of the world, it is doubtful whether any other large land was changed so quickly by the arrival of a new animal.

Sheep reached Australia in 1788 in the ships of the First Fleet. They came mainly from South Africa and Bengal, and were small and scrawny by today's standards; they were valued for their mutton rather than their wool. A few Spanish merino sheep were imported in the 1790s but the quality of their wool, occasionally shipped to England in barrels, was suspect: no manufacturer of good cloth would have touched it. The Macarthur family was the first to take sheep seriously, owning about 5,000 sheep in 1806. The husband, John, did much to promote Australian wool in England – after the finest wool from a tiny minority of the sheep became saleable – while his wife, Elizabeth, remained with the family's sheep, becoming Australia's first stud-master. Another vigorous supporter of wool was a colonial chaplain, the Reverend Samuel Marsden, who visited Yorkshire and had his own Australian wool made into fine cloth, from which a suit of clothes was made for King George the Third. No sermon he preached from the pulpit to convicts could have been more influential than the secular sermon he preached in England: Australian wool is as excellent as the best German and Spanish wool.

More and more colonists began to graze sheep in New South Wales and Tasmania. By the 1820s the export of wool was important. By the 1830s the sheep population was exploding, and in almost every year an area of grassland about the size of Ireland was occupied by sheep and shepherds moving into new country, with the governor in Sydney almost powerless to control them.

It seemed that almost everything in Australia was ready to welcome the sheep. On the dry inland side of the low spine of mountain ranges that followed the Pacific coast were sweeping grasslands which, first glimpsed in 1813, could feed even more sheep than lived in Europe. Even on the grassy slopes of the higher mountains the winter was not so cold that sheep had to be placed in shelter and fed with hay, and so the early Australian sheep farmers, unlike those in Germany and England, did not have to spend much of the summer cutting hay and carting and storing it. Most varieties of Australia's climate, except for the tropics, favoured sheep. Another advantage was that the only native animal capable of killing full-grown sheep was the dingo, and with care it was eventually defeated. Fortunately Australia suited one of the finest breeds of sheep, the merino, which had originated in the similarly dry climate of Morocco and north-west Africa.

By 1820 the industrial revolution was gathering pace in northern England, and clever machines improved and cheapened the production of woollen cloth and garments, flannels and blankets at the very time when the rapid growth of population was demanding more. In the tall stone mills of Yorkshire, their waterwheels turned by fast streams, the demand for fine wool was rising. It so happened that wool was one of the high-priced commodities of the modern world, and therefore a wool-grower could afford the high expense of carting the wool by bullock-drawn dray to Australian ports and the cost of sending it in sailing ships to the other side of the world, and still retain a profit. In contrast, the imported cattle that multiplied in early Australia produced only hides for export, and they did not command a high price. The cattle's main product, the meat, could not be exported to Europe's huge population until the dawning of the era of refrigeration.

2

The flocks of sheep now grazing far from the coast needed thousands of shepherds to watch over them. It would have been hard to recruit free immigrants to live a lonely and sometimes dangerous life far from the bright oil lamps of the ports and their taverns and shops. Nor would their wives have been eager to follow them. Convicts and ex-convicts, however, could be compelled to watch the sheep. That task was not difficult. As sheep liked to stay together, the convict shepherd could normally sit under a tree for part of the day while they grazed, and then towards sunset he could drive them slowly back to the vicinity of the hut where his mate, the hut-keeper, erected a fence made of wooden hurdles. This movable prefabricated fence formed a yard around the sheep, which were crowded together, and helped to protect them from dingoes prowling at night. If the hut had to be moved, the yard and fences could be moved too.

The shoppers in Europe who bought garments made from Australian wool would have blinked in surprise if they had seen the sheep just before dark. Often the makeshift yards where the sheep were kept together at night were dusty, and the smell of greasy wool and sheep dung was strong. After dark a dog was tied to each corner of the sheep yard to frighten away dingoes. The hut-keeper acted as watchman during the night, sleeping in a portable wooden watch-box placed near the sheep fold. In the morning, after the shepherd had drunk his hot black tea and eaten his cooked mutton and flat flourcake made without yeast, he drove the sheep out to graze. In the early green of spring the scene of off-white sheep dotting the grasses seemed idyllic. In many districts in early summer the sheep could hardly be seen, for the kangaroo grass stood high, its brown seeds waving in the breeze like heads of wheat.

The flocks and herds were driven far beyond the most remote made road and the most remote building with glass windows. By 1840 they extended in a sweeping arc all the way from the downs of southern Queensland to the dry country north of Adelaide and to the cooler pastures of Tasmania as well. Sir George Gipps, the governor of New South Wales, knowing the edges of his territory were almost ungovernable because people were so dispersed, could see no way of halting the exodus. In Sydney, just six days before Christmas 1840, he took up his pen and wrote privately to London that he was powerless. He said it would be as futile

> to confine the Arabs of the Desert within a circle, traced upon their sands, as to confine the Graziers or Woolgrowers of New South Wales within any bounds that can possibly be assigned to them; and as certainly as the Arabs would be starved, so also would the flocks and herds of New South Wales, if they were so confined, and the prosperity of the Country be at an end.

As a temporary measure Gipps legalised the new graziers or 'squatters', giving them leases over the vast areas where they squatted.

It was a rare woman who went to live on the furthest sheep runs. In 1839, Katharine Kirkland and her young child went from the new town of Melbourne to her husband's sheep run 150 kilometres in the west. Arriving after about a dozen days spent in the swaying, bruising dray, she was soon living contentedly in a three-roomed hut amongst the sheep. She noticed how few men washed themselves and their clothes. She was shocked to see that so much mutton – it was very cheap food – was wasted and thrown away. She marvelled at the ways of the Aborigines, many of whom would peep through the window to look at the inside of her hut. For three months her hut had a doorway but no door. When she decided to go to Melbourne for the birth of her next child, she travelled in a dray fitted up like a covered wagon. She had become so accustomed to the bush, so familiar with the male conversation which revolved around sheep and horses, that when she briefly rejoined the company of Melbourne ladies she hardly knew what subject to select for conversation.

Her new baby was delicate but thrived during the long journey home on the rough bush track. The sheep and lambs that almost everywhere were sprinkled over the park-like landscape reminded her of the biblical saying, 'God tempers the wind to the shorn lamb', and she felt that she was in God's care. She knew she was close to home when four or five kangaroo dogs ran up and, half playful, almost tore her dress to pieces.

After the annual shearing of the sheep and the washing away of the grease that had added about one-quarter of weight to the wool, the small bullock drays were piled high with big bales of wool. So they set out, top-heavy and swaying slightly in the wind for the nearest port. Britain, the world's great importer and manufacturer of wool, bought more wool from Australia than from Germany, Spain and the rest of Europe combined in the late 1840s. And yet Australia's wool industry, already covering a vast area, was still an infant. The heavy square bales of packed wool that were loaded onto sailing ships for the slow voyage to English ports increased in number in all years except those of acute drought. Between 1850 and 1890 the annual output of wool was to be multiplied by more than ten. Much of the increase came from the breeding of sheep more suited to Australian conditions.

The first sheep were more like large dogs than today's fat, waddling woolly creatures. Like dogs, the most prized sheep wore collars. Dozens of sheep-breeders used their powers of observation more than scientific theory to breed sheep that were heavier and woollier. By the 1860s in the dry saltbush country of the Riverina, the Peppin-style merino was distinctive, and in dry country in South Australia the Hawker family and its gifted shepherd, John Noble – with a faraway look in his eyes – were breeding sheep that were merino only in name. Their heavy body and bulky fleece dwarfed the merino of coastal Sydney in the convict days. They differed almost as much as the German shepherd dog differed from the spaniel. Elizabeth Macarthur, had she lived long enough to see them in their paddocks in 1900, would have realised that they were about seven times as heavy as her original sheep. Indeed she might have asked herself, 'Are they really sheep?'

The astonishing rise of the wool industry changed Australian life. It tied faraway Australia's economy to Europe, for wool was primarily worn in the northern hemisphere. In contrast Australia during its first half-century had made numerous links with nearer Asia. Isolated Sydney had bought most of its emergency supplies and most of its early sheep from British India. Rum was the strong drink of the early Australians, and it came not from the West Indies but from Bengal. English ships, after their convicts and supplies had gone ashore in Sydney and Hobart, mostly set sail for China, there to take on cargoes of tea for England or, increasingly, to bring it back for Australians who were soon, for each head of population, the thirstiest drinkers of tea in the world. In architecture the Australian house verandah seems to have been adapted from India. Indeed the Anglican church, the dominant church in early Australia, was initially part of the diocese of Calcutta, though its bishop could never spare the time to visit his remote Australian flock.

Some of Australia's earliest exports – sealskins from Bass Strait, coal from Newcastle, sandalwood from Western Australia and the food delicacy bêche-de-mer (or trepang) from the shallows of tropical Australia – had been shipped to India and China. On the other hand, wool rarely was shipped to the Orient. Wool in its new dominance did more than anything to turn the economy back towards Europe. Between 1835 and 1975, a total of 140 years, it was Australia's main export in all but a score of years.

3

The Aborigines were the silent victims of the sheep moving further inland. Having never seen a white person, let alone a sheep or horse, they were suddenly confronted with these puzzling intruders on the very lands they had inhabited long before the time of Moses – indeed long before the time of Adam and Eve, according to the Englishmen's own chronology. As the sheep were driven further into new districts, new clashes with Aborigines broke out. Even with goodwill, clashes were difficult to avoid. From one side the story was plain: Aborigines killed sheep and cattle, stole from the shepherds' huts, murdered shepherds and hut-keepers, and occasionally ate some of the victims' flesh. On the other side the story was equally clear. White men knowingly occupied black lands, waterholes and springs, and unknowingly let their sheep and cattle trample on sacred ground. Some took Aboriginal women by force, raping them or maltreating them in other ways. A few groups of white men on horseback, some carrying the new double-barrelled gun, pursued Aborigines, cornered and shot them.

In the turmoil some Aborigines turned on their old tribal enemies. Payback prolonged the bloodshed. Small numbers of newly arrived Europeans or big numbers of Aborigines were killed in individual massacres and fights. In less than a dozen years in the sheep country of western Victoria, at least thirty-four European men and a three-year-old child were killed by Aborigines but perhaps ten times as many Aborigines were killed, including at least twenty-seven women and ten children. In northern New South Wales, many Aborigines were killed in a massacre on Australia Day, 1838. In the same region later that year twenty-eight Aborigines were slaughtered at Myall Creek and, as a penalty, seven Europeans were convicted and hanged: rarely were Europeans sent to trial for the death of Aborigines.

In some districts, harmonious relations emerged after the trickle of blood. In other districts the blood continued to flow. J. H. Wedge, writing in 1838 from Shady Camps to Lord Glenelg in remote England, concluded that even if all the soldiers and police of New South Wales were sent inland to try to prevent 'the aggressions of the Stock keepers on the one side, and the attacks of the Natives on the other', they would not succeed in making the two sides live in peace.

The typical outback settler probably killed or wounded no Aborigines. On the other hand, the lawless settlers might have numbered several hundred in New South Wales in the 1830s and 1840s. Many settlers despised the Aborigines; even more feared them. While many saw the blacks as the lowest of the low on a ladder of the human races, many respected their ability. Captain George Grey, observing hundreds of Aborigines while exploring in Western Australia, concluded in 1840 that they were the prisoners of a barbarous culture but still a people of talent: 'They are as apt and intelligent as any other race of men I am acquainted with; they are subject to the same affections, appetites and passions as other men, yet in many points of character they are totally dissimilar to them'.

Goodwill and effort went into schemes to harness or cultivate the abilities of Aborigines – 'to civilise them' was the phrase – at the very time when sporadic energy went into killing them. While settlers on the frontier did the killing, those sitting at the official desks, whether in Sydney, Hobart, Perth or London, sought humane solutions. Some thought Aborigines should be kept apart, for their own interests, and some thought they should be absorbed into the new settlers' society. It was hoped that if only Aborigines could cease to move about, and became farmers and labourers instead of hunters and gatherers, all would be well. Perhaps they could be persuaded to wear clothes, to read and write, and to accept Christianity. It was not yet appreciated that the gap was unimaginably wide between the Aboriginal and the British attitudes, values and ways of life.

From time to time there came a surge of hope that Aborigines would abandon their old ways. Reverend Robert Cartwright, a colonial chaplain, hoped in 1820 that here and there an adult Aborigine could 'be completely weaned from his roving habits', thus setting an example for others. He believed that the children could be educated first and then they could teach their parents the advantages of more civilised life. Governor Macquarie decided in 1814 that local Aborigines he had met, though indolent, were promising. Honest and open, they seemed to lack the traits of 'Trick and Treachery' and the cannibal ways which, in his view, characterised the Maoris of New Zealand. If only some could be persuaded to settle down as semiskilled tradesmen in the town, they might soon prefer to live on the results of their labour than on 'the Wild and precarious Pursuits of the Woods'. Many observers were surprised to see the speed with which black children could learn. Cartwright thought the day would come when, at the annual awarding of prizes to the colony's best students, 'these sable Australians' would outshine what he called 'Albion's Sons'.

Incentives were offered to little black children. Sometimes a block of land was offered to adult Aborigines in the hope that they would plant crops. Large reserves of thousands of hectares were set aside for experiments. One advantage of a reserve where only Aborigines lived was that they could not be influenced by the more depraved convicts.

Thus in 1820 Governor Macquarie set aside rural land on the outskirts of Sydney as a reserve where Aborigines might adopt the new ways. The experiment failed, the Aborigines preferring their old ways.

Missionaries came from Europe and founded settlements. They attracted the remnants of lost tribes with the promise of weekly rations of flour and sugar, and taught some adults and children to read and pray. Then one Sunday the pastor would appear in the wooden church or the shaded hollow where normally he preached, only to find that most of his seemingly devout congregation had resumed their old 'wanderings'. Aboriginal children who showed brilliance at arithmetic and the Old Testament were hailed as the potential saviours of their race after they recited word-perfect their lessons in the presence of the governor and other visitors, but they died while young or vanished from the schoolroom. It was unbelievable and saddening to their teachers.

If, by chance, groups of white Australians in the 1840s had been forced to try to adopt Aboriginal culture in its entirety, they too would have finally rebelled or copied only fragments. Similarly there was little chance that the Aborigines could change their ways quickly. With such different attitudes to family, kinsfolk, the devil, the deities, and land and private possessions and personal knick-knacks, Aborigines could see no point in the British ways. They might adopt them briefly but usually for the sake of novelty or temporary gain. Moreover, they met two contrasting kinds of behaviour – kindness from some white people and brutality or indifference from others.

If the Aborigines had been quick to adopt British ways, they would have won esteem or respect. Some would have acquired large areas of farmland and even sheep runs. It is a modern myth that initially the Aborigines were universally despised: Captain Cook and Governor Phillip were two who respected them. That no Aborigines had the right to vote until the 1960s is another myth. In the two big colonies, Victoria and New South Wales, most Aborigines were to receive the right to vote under the democratic constitutions of the 1850s, but few had an interest in the ballot box. When many Aborigines were later deprived of vital civil rights, it was largely because they, understandably, had not earlier accepted the chance to become Europeans in attitudes and way of life.

A few Britons who came to Sydney in 1788 saw nobility and dignity in the Aborigines. Those who came to the settled districts fifty years later saw them in decline, with some begging for clothes and money, some drunk, and many others accepting paid work for only a few days at a time, thus forming only a small core of the continuous workforce. In theory their freedom remained but in practice it was lost because in the extensive rural districts their old food-gathering grounds were now occupied by the multiplying sheep and cattle.

Beyond the furthest sheep station, life went on almost as before, but sickness was arriving ahead of the white settlers. New diseases were the main killers of the Aborigines in towns and sheep districts, and even in places which no white man had reached. Influenza, measles, smallpox, venereal and other diseases – far more than guns and rifles – were the killers. Alcohol compounded the assault on Aboriginal health. Rum and other hard liquor, not beer, was the drink of the outback, and those Aborigines who liked the solace of alcohol drank it in potent form. Amongst some Aborigines, alcohol was as virulent as disease. Even the will to live faded away, as the secure old Aboriginal world crumbled.

It was believed that the Aborigines would all die out. While those of mixed European and Aboriginal blood multiplied, the 'full-blood Aborigines' declined with speed. The eager search, in the nineteenth century, to record their languages before they were spoken no more, and to take permanent note of their manners, skills and beliefs, was hastened by the fear that time was running short. The belief in the early extinction of Aborigines was reinforced by evidence that so many were dying even when they were fed, clothed and cared for.

The pessimistic belief was propagated by distinguished scholars. Perhaps the most famous scientist of the nineteenth century was Charles Darwin, who concluded that the full-blood as distinct from part-Aborigines might die out. It was part of his theory of biological evolution, of the survival of the fittest, whether of human races or plant species. Darwin, however, was not just a theoretician. One of the few European scientists who received an opportunity to observe Aborigines, he described them in 1836 when he crossed the Blue Mountains on horseback. He marvelled at their skill in throwing a spear through a man's cap from a distance of some thirty metres away. But he regretted that the Aborigines were now so few. He correctly assumed that disease, alcohol and the loss of hunting grounds were mainly wiping them out – he did not know of the additional work of the musket – but he thought that there must be another 'mysterious agency generally at work' to hasten their decline, a factor he admitted that he did not quite understand. He concluded that Maoris as well as Aborigines would eventually vanish: 'The varieties of man seem to act on each other in the same way as different species of animals – the stronger always extirpating the weaker'. Most scholars accepted his prediction until perhaps the 1920s when evidence showed that tribal Aborigines in the outback were not declining.

A few early settlers were not so sure that the Aborigines must die out. Edward Curr, a young Victorian squatter who was sympathetic to them, argued that they were the victims of unwise policies and attitudes, and sometimes of too much kindness. 'That they must die out is, I think, a foregone conclusion', he told a royal commission in Victoria in 1877. But he argued that there would be no prospect of them dying out if they 'were as valuable commercially as short-horned cattle, or merino sheep'. Ways would then be found to save them, he argued.

4

The eclipse of the Aborigines was tragic. Could it have been averted? It could have been prevented for a time if no British settlers had landed, but eventually people of other European or Asian nations would have come in and occupied much of the land. The eclipse of the Aborigines could partly have been avoided if the expansion of the sheep had been halted, say in 1835, and if the remainder of Australia had been declared out of bounds. The governments, however, could only have policed the new boundaries at heavy expense, and their policing often would have failed. Such policing would also have curtailed the increasing output of wool that was eagerly wanted in Europe, where sheep pastures were being converted to farmlands to feed an expanding population. In essence, wool now was too big an economic interest to be thwarted.

Another fact or opinion – rarely stated today – was widely accepted. The world's economy and population were advancing rapidly and, by the latest standards and goals, the Aborigines had to be judged as poor custodians of their huge resources. They were occupying a rich resource bowl but wasting or under-using it. Today Aboriginal advocates explain that their ancestors were great and responsible custodians of nature. The other side of the coin is that they had monopolised a land that was now capable of feeding, clothing and sheltering a population many times larger.

The British did not doubt that their civilisation in the widest sense was superior to that of the Aborigines. Materially it was far ahead; and many Aborigines actually clamoured for British goods, including iron, flour, sugar, tobacco and rum. If, however, British civilisation was to be judged mainly by the behaviour of its members who guarded the flocks and herds and confronted the Aborigines, it could not be judged superior. Sometimes it was patently inferior.

In hindsight, other solutions might have been applied to the chaos and misery arising from the historical anachronism of a modern society confronting a long-quarantined and vigorous survivor of an era long past. But no solution would have been effective. The multitude of deaths through disease could not have been avoided. In 1992 a solution was offered in hindsight. The High Court of Australia decided that much of the outback land, though not the cities, probably still belonged to Aborigines and that a grievous wrong had been inflicted on them. How to redress the wrong in practical terms, however, continued to defy judges and law-makers.

While strong arguments can be mounted for and against the court's decision, one conclusion is clear. Even if compensation had been paid in, say, the 1830s to each Aboriginal group which lost land, that sum would have been initially handed to white trustees to spend in what they thought were the interests of each group of Aborigines. Usually the trustees would have spent it in making Aborigines abandon their own wandering ways and the religious and cultural views so dear to them. The compensation would simply have been another way of depriving them of their culture in addition to their land. As for the parallel idea that large permanent reserves should have been set aside for Aborigines in the 1830s so that they could pursue, without interference or supervision, their old way of life, even that dream could not have been fulfilled in the long term. Too many Aborigines would have left those reserves. The food, bright clothes and glitter of the outside would have been too seductive.

The shrinking world was becoming too small to permit a whole people to be set aside in a vast protected anthropological museum where they would try to perpetuate the merits and defects of a way of life that had vanished elsewhere, a way of life that – so long as it continued – would deprive millions of people in Australia and other lands of the food and fibres and minerals that could be produced on their land. And yet the grievances of the Aborigines were deep and legitimate.

The fading of the yellow flannel

In the winter of 1824 the ports of Australia were few. Crews of ships that ran aground were forced to row along the coast for weeks, and they might travel 5,000 kilometres to the nearest port without seeing one lighthouse or jetty. The main harbours were Sydney and Hobart, followed by the small river-ports of Launceston and Newcastle. On the long coast of tropical Australia was not one wharf or jetty.

Those sea captains who occasionally called at the few ports saw a remarkable change during the following dozen years. Four of Australia's five largest cities were founded along a wide stretch of coast. Brisbane, the first of the new, was a small convict port beneath the hot sun and did not begin to grow rapidly until it became the capital of the new colony of Queensland. Perth began as a free town in 1829 and slumbered on its peaceful estuary for some sixty years, to be awakened by the western gold rushes. Melbourne began in 1835 as a free village at the foot of a rock bar across a river, and made its living from wool. Born free, or almost free, it was a quick success, and was soon to challenge Sydney.

2

Adelaide, the last of the four cities of the future, was a free town, hoping to thrive on its people's talents. Settled directly from England, it possessed probably the most skilled, most literate population so far assembled in one Australian town. In its sense of purpose and its religious intensity it had some likenesses to those Puritan religious settlements founded in North America nearly two centuries earlier. Adelaide was intensely proud to be untainted by convicts though, ironically, its English founders were much influenced by the theory of the economist Edward Gibbon Wakefield who, convicted for abducting and marrying a girl under the age of 16, had used his time in Newgate prison to write a book about colonisation.

In the first decades Adelaide and the colony of South Australia had geography on their side. Their wheatlands were conveniently close to the sea. Moreover, to harvest the grain, they devised one of the first mechanical harvesters in the world. Ridley's stripping machine, drawn by bullocks, stripped the grain so quickly from the wheat stalks that farm labourers lamented that the monster would deprive them of work. In almost every year between 1853 and 1896 South Australia was to sow more wheat than any other colony. No less important, Adelaide was the earliest Australian town to sit near to those ancient Precambrian rocks that are relatively rich in minerals. In 1842, not far from Adelaide, rich copper was found. It was discovered simultaneously by a boy picking wildflowers and by a sheep owner who was searching for a flock straying a thunderstorm. Known as Kapunda, it was the first of the rich metal-mining fields to be worked in Australia. It so galvanised the sleepy economy that one observer predicted in 1845 that South Australia would become 'one of the brightest gems in the imperial diadem of Britain'. After the rich copper of Burra was found further to the north, the colony began to overtake Cornwall as a miner of copper, indeed luring away so many of its mining families that it became the Cornish corner of Australia.

Adelaide also possessed the most central position of the capital cities. Lying on the deepest indentation in Australia's long south coast, it was a springboard for those exploring the interior and was the first to employ camels as help in exploring dry country. Adelaide was also close to the mouth of the skinny Mississippi of this driest of continents, the River Murray. There in the 1850s were launched paddle steamers that chugged far inland along the narrow winding waterway. From the 1860s, Adelaide governed the remote Northern Territory, and in the absence of an overland road it had to send its policemen, surveyors, customs officers and teachers in steamships by way of Sydney and Torres Strait to Darwin. Late in the century, South Australian investors were initially to win control of the largest mining fields of that era, Broken Hill and Kalgoorlie. All this was a tribute to the enterprise of these colonists and their determination to compensate for the relative dearth of fertile farming land.

In 1836 there was no inkling that such assets were waiting to be plucked. The first settlers clung to Adelaide's grid of wide streets, and in the first years many of Adelaide's pioneers did not even travel more than fifteen kilometres from their own front doorstep. South Australian settlers, more than those of any other early colony, displayed that tendency to cling to the capital city. Staunch urbanisation is actually a stronger tradition in Australia than in North America. South Australians were the first take pride in a settled home life, for they had no wide disparity between the numbers of adult males and females. Their religious life was vigorous: the silent Sunday streets were proof of that. At a time when churches in other colonies depended on government aid, South Australia was able to withdraw such aid.

The founding of Adelaide as a British town was one of the far-reaching events in the history of Australia, though nobody realised it at the time. Here virtually vanished the last opportunity for another European power to place a colony.

At first sight it is strange that the whole continent was to become the possession of one nation. After all, Australia possesses an exceptionally long coastline, which is navigable the whole year round. Therefore the opportunities stood out for other European or Asian powers to occupy part of that coast.

In contrast the coast of Africa and America sustained a variety of European colonies, especially along the Atlantic seaboard of North America. By the year 1750, the coast between the St Lawrence estuary and the Gulf of Mexico had seen the flags of many colonising countries, flying side by side. The French held Canada, the English held New England, and the Dutch pioneered the Hudson River and were the first to settle New York. The Swedes briefly held Delaware, the English held Virginia and most of what are now called the southern states. Spain held Florida, and France founded New Orleans. Whereas Europe's colonial powers jostled one another for a corner of North America, they did not jostle one another for a corner of Australia.

Why did they largely ignore Australia even after navigators showed that a few regions were very promising, and even after the British pointed the way by settling Sydney? The old colonial and naval powers – Spain, Portugal, Holland and Russia – were not interested because they already possessed more colonies than they could cope with. The infant United States was not yet interested in extending itself outside North America.

As a potential coloniser of Australia, France was the main rival to Britain. It was already a colonial and naval power of the first rank. A Frenchman, Jean de Surville, had been almost within sight of Sydney Harbour, five months ahead of Cook. Other Frenchmen landed on the coast of New Zealand and Tasmania. Two French naval vessels under the command of la Perouse actually visited Botany Bay only days after

Britain's First Fleet arrived in January 1788. That was an emphatic sign of the French interest in colonisation. But the French Revolution, beginning the following year, and the drawn-out wars in Europe, served to weaken or postpone any French desire for new colonies. After the end of the war in 1815, however, France had an incentive to plant new colonies in the Pacific or Indian oceans in order to compensate for those important possessions, especially the islands of Mauritius and Reunion, which she had lost to Britain.

In Australia even in the mid-1820s several important harbours were still there for the taking. As late as 1825 a French expedition could have reached Western Australia and colonised the vicinity of Albany or Perth. A French fleet could have sailed further east and occupied the attractive sites of Adelaide and Melbourne. Possession is nine-tenths of the law, the international law, and Britain at that time did not physically occupy and positively possess more than a few of the line of attractive harbours on the Australian coast. Naturally, Britain might have protested against any French incursion, but it would have taken no firm action. Australia at that time was hardly worth fighting about. By 1840 France was eager to establish colonies in the south-west Pacific, but the time was almost too late. So France had to content itself by annexing New Caledonia and Tahiti in mid-century and later the New Hebrides. On the other hand the whole coastline and interior of Australia remained in British hands. For the first time in history a whole continent was in the hands of one nation.

3

The rise of Adelaide and Melbourne and the growth of Sydney and Hobart and the older Australian towns owed much to the free migrants. Before 1831, a grand total of only 7,000 free migrants had come to

Australia from the British Isles. Now, however, the convict ships were outnumbered by sailing ships carrying free migrants. The white population of Australia, growing swiftly, almost trebled in the 1830s and doubled again in the 1840s. By 1850 there were over 400,000 white people, nearly half of them living within what are the present boundaries of New South Wales, with the other half divided in almost equal parts between Victoria, Tasmania and South Australia. The new settlers were concentrated in the south-eastern corner of Australia. In contrast, stagnant Western Australia, occupying one-third of the continent, held only 6,000 white people and a large, uncounted number of Aborigines.

Most of the free migrants coming out had initially been tempted by the United States. The fare across the Atlantic was cheap, the voyage occupied less than a quarter of the time, and the climate was closer to Britain's. Instead they were enticed to Australia by a simple lure. In the face of trans-Atlantic competition, the Australian colonies paid the fares of most migrants and fed them throughout the voyage.

Money spent in subsidising the fares came from the sale of land. The price of Australia's virgin land rose in quick leaps, becoming much dearer than virgin land in most of the new regions of North America. In many years half the revenue from the sale of land was spent in bringing out migrants. In the long period extending to the 1960s, over half the migrants setting out for Australia and New Zealand paid little or nothing towards their fare. So, by the early 1830s, was established one of the main social differences between Australia and North America.

An official agent in the British Isles usually selected the migrants, the public purse paid most or all of their fare, and after they stepped ashore they were often housed or cared for by the government during the first weeks, especially if new jobs were scarce. As most migrants were subsidised, they tended to lean on the government that initially cared for them. Self-help dominated American attitudes, but a preference for the welfare state was to be a common Australian attitude. Whereas North America's immigrants largely selected themselves, Australia's were chosen partly to serve the needs of the country they were settling in. So the young were preferred over the old, the fit over the unfit, the skilled tradesman over the labourer, the British over the foreigner, and often, to correct the shortage of women, the female over the male.

Women were reluctant to migrate to Australia: it was remote and strange, its daily way of life was often hard, and it carried the convict taint. As women were outnumbered in Australia, the British officials went out of their way to try to find women of marriageable age. Many orphan girls were chosen from Irish workhouses, and in the late 1840s at least 4,000 landed in Sydney. Some were cheeky and slovenly but others were eager to please the mistress of a house or the owner of a hotel. From Sydney in February 1850 a party of 105 Irish girls, fresh from their ship, set out in bullock-drawn drays for the inland town of Yass. Thirteen days they spent on the hot dusty road. Reaching Yass on Saturday evening, all but one attended mass the next morning, their clean hands and clothes and their good conduct winning quiet admiration from those who believed in such qualities. In the afternoon, women in search of a servant and men in search of a wife arrived at the recreation ground, there 'to feast their eyes on the dear creatures', said the newspaper, 'as they promenaded and gambolled arm-in-arm'.

For most of the century – except during the gold rushes – Australia tended to attract those migrants who were slightly less willing to stand on their own feet than those going to the United States. Australia received many migrants who came from cities and wished to continue living in a city. Moreover the dearness of land and the erratic rainfall did not help Australia compete with North America as the goal for rural migrants. A would-be farmer was less likely to sail to Sydney than to New York. Australia-bound migrants increasingly came from London, Manchester and other cities and towns.

There was rarely an attempt to pay for foreigners to come as migrants. The Germans reaching South Australia in the 1840s and the Chinese entering Victoria in the following decade paid their own fare or borrowed the money. So Australia remained primarily a haven for British settlers at the very time when German migrants, followed by Italians, Scandinavians and eastern Europeans, poured into New York and Boston. Nothing did more to give Australia an ethnic unity than the practice of selecting and subsidising the migrants. This sense of unity was to encourage later generations of Australians to fight in Britain's wars on the far side of the world. In contrast, in the United States the ethnic disunity helped to deter that nation from fighting in foreign wars. Thus Australia's distance from Britain, and its consequent need to woo migrants, shaped another of the characteristics of the Australian people.

The long voyage was made safer by a widening web of regulations. A passenger had to be vaccinated against smallpox – many of course were vaccinated naturally because they had experienced the disease, as their pocked faces revealed. A list of clothes was specified for each subsidised immigrant about to sail to Australia in 1850. Thus a woman, in addition to her sheets and towels and two pounds of soap, had to carry in her luggage at least two gowns, two pairs of shoes, six pairs of stockings, two flannel or woollen petticoats and six shifts. Unless they arrived at the British port of embarkation with sufficient clothes for both the hot and cold parts of the voyage, they were not allowed to board the ship. The ship of course provided food, cooking equipment, cutlery and plates, and medical aid. It even provided mattresses and blankets, which could be finally claimed and taken ashore, free of charge, by those migrants who had 'behaved well on the voyage'.

Migrants offered a free passage had to be healthy, be willing to work initially for wages, and preferably had to possess a useful skill. People likely to be a burden on the government in Australia were not selected.

• • • • • • • • • •

In the early 1850s, subsidy was refused to any widow or widower bringing out children because, if the sole parent died, 'the children would be left friendless and destitute in a strange land'. Families with more than four young children were not eligible for a free fare on the grounds that too many children travelling in the same ship increased 'the risk of disease and mortality'. A migrant ship then, even more than a cruise liner today, was an incubator of ailments.

To be present at a funeral service was a normal part of a passenger's experience. Babies, toddlers and children to the age of about seven were very vulnerable to infections. In the 1850s in a typical ship carrying 300 or so migrants, six or seven babies might be born at sea; and they were also vulnerable to infection. The food available in ships was partly blamed for infants' deaths. Eventually it was decreed that special food and liquids, including preserved soup and eggs, be supplied to infants between the ages of four months and two years. On the long voyage the eggs for babies were not always fresh. A daily allowance of water and a quarter of a pint of milk also had to be set aside for each infant at sea. By this time, at least one cow was kept in a pen in each migrant ship.

4

As the flow of free migrants increased, the rights and liberties of a free society were granted to new settlers. Trial by jury in a civil lawsuit had been introduced as early as 1823, but in criminal cases it had to wait another sixteen years. By the mid-1830s the press was relatively free, and its owners had the privilege of posting, without paying postage, copies of newspapers to subscribers in outlying districts. In fact the press in Sydney was more free than in England where a heavy tax was still imposed on every copy of every newspaper printed.

A version of self-government slowly appeared, eating into the power of the resident governor and the government sitting in distant London. By the early 1840s the main cities gained their own municipal councils. In 1843, New South Wales had its own legislative council with twenty-four elected members and twelve nominated by the governor. While the governor had to approve all laws that were passed, the council had its right of veto. It was a hesitant half-step towards self-government. That step was to become more positive in the more prosperous, populous colonies. Australians who wanted more say in their own future clamoured for self-government, but the victory was really won for them by the Canadians. The Canadian rebellion of 1837 eventually won self-government for most parts of Canada. Nova Scotia, with a population about as large as that of New South Wales, became in 1848 the first British colony to govern itself in most matters. Two years later the main Australian colonies were invited to take the same path, and to submit to London, for approval, a draft of a constitution determining how each should be governed. It is said, sometimes with barely concealed regret, that Australians largely won their independence without the aid of a revolution on their own soil. It is little known that Canadians, mainly French Canadians, fought and won that revolution for Australians.

New technology was as important as new freedoms in enabling Australians to shape their future. More and more ships entered the England–Australia run, and the sailing time was reduced to about four or five months, speeding the flow of new ideas and products to Australia. One of the great discoveries in the history of the world, the use of anaesthetics to relieve pain, almost flew to Tasmania in 1847. In Launceston a doctor, inspired by an article in the latest issue of the *Illustrated London News*, made an apparatus through which to transmit ether to a suffering patient; and quickly he pulled out two double teeth from 'a young female who, for upwards of two years, had been suffering from disease of the lower jaw'. She then walked home – a testimony to the miracle.

Launceston, then Australia's fifth-largest town, was a mirror of the pace of change. Convicts could still be seen in the streets and workplaces; but the town formed its own savings bank to encourage thrift amongst the working people, and a brass band – perhaps the first in Australia – was financed by the advocates of temperance in the hope of providing sober amusements for the citizens.

Australia began to catch up to the British Isles in its institutions and amenities. Religion and education had long been neglected. Richard Johnson, an Anglican, had come to Sydney as chaplain with the First Fleet, giving his first sermon to assembled marines and convicts on the second Sunday ashore and realising that nearly all his words fell on stony ground. Reverend James Dixon, transported after being convicted of sedition, became the first Catholic priest. Such was the neglect of religion that in 1809 eastern Australia held 9,000 Britons but only one ordained clergyman. Six years later the first permanent Methodist clergyman arrived, followed eight years later by a Presbyterian. In the scarcity of clergymen the governor of a colony continued to fill several of the functions of a church leader. When drought set in, he might publicly set aside a day on which all colonists were asked to pray for rain. Governor Sir Richard Bourke had quick success, rain falling nine days later.

More churches were built, and more clergymen – even a bishop – came. John Polding arrived as Catholic bishop in 1835 and William Broughton as Anglican bishop a year later, making a grand total of fifty-eight clergymen in eastern Australia. In 1836 Governor Bourke made all denominations equal, to the disappointment of the Church of England. He poured money into the building of Anglican and nearly all other Christian churches, and as the Anglicans had the most adherents they were the main gainers. In Tasmania the governor also decided to pay for new churches and clergymen's salaries. By 1850, a sign of the revival of religion, it had more clergymen in relation to population than it would possess a century later. The spread of primary schools next door to the churches was another sign of the new religious vigour.

While many of the new churches built in suburbs and country towns were far too big for their existing congregations, a church building in the bush or outback was unusual – except where Scottish settlers gathered. In the 1840s one New South Wales squatter complained that he was visited only once a year by a Protestant clergyman, a 'flying visit' which allowed no time for divine service. His servants and shepherds were unlikely to see even the 'passing shadow' of that parson on his galloping visit. The same rural district supported six public houses but no church.

In political and intellectual life in the late 1840s many of the clergymen were the leaders. In New South Wales two Anglicans, Rev. R. L. King and Rev. W. B. Clarke, were the experts on Australian insects and geology, while in Tasmania the Reverend John West, a Congregationalist, was writing a large and learned volume, *The History of Tasmania*, which – a tribute to his literary and scholarly skills – is still read by historians. In many of the political and social crusades, clergymen spoke up, and West was one of many who denounced the continuing arrival of convicts.

5

The flood of free migrants endangered the old convict system. The two could not co-exist much longer. The taint of convictism, and the knowledge that most of the violent crimes were the work of escaped convicts or ex-convicts, convinced many free settlers in Tasmania that convictism was a curse. In New South Wales the sheep industry was now almost rich enough to provide the colony with the revenue and economic momentum once provided by the annual arrival of thousands of convicts and the funds that the British government sent to support them. Many squatters still wanted to employ the cheap labour of convicts, but they were not convinced that society as distinct from the economy gained from the presence of a vast open-air gaol operating inside and alongside a free society.

In the British parliament the critics were pointing out that the threat of 'transportation' did not necessarily deter their citizens from committing crimes. Nor was it always a satisfactory system in Australia, where it could corrupt rather than reform the convict. Moreover the punishment was a lottery. Criminals might become the servants of a kind Australian family, with more food and leisure than in England, and some convicts might become rich merchants and, from their high carriages drawn by stylish horses, look down on the governor in his ornate uniform, and congratulate themselves that they earned ten times his income. Probably in our eyes convictism, and especially the floggings, seems a harsh punishment; but the treatment of convicts conformed to the standards of an era when Europe's soldiers, sailors and schoolboys were treated to floggings often similar in harshness to those endured by convicts in Australia.

On the other hand an English parliamentary committee noted in 1838 that a convict could virtually become the slave of a harsh master: 'Compelled by the lash to work, until driven to desperation, he takes to the bush, and is shot down like a beast of prey'. In London, humanitarians thought it strange, in the very decade when they voted to abolish slavery in distant colonies of the British Empire, that another cruel form of servitude was practised on members of their own race in the distant convict colonies. The testimony against the convict system at its worst was sobering. Reverend W. B. Ullathorne, a young Catholic priest from Yorkshire, reached Sydney in 1833 as vicar-general and, travelling widely, saw the humiliation of convicts, many of them belonging to his own flock. He told how several prisoners, about to be hanged for further crimes which they had committed in the colony, 'dropped on their knees and thanked God that they were about to be delivered' from their misery.

Another high-security prison for those convicted of further offences was set up in Norfolk Island, a kind of Devil's Island. About 1,200 prisoners living there in the early 1840s were supervised not only by the official guards but by a 'Ring' or Mafia consisting of top-dog prisoners who rivalled the worst guard in cruelty. They would bite off part of the nose or ear of a disobedient convict. Captain Maconochie, reaching the island as commandant in 1840, addressed all the prisoners for the first time and, gazing at the heads turned towards him, realised that he had never seen such wild, demoniacal faces.

The English reformers who were determined to end the convict system won their first victory in New South Wales. The last convict ship – or so it was hoped – anchored in Sydney Harbour in November 1840. In New South Wales the number of convicts quickly fell away, as one by one their sentences expired. In 1845 there were still 16,800 convicts but a year later that number had declined to 11,200. Not everyone rejoiced to witness this decline. Many squatters lamented the loss of cheap labour and hoped that a new form of transportation would be adopted; and briefly it was in the late 1840s.

The gold rushes were finally to undermine the practice of sending British convicts to Tasmania. Why send them – as a punishment – to an island from which, once their sentence was completed, they could cross a narrow strait to the goldfields and either make a fortune or rob someone else of his? Tasmania received its last convicts from Britain when the ship *St Vincent* reached Hobart in May 1853. To newcomers the convicts were still one of the strange sights of this city of more than 20,000 people, and William Howitt described them 'in their close dresses of yellow flannel and leathern caps, working in different places about the streets, some of them wearing chains, some dragging trucks'.

• • • • • • • • • •

In 1855 the last convicts were transferred from Norfolk Island to Tasmania, which continued to guard those serving out long sentences.

The last colony to receive convicts fresh from the British Isles was Western Australia. Failing to attract free settlers, in desperation it became a convict settlement in 1850 in the hope of winning cheap labour and a subsidy from the British government. In January 1868 the last British convicts were landed in Western Australia. A few of these convicts, their sentences having long expired, were no doubt living anonymously as late as the time of World War I. It is statistically possible that at least one former convict was alive as late as World War II, when he would have been in his early nineties. Probably no record of his death will be found in the newspapers, because most convicts hid their past.

A total of 163,000 convicts had come to Australia since the arrival of the First Fleet. Some became law-abiding and shrewdly concealed their past from prying neighbours. One former convict was even elected to the first federal parliament in 1901. Some became the pillars of their bush church, and gravely handed around the collection plate, while others were living on the fruits of new robberies, or planning them. Years after the end of transportation a high proportion of the graver crimes committed in the free colonies were the work of former convicts.

The whole nation felt embarrassed by its convict past. In folklore the tendency was to magnify the brutality of the guards and to emphasise the original innocence of the convicts. For many decades, average Australians received their vivid picture of the convict era from Marcus Clarke, whose novel *For the Term of His Natural Life* originally was printed as a serial in a newspaper in the 1870s. A fluent painter-like writer, he loaded the dice in favour of the convicts and against the men who ruled over them. The hero, Rufus Dawes, transported to Tasmania for a crime he did not commit, becomes a prisoner at the terrible island prison at

Macquarie Harbour on the west coast of Tasmania. Marcus Clarke's celebrated book exaggerates the deaths in that island prison, reporting eighty-five in one year when actually they occurred over eleven years. One hundred lashes is the normal flogging in the novel; it is twenty-five lashes in the prison records. The novel, with dramatic licence, tells of two boy prisoners at Point Puer near Port Arthur, preferring to suicide by jumping off a high rock rather than go on living in utter misery. No such suicide is recorded in the prison's records.

More than a century later, Robert Hughes's wonderfully written history of the convicts, *The Fatal Shore*, was to entice more readers than any other book on Australia's history, but he loaded the dice when he likened the convict system to the Gulag Archipelago in the Soviet Union. From the Gulag, convicts did not emerge full of go, later rising to become some of their country's richest citizens. Hughes was also mistaken in his conclusion that a colony or region settled with convicts was doomed, long after the last convict came, to economic stagnation. The colony of New South Wales, originally occupying until 1851 all of that huge area stretching from Bass Strait to Torres Strait, was the main receptacle for convicts; it flourished as a convict colony and flourished when it ceased to be a convict colony. Queensland, beginning as a convict outpost, boomed once it became a home of the free.

. . . .

part two

'The Land I Love'

• • • • • • • • • •

The first gold rushes

Edward Hargraves, a lethargic young man on a slow horse, was the hero of Australia in 1851. He found gold, or at least persuaded others to find gold, beyond the mountain road that wandered west from Sydney. Perhaps no country in the modern world has opened a new half-century with such a momentous event.

He had worked at Gosford near Sydney, a kind of rolling stone, before he joined the rush to the goldfields in California in 1849. Thousands of Australians crossed the Pacific at that time, some of them former convicts who became notorious in California as thieves, thugs and 'Sydney Ducks'. Hargraves returned to Sydney with a few ounces of gold dust and the intuition that payable gold would be found somewhere in the interior.

While watching their flocks, shepherds had already found gold in the white quartz rock that obtruded above the ground in many places. Some shepherds had extracted small lumps of gold, selling them to city jewellers, and Hargraves realised that large patches of alluvial gold must lie buried near these rocks. This was gold which, over the ages, had been separated by attrition and erosion from the white quartz rock. It was easy to work, if anyone knew the Californian technique of extracting or washing the heavy gold from the lighter gravel by shaking the gold-bearing gravels in a wooden rocker or cradle. On the western side of the Blue Mountains early in 1851 he inspired three rural lads to look for specks of gold, which they finally found in a small creek – really a chain of waterholes – at the foot of steep hills. Hargraves, a remarkable publicist, christened the place Ophir. Those Australians who read the Old Testament knew that another Ophir, long ago, had sent vast amounts of gold and precious stones to King Solomon.

In the winter and spring of 1851 a chain of richer goldfields was found a few days' ride from Melbourne. During the following ten years Victoria supplied more gold than King Solomon had ever seen. So much gold was being mined in Victoria and California that London bankers predicted that everywhere the prices of all commodities would soar. They were correct: here was the fastest episode of inflation that the world experienced in the hundred years between the end of the Napoleonic Wars and the start of World War I. In Australia inflation was swifter than almost anywhere else.

2

Most goldfields lay more than 120 kilometres from the nearest port. There could never be enough inns or lodging tents for the crowds on the way, nor could most diggers have afforded them. In the first light of morning a horseman hurrying up-country would pass dozens of little camps where 'fires are blazing, steaks and chops are frizzling, pannikins are clattering, tea-kettles fizzing'. A few gold diggers rode horses but most walked. Those who crossed the seas to dig for gold felt their limbs and shoulders aching at the end of the first day on the road because they had been idle at sea for three or four months – the longest period of idleness in their working life. Right from the start men set out with loads heavier and more awkwardly packed than their backs and legs could stand. At the first rush to Buninyong in 1851 one man arrived 'wheeling a bag of flour' in a barrow. Soon, thousands of drays drawn by horses or bullocks were on the rough roads to the gold towns. Carriers and shopkeepers – the suppliers rather than the gold diggers – won the first small fortunes.

A few women dug for gold or opened shops in oblong tents with a flag flying from a tall pole to advertise their whereabouts in towns without the luxury of street-signs. An Englishwoman said she could usually tell when a woman was looking after a tent or hut: the tin plates and pannikins were clean and shining, the beds had sheets as well as blankets, and the bare earthen floor was covered with a stretch of carpet or a dry sack which might have once carried bran or flour. On the diggings, when husband was away, a pet cockatoo chained to a perch might serve as companion.

The first gold rush filled many old colonists with fear. Would law and order break down? Would a glimpse of so much gold being carried along the rough highways convert former convicts back into robbers? California in the grip of gold-fever was renowned for lawlessness and New South Wales could not expect to be less so. And where would the squatters find shepherds to replace those who had vanished to the diggings? Everything suddenly was upside down. A Sydney gentleman confided in 1852 that a brother of the Duchess of Marlborough could be seen at the gold diggings wearing a blue flannel shirt and working with dirty hands alongside a former convict. 'All the comforts and many of the decencies of life', he sadly added, 'are abandoned or disregarded.'

The rushes were a remarkable turnaround in the allocation of resources. Australia's first big resource, the grasslands, had been allowed to pass temporarily to maybe less than a thousand squatters; thereafter the task of legislators was to cut up those domains and divert much of it to small farmers. In contrast, in 1851 the potentially gold-bearing ground had been cut into tiny plots. Therefore everyone who reached a goldfield would have a chance of finding it, and therefore be less tempted to riot or to steal. A gold digger usually was allowed to peg out a surface area no larger than the average bedroom of today's Australian house. This meant that the gold was apportioned into tens of thousands of hands, with no fortune being dug by just one man. Whereas the first wool rushes favoured the accumulation of wealth in few hands, the first gold rushes distributed the grains of gold into a host of hands. In effect the gold rushes were astonishingly democratic.

A new country often faces a crisis when a new resource, whether land or gold, is suddenly thrown open, or the rules of access are suddenly changed. Even wise rulers could rarely cope with such unexpected events as the dynamic dispersal of the squatters and their sheep, the discovery of gold, the later land-craving of small farmers, or the demands for the return of vast lands to Aborigines in recent times. The crisis of 1851, however, was handled by the government in Sydney with a blend of flair and common sense. All people willing to handle pick and shovel were given, once they paid a large monthly fee, the right to dig for gold on a small area of promising ground. If they could not afford the monthly fee they had to return home. By 1854, however, the solutions of three years previously were hopelessly inept for the deeper mines at Ballarat. Many miners spent up to eight months sinking a shaft of perhaps 50 metres depth in their search for gold, and in that time they received no income. Why they should they pay a high sum for a monthly licence. Those who governed Victoria did not understand the new mining conditions.

Miners resented the dear and discriminatory tax they had to pay and the high-handed tactics of the police and other authorities. On the

Ballarat goldfield in 1854, amidst rising tension, thousands of protesters gathered beneath a handsome revolutionary pennant of dark-blue and white. Called the flag of the Southern Cross, it remains to this day a radical and republican symbol. It is now a secular symbol though it looks more a Celtic and Christian cross than the familiar, straggling constellation in the night sky. Irish miners were very prominent in the uprising. The leader, Peter Lalor, had recently arrived from Ireland, and the site of the armed rebellion was squeezed into vacant land between the deep shafts worked largely by Irish teams of working owners.

Behind a makeshift barricade or stockade, the more dedicated of the agitators hoarded firearms and manufactured iron pikes. They proclaimed themselves as rebels, swore an oath of loyalty by the Southern Cross, rather than the British flag, and burned their gold licences, which were in effect identity cards. The Victorian government had to respond. At dawn on Sunday 3 December, on foot and horseback, its forces stormed the stockade. At least thirty miners and five soldiers were killed. Peter Lalor lost his left arm. A selection of rebels was sent to Melbourne to face the serious charge of treason, but the juries refused to convict them.

The Eureka Stockade still fires the imagination of many Australians. Until World War II it was frequently commemorated by orators and poets as the only battle fought on Australian soil, though this claim overlooked the earlier battles fought between Aborigines and the later battles between Aborigines and European settlers. Eureka indirectly promoted democracy in Victoria. It is said to be the birthplace of Australian democracy and is fervently acclaimed by scholars who believe that revolutions can work wonders; but that is not a persuasive argument when applied to Australian history. Australia's democracy was born in the parliament on the banks of the River Thames as well as in the stockade at Ballarat. Moreover, the democratic impetus was strong in Adelaide, Sydney, Melbourne and Launceston as well in the Victorian goldfields. Indeed an early citadel of democracy was respectable, law-abiding South Australia, which so far had experienced no gold rush.

One result of the Eureka uprising was the allocating of a larger area of gold-bearing ground to each miner and syndicate in Ballarat. Increasingly miners were to join together to form co-operatives and companies, sink deep shafts, and erect big stamp mills to crush the gold-bearing rock. The rebellion paved the way for capitalism on the goldfields.

In the first years thousands won a small fortune from shallow gold dug with pick and shovel. A procession of lucky ones returned to Europe by way of Cape Horn in fast sailing ships, their own gold stowed in the ship's strong room. They astonished British friends with the gold they displayed. The hardships of their life were not always reported: days of working in holes where the water covered their boots, sleeping in wet blankets, bouts of dysentery, and eyes sore in a long dusty summer. Many who went to the diggings were crushed by earth falls, murdered by unknown persons on the road, or run over by drays – a common cause of death for those who drank heavily and fell asleep on the road. Occasionally the government would publish a long list of people who had died, leaving behind gold and other possessions but no known relative in Victoria. The larger post offices held thousands of letters, mostly from England, and still not collected after six months. The person to whom the letter was addressed might not have died, but have simply moved on. Here was a land of missing persons.

3

Gold was found on grassy sheep runs, in the forests and in steep valleys. Sometimes 30,000 Victorians would rush to a new find, and a tent city or bark village would arise, quickly declining if the field proved shallow. By the mid-1850s thousands of men were busily searching for new goldfields. They worked in secrecy, covering their new-dug holes with branches for fear that a passer-by might come across their find and take up ground alongside before they could decide which area was likely to be richest. Andrew Thunder's experience at Beaufort, which now stands on the highway between Adelaide and Melbourne, demonstrated the reasons for secrecy. A digger, he was out strolling when he heard the unmistakeable sound of the digger's cradle, rocking up and down the wet gold-bearing dirt and gravel; the tell-tale sound he described as 'dumpedy dump'. He soon saw a man and three lads working the cradle and carrying up buckets of water from a creek nearby. Their hearts must have pulsed when Andrew Thunder suddenly appeared and posed that question which must have been asked a million times in the 1850s: 'Hello, mate! What luck?' The question was answered by silence. Thunder instantly knew that they had found gold. He took up ground nearby and began to sink a hole.

Once a discovery was known, the word spread like a bushfire. Butchers and bakers, grocers, blacksmiths, gold-buyers and sly-grog sellers set up shops for the stampede of diggers. At one time 15,000 people were said to be at Beaufort, alias Fiery Creek.

The big goldfields were memorable after dark. Outside many huts the small log fires were burning, with sitting or standing men silhouetted against them. There was a sound of dogs barking, the crisp music rising from a long axe splitting firewood, perhaps shotguns and revolvers being fired as a sign of high spirits or, occasionally, bad spirits. Late on Saturday nights came the shouts of revellers trying to find a path through the honeycombed ground to their own tent. And, at last, the silence.

After a goldfield had been working for three months there was an air of devastation. The ground was overturned, the trees chopped down, and the creeks clogged with silt discarded by the gold-washing appliances. Like locusts the diggers devoured wood. They burned it, they built huts with it, they lined their deepening shafts with it, and in winter they laid long saplings side by side to form a road over muddy patches of ground. Soon hundreds of firewood cutters and carters were making their living. On a goldfield, nine of every ten men were diggers, but eventually they were outnumbered by those who served and supplied them.

Victoria could not produce more than a fraction of the food and other goods demanded by the gold diggers. Flour came from as far away as Chile. Hay for the horses came in shiploads from South Australia, palings and fence posts from Tasmania, and beer and brandy, boots and bonnets and lollies from England. Ornate buildings of iron – houses, churches, schools and even a theatre – came in prefabricated pieces from England and were assembled in Melbourne where the sun beating down on the iron turned the rooms into hothouses. Sailing ships arrived from Boston with cargoes consisting entirely of ice, much of which had melted during the voyage through the tropics. From Melbourne the ice was rushed in carts and coaches to local hotels and up-country dining rooms and served as a luxury. Melbourne's average income was probably the highest of any city in the world while the gold was arriving from the new diggings.

It was astonishing, in this once-isolated country, to see so many ships arriving from distant ports. Each week throughout 1853 an average of five British sailing ships set out for Melbourne, commencing a voyage in which, after the shores of England or Ireland sank low on the horizon, no further land was glimpsed for another two or three months. In the course of that long voyage few passing ships were seen by passengers. In the wild seas of the roaring forties or fifties of the southern Indian Ocean, a few passenger ships were swamped by giant waves or crushed by icebergs. More were wrecked when they came in sight of Australian shores.

The first gold rushes

• • • • • • • • • •

Other ships came, crammed with Chinese. In 1855 more than thirty of these ships reached Melbourne, and the Cantonese passengers went on foot to the goldfields. Perhaps the largest Chinese town arose at the foot of the long basalt plateau at Guildford, where some 6,000 migrants – nearly all Chinese and nearly all men – could pay for the services of Chinese stores, shoe-menders, barbers, herbalists, restaurants, a theatre and temple as well as fortune-tellers. The Chinese seemed too strange, in dress and eating habits, language and rituals and religion, to be easily welcomed by most diggers. When in 1858 they numbered more than 40,000, or close to one in ten of Victoria's population, the common fear was that the inrush might never be halted.

Victoria imposed a tax on incoming Chinese, who then opened a back door by walking overland in long crocodiles across the plains from South Australia where at first no landing tax was collected. The spearhead of the gold rushes was to dart around the rim of the continent in an anti-clockwise direction, the first exciting Queensland rush being in Gympie – near the present Sunshine Coast – in 1867. One by one the other colonies imposed taxes on Chinese, with Western Australia going the furthest in 1886 by virtually banning Chinese from working on new fields.

Gold set in motion an economic and social revolution. The population, which numbered 405,000 in 1850, was to exceed 1,000,000 in 1858. The inflow of gold-rush migrants in just two years exceeded the grand total of convicts who had arrived in the eighty years of transportation. For the very first time Australia could stand some kind of comparison with the United States. Twice as many migrants came to Australia in the 1850s as went to the United States in the three decades from 1800 to 1830.

Golden Victoria was the main goal for these migrants, and its population jumped in ten years from 76,000 to the astonishing total of 540,000, making it much the biggest colony in 1860. For a year or two Victoria held over half of Australia's population. For more than a quarter of a century Melbourne and the small gold cities of Ballarat and Bendigo were three of the country's five main cities. Melbourne itself outgrew Sydney. By the 1860s several Gothic spires and church steeples capped its skyline, the head offices of the banks were grand, the new university ran the country's first medical school, and a remarkable public library was the envy of most North American cities. A torrent of fresh water was carried along an aqueduct to the city from a reservoir at the foot of a wooded mountain, and the busy streets were lit by gas. On almost every night the live theatres were open, and opera had its season. Stirring preachers were eagerly heard in churches which now provided enough seats for at least one in every three people living in Victoria.

In the leading colonies the progress that might normally have been spread over three decades was – through the impact of gold – squeezed into one. In the 1850s the first railways were built, a telegraph line linked Adelaide and Melbourne and Sydney, the first paddle steamer went from South Australia far up the Murray River, and the fast horse coaches of Cobb & Co ran their passenger and mail services to inland towns on a tight timetable. The world's fastest sailing ships, including the clippers *Lightning* and *Champion of the Seas*, cut weeks from the average journey between Liverpool and Melbourne, and the first overseas steamships – with the aid of sails – plied between England and Australia.

The economy was strengthened because it now possessed two powerful exports – gold and wool – instead of one. Gold output probably peaked in 1856 and slowly the shallow diggings gave way to deeper mines worked by companies whose shares were traded on the dozens of stock exchanges, of which at least one could be found in each large mining town. Wool recovered from the labour shortages of the first gold years, but not until 1870 did it again challenge gold for the title of the main export.

The population map of Australia was lopsided, because nearly all people were concentrated in the cooler south-east corner. It was like a Europe in which Scandinavia possessed nearly all the towns and wealth. And yet it was logical to expect that other parts of the huge continent would prove to be just as attractive. As the remote interior was not yet explored, perhaps other fertile regions might be found; and hardly a year passed without an exploring party setting out from the coast. Surely an inland sea surrounded by fertile soil, surely some mysterious Nile, must exist. Ever since the 1820s these parties, with their bullock carts and riding horses and often their Aboriginal helpers and guides and interpreters, had set out to the sound of three loud cheers from those farewelling them. John Oxley, Allan Cunningham, Charles Sturt, Hume and Hovell, Edward Eyre, Major Thomas Mitchell, Ludwig Leichhardt, Augustus Gregory and many more strode or rode across lands which Aborigines had settled thousands of years earlier. Sometimes they carried wooden boats just in case they found the inland sea. Many explorers were disappointed. In ideal seasons they saw fast-flowing creeks and waving grasslands, which had often vanished by the time the next Europeans arrived.

4

The unquenchable desire to find new pastures for livestock, the hope of finding gold or silver, and the wish to find an overland route from southern to northern Australia, spurred another burst of exploration in 1860. There was also sheer curiosity to unravel the wonders of what Governor Barkly of Victoria called 'this most exceptional and extraordinary portion of the globe'. From Adelaide bold John McDouall Stuart made three attempts to travel from south to north. His right eye was so damaged that, he recorded pitifully, 'I now see two suns instead of one'. On his third attempt he reached the warm northern sea just to the east of the site where Darwin arose a decade later. His route was followed in 1872 by the telegraph line which, linking Adelaide and Darwin, carried telegrams over the land and under the sea to distant Indian and European cities.

The winner and loser of the contest to cross the continent was the fatal expedition led by Burke and Wills. Late in 1860, after travelling from Melbourne, it reached Cooper's Creek in south-west Queensland. With two other men, Burke and Wills loaded camels and decided, travelling lightly, to make a dash to the Gulf of Carpentaria and back again. Another four men, left behind to guard the supplies until Burke and Wills returned, built a little stockade of boughs and tree branches. Inside they pitched a tent to hold guns and ammunition. They spent the next four months there, nervous of nearby Aborigines and racked by the heat which once tipped 47 degrees Celsius in the shade of the tent. Eventually the caretakers decided they had waited long enough in their stockade. Packing most of their possessions, they rounded up their horses and camels and went south towards civilisation.

Burke and Wills, having reached the Gulf and turned for home, were dismayed by the intense heat of midday. When the moon was bright they travelled in the cool of night. Perhaps no previous explorers had been forced to 'explore' so often by the light of the moon. At last, on Sunday 21 April 1861, in the hope of speedily reaching their own stockade in the interior, the three surviving explorers threw away surplus supplies so that they could ride rather than walk. That day the two weak camels walked a remarkable fifty kilometres. Their riders did not realise that on the same morning the caretakers had abandoned the stockade and were retreating to the south.

In the moonlight Burke on one camel and Wills and King sharing the other felt confident that a welcome awaited them at the stockade. From his high seat on the camel Burke could almost see the stockade in the distance. In the eerie light he called out that he could see the tents of his waiting men. There were no tents.

After Burke and Wills died, far from help, it was widely assumed that Australia's interior would always be frustrating. It was not the whole truth. Sheep-owners were soon occupying land the explorers had traversed, and in lush years their sheep even grazed near the site of the stockade at Cooper's Creek. A century after their death a major field of natural gas was found not far from the site of the stockade, and today its gas is piped to Adelaide and Sydney. The capacity of the continent to surprise is as characteristic as its ability to destroy.

Some were keener on prospecting the heavens than the earth. One of the finest astronomers of the century, John Tebbutt, lived in obscurity in the valley of the Hawkesbury River, where his father was a farmer. John attended no university and never set foot outside Australia. His love of astronomy came from a village schoolteacher. He himself learned enough French and German to read foreign journals, and with the aid of a telescope and other instruments he made discovery after discovery that brought delight to readers of those journals. He lived until World War I but more than half a century previously, just before his twenty-seventh birthday, he made a discovery that every astronomer of Europe would love to have made.

Six comets of exceptional brilliance were found in the sky in the nineteenth century, but Tebbutt's own comet was vowed by some scholars to be the most startling. He first saw it in the night sky on 13 May 1861 – perhaps Burke and Wills also saw it in their last days. At first the comet was hardly worth noticing but it became elongated, and at its most dazzling its tail was a thin luminous trail stretching across the sky for more than 80 degrees. On 30 June it was first visible in Europe and caused a stir. For decades Tebbutt was to find what no others had yet seen in the night sky. Long after his death he was allowed to sit on one side of Australia's one hundred dollar note, so receiving more fame than he enjoyed in his lifetime.

In the capital cities, Australians – mostly the new migrants – were making a less dramatic kind of discovery, but no less difficult. In the mid-1850s they were discovering how to organise free large-scale elections and to conduct a parliament. A few years previously they had been promised the right to govern themselves – except in foreign policy – but would all men or only a small minority be allowed to be the governors?

In 1850 the British government made the initial decision that thereafter the new Australian parliaments could alter if they wished. In a remarkable decision Britain decided that any male Australian who owned a small property or any householder who paid a rent of ten pounds a year could have the vote. After gold was found in Australia a year later all prices and rents soared, and soon nearly everyone who lived in a town was paying an annual rent of at least ten pounds and was therefore entitled to vote. By 1856, 95 per cent of the men in Sydney were entitled to a vote, though in rural districts and goldfields fewer men qualified as voters because tents and huts were the norm and rents and values were low. In New South Wales the new parliament in 1858 went a step further and theoretically gave every man the right to vote. The historian John Hirst calls it 'the most rapid political transformation in Australian history'.

The new parliaments in Victoria and South Australia were even quicker to grant to all men the right to vote, at least for the lower house. South Australia granted the vote even though it was under no pressure from a swarm of gold diggers who saw the vote as an answer to grievances. The most exclusive colony, it held probably the most educated and certainly the most devout and law-abiding population. It also had perhaps the most cohesive population, consisting largely of English with fewer Irish and Scottish. Many of its citizens probably believed – more than is believed today – that democracy required in its voters a strong sense of civic responsibility as well as a quota of self-interest. They did not fear that democracy would give too much power to the irresponsible. Such people, in their view, were less likely to be found in South Australia than in the other colonies and indeed than in the British Isles.

Every colony had influential citizens who did not want democracy to be extended to all men. They were willing to go further than England's democracy, where less than one in five men had the right to vote, but they were wary of going too far along a path paved by raw public opinion. They knew that a minority of the potential Australian voters could not read or write, and many were ex-convicts. Moreover the year 1848 had seen many revolutions in Europe: government by the mob was a living fear.

Richard Dry, an experienced Tasmanian politician, clearly expressed this hot-cold vision of what colonial democracy should be. The lower house should represent the views of 'the great mass of the people'. For that house every loyal male should have the right to contest an election. After all, that was already the law in Scotland, though not in England. Almost every man should also have the right to vote in such elections – except 'the class which it is absolutely desirable to exclude, namely the dissolute and improvident'. In contrast the small upper house or legislative council was to consist of older men and they were to be elected – each for a long period – by those who owned property in Tasmania. The lower house was to be the home of 'innovation' while the upper house was to be a small forum displaying caution, experience and moderation. In every colony the upper house was initially seen in this light.

Australia now is possibly one of the three oldest, continuous democracies in the world. Even in 1860 it could make a claim to be a rare stronghold of democracy. Nine of every ten Australians lived in colonies where every man had the right to vote, where politicians in the lower house had to stand for re-election no later than every three years, and where voting was conducted by that revolutionary secret ballot, known later in America as the Victorian or Australian ballot. Even the Aborigines living in the more populous colonies had the right to vote, though few entered a polling booth. At this time Australia was more democratic than the United States, where slaves, existing in their millions until 1865, had no right to vote. Admittedly, democratic France was sometimes compared favourably with Australia, and every Frenchman now had a vote for the lower house; but a gap of six years separated elections, the French press was censored, and many stalwarts of the opposition were forced to live in exile.

At the same time there were brakes on democracy in Australia. In each colony an elected upper house, consisting mainly of propertied men, could thwart the will of the lower house, for every bill had to be passed by both houses. Occasionally, bills passed by both houses were delayed or rejected by London, especially if they dealt with foreign policy which, strictly speaking, was the preserve of the British government. And yet each colony soon had complete economic autonomy. Victoria from the 1860s could place duties on British imports, which it did with pleasure. In essence, economic independence came quickly to Australia – except to the convict colony of Western Australia. Full political independence, if there is such a state of being, did not come until the next century.

Australians had achieved an advanced form of democracy mainly by peaceful activity. It came easily. But it was not so easy for the newly elected parliaments and ministries to legislate and govern, what with the fast growth of population, the mobility of people in search of gold, the need to set up free institutions so quickly, and the fierce inflation of the 1850s which made it hard to run a colony's finances. Even the finest 200 politicians in the free world – and Australia can have possessed only one or two of them – would not have coped easily.

• • • • • • • • • •

From England, in cottages and castles, the brave democratic experiment was looked on with mingled delight, awe and alarm. Would it really succeed? Most of the Australian politicians who became ministers of the crown had had no experience of governing: most did not even have the right to vote before they emigrated. Bribery of politicians was probably widespread in the first years though it was to become abnormal, so far as we know. The Unitarian clergyman, John Martineau, heard in the late 1860s that any bill might be passed by the parliament in Melbourne if the sum of 15,000 pounds was 'judiciously expended in bribes'. He privately passed on this opinion to an experienced politician who promptly replied that much less than 15,000 pounds was needed. It was almost a miracle that democracy, launched in such a tumultuous era, worked well.

The age of the marvellous

Almost everyone in Australia was aware of a momentous change taking place by the 1870s though few foresaw how far it would extend. It would reshape Australia, swiftly in some places and slowly in others, because it transformed work, leisure and travel. It was first called steam power though significantly it was measured in horsepower, a tribute to the animal it was to supersede.

Australia hitherto depended heavily on the patience and strength of animals. While cattle produced milk for drinking, beef for eating and hides for the making of leather, they were also vital for power. Drays pulled by bullocks carried bales of wool on the long journey from shearing shed to wharf, the bales stacked so high that in gusty weather the drays crossing the plains resembled little galleons in the wind. The bullock was the long-distance carrier, with the horse a poor second. To the mountain goldfields a procession of packhorses carried supplies. At the mines were workhorses, on the surface or far below. On the farms the heavy horses pulled the plough and also the harvesting machine, and for a time Tasmanians favoured the Shire horse, the Hunter Valley favoured the Suffolk Punch, and the German farmers of South Australia favoured the Schleswig. Later the noble Scottish horse, the Clydesdale, dominated wheat farms.

A dozen occupations, ranging from farmer to harness-maker, centred on the needs of horses. On long mail routes the fast horses drew the mail coach. In cities the street trains and omnibuses as well as the delivery vans were drawn by horses. So was the early taxi, the two-wheeled hansom cab. The first big-selling crime novel in the English language, written by young Fergus Hume and published in 1886 under the title of *The Mystery of a Hansom Cab*, began with a man in evening dress hailing a cab outside Scots Church in Collins Street, Melbourne. From the 1830s to the 1930s the country exported half a million horses, mostly geldings, to India where they were seen in parades of British cavalry, on the polo grounds and on the racecourses, everywhere being known as 'Walers' because they originally came from New South Wales.

Dogs were work animals whereas today they are more often city pets. At first the 'kangaroo dog' was a vital servant in rural areas. A hunting dog, it was usually part deerhound or greyhound, often of Scottish ancestry, with perhaps a dash of mastiff or even bulldog. It hunted kangaroos and later English rabbits, which were imported too successfully. Explorers usually set out with a dog or two, and in 1845 when Charles Sturt left Adelaide for the unknown interior he had six dogs and eleven horses. On the vast newly fenced plains in the 1870s the sheep dog became vital. It was bred mainly from the short-haired Scotch collie and, some say, the dingo.

2

Economic life would have almost collapsed without the animals, but animal power was now challenged by steam. In the conveying of goods and passengers, the steam engine intruded into the domain of bullocks and horses. In lifting heavy weights the engine was supreme. It carried miners and small hand-trucks of golden ore from the depths of the earth, thus enabling mines to go deeper. In 1880 at Stawell in Victoria the Magdala gold mine was nearly a kilometre deep. In Stawell's mines were nearly fifty steam engines, puffing and throbbing. Steam also operated pumps for irrigation, heavy hammers in the foundries, rollers in the biscuit factories and flour mills, and the saw in the timber mills.

David Syme's Melbourne *Age* and other penny newspapers owed much to the steam-driven printing presses. In wheat districts a threshing machine with its steam engine lumbered along the roads to farms where it separated grain from straw. The steam engine made artificial ice and froze food: Geelong newspaper editor James Harrison was a world pioneer in refrigeration in the 1850s. Three decades later F. Y. Wolseley installed steam engines at the outback shearing sheds where his shearing machine began to supplant the blade shears. On many city wharves the cumbersome steam cranes lifted cargo from a ship's hold, though the procession of wharf labourers carrying heavy bags of coal or wheat on their shoulders was to be visible for decades.

Nothing did more than steam to change daily life in the years from 1860 to 1900. It altered men's work but women still lacked mechanical help in their daily tasks of cooking and preserving food, in sweeping and cleaning, the washing and drying of dishes and polishing of lamps, the scrubbing of wooden floors and wooden tables, and the ironing and starching of clothes. The gas lamp, gas stove and electric refrigerator and washing machine were to be among their liberators. The steam engine – and its suitability for heavy manual tasks – helps to explain why the shorter working week came to men long before it came to women.

The era of steam depended on cheap firewood, and so the cutting, carting and stacking of firewood might well have been the biggest single employer of labour in Australia. In contrast, the steamships – except Murray River paddle steamers – and foundries and certain engines preferred coal. Ports began to reek of coal smoke. On blue days in the late 1880s, when travellers stood on deck as their ship slowly steamed up the harbour towards Adelaide or Sydney, they saw, above the skyline of ships' masts and church spires and tall trees, the haze of smoke. Surviving photos of the cities rarely capture the smoke haze or the smoke rising from hundreds of chimneys in factories, hospitals, gasworks, railway yards and docks. A photographer who was determined to snap a view of the expanding cities in all their glory waited until Sunday or a public holiday when less firewood and coal were burned.

By the 1880s most migrants came in steamships. With the aid of the Suez Canal, the voyage took less than seven weeks. At each Australian port the heavy canvas bags of overseas mail were unloaded, and the main post office flew a special flag on its tower to announce that the overseas mail had arrived. When the ship was about to leave again for England the clerks in banks, importing houses and government offices were dipping pen into inkwell almost until the hour when the ship sailed, all urgently completing their reports for London. The handwritten letters from British-born colonists, especially from women, filled many of the outgoing mail bags. A postage stamp, however, was still expensive. A labourer might work for thirty minutes, a female housemaid for one hour, in order to pay for just one letter to be posted to England.

Steam worked miracles on land as well as sea. Politicians believed that the steam train could convert their continent into a second United States. Thomas McCombie told the parliament in Melbourne in December 1856 that 'the period would soon arrive when that mighty civilizer, the railway, would be carried throughout the length and breadth of this vast continent'. Victoria so far had only one short railway running from Melbourne to its port, but many other politicians and merchants shared McCombie's confidence that the railways would create a chain of inland towns that traversed the continent.

To build railways was expensive because the wages of Australian labourers were high. Moreover the first railways were designed to impress with their fine stations and, often, two parallel tracks where one would have sufficed. The 1870s and 1880s saw the first boom in constructing railways. In some years, along the routes of new railways, there must have been close to 30,000 railway navvies and a few thousand women and children camped in tent villages. Today there is hardly a trace of most of these towns and their narrow main street of grog shanties, general stores and portable schools, though an excavation would no doubt find plenty of buried liquor bottles, all empty.

One stretch of railway in New South Wales was especially admired. Running along the western shoulders and sides of the Blue Mountains, it was known as the Lithgow Zig Zag and was sometimes described as 'stupendous'. It enabled trains to descend into the Lithgow valley, following cuttings and tunnels blasted from rock, crawling along narrow ledges, and crossing ravines on bridges made of many arches. For about eight kilometres, the train slowly descended in a series of ramps designed like a zigzag, so that along one ramp the locomotive would pull the train and along the next ramp it would push the train, eventually reaching the bottom at Bowenfels. Before most of the trunk railways had been constructed across the alps of Switzerland, the Zig Zag was seen by proud Australians as one of the world's eye-opening projects in engineering.

It did not provide a speedy journey. The early trains took six hours to travel from Sydney to Lithgow, less than 160 kilometres away. While Sydney engineers took pride in the Zig Zag, the Victorians took pride in their railways built on a gauge broader than Europe's and the locomotives and carriages built at the big Phoenix Foundry at Ballarat and at the government's workshops at Newport.

Between 1871 and 1891 the length of railways open in Australia was multiplied by nine. Considering the vast distances and the small population, Australia was perhaps the most impressive builder of railways in the world. The cost was high, and about 100 million pounds had been spent by the early 1890s. The paying of the interest on these long-term loans tended to dominate the annual budgets of most of the colonial governments. But the cost of cartage from the hinterland was revolutionised. Without railways the wheat belts could not have been opened, far-off mining fields would have been less productive, and drought would have been more damaging to the pastoralists.

At last passengers could travel in a train all the way from Adelaide through Melbourne and Sydney to Brisbane. The final link in that long route was the completing of the railway bridge across the Hawkesbury estuary in 1889 − the bridge's surviving pillars can be seen from aircraft flying into Sydney. It was still impossible to go to Western Australia or to central and north Queensland by train. The longest train journey available commenced at the new silverfield of Broken Hill, in the far west of New South Wales, and proceeded to Adelaide, Melbourne, Sydney and Brisbane and then some 800 kilometres westwards to Charleville, on the plains. Depending on the timetables, it occupied about a week.

On a long journey there were many delays and much transferring from train to train. Perhaps no journey was possible in the same train for more than twenty-four hours. Passengers reaching a capital city in the morning usually had to wait there until evening when the all-night express was ready to leave for another capital city. One cause of delay for passengers was the need to change trains at border towns because of the break of gauge. The busy stations where everybody had to change trains, moving themselves and their luggage from one side of the platform to the other, included Albury on the southern border of New South Wales, Wallengara on the northern border and various inland towns in South Australia.

South Australia and Victoria had built most of their railways on the very wide gauge, at a width of five feet three inches, New South Wales chose four feet eight and a half inches, and all other colonies deliberately selected the narrow gauge of three feet six inches. On the long plains and in the mountains, the narrow gauge allowed the building of a cheaper railway. By the 1890s nearly half the railway lines were narrow in gauge.

Now it is common to chastise engineers for building railways which could never form an efficient working system for a nation; but the engineers were not as silly as they are portrayed. Their aim was to link each port with its back-country rather than to form a national grid linking the main cities. As the capital cities were all on the coast and connected to one another by sea, and as a ship could still outbid a train in cheaply carrying freight and passengers, the inter-city expresses were favoured only by the wealthy and the express mails. Later, as coastal shipping lost its efficiency, inter-city railways became vital. Only then did the break of gauge become a cause of recrimination.

An excited, even a jubilant, buzz was heard in the main street when news arrived that parliament had approved the extending of the railway to that inland town. A daily train reshaped nearly every facet of personal, social and political life, especially in towns that were more than 300 kilometres from the sea. The train brought the latest city and overseas newspapers and the heavy bags of letters and parcels, perhaps twelve or twenty-four hours ahead of the time when they previously arrived. At Christmas time the train carried relatives and friends who previously had refused to endure the long and very expensive journey in a horse-drawn coach. In a drought the goods train arrived with hay from a district where rain had fallen. To the distant port the train carried away wool and wheat at lower prices.

When the local doctor treating a feverish patient called for a special medicine or perhaps a small consignment of ice, the train brought them with speed from a bigger town. If the patients did not recover, there was now a prospect that their relatives elsewhere in the colony could arrive in time for the funeral: in the era before refrigeration, a funeral was held only one or two days after the death.

Not everything arriving in the new trains was welcomed. The trains cut the cost of transport; and so the owners of the towns' little brewery – with its three employees – suddenly realised that barrels of beer arriving cheaply on the new railway from a big city brewery outsold the local barrels and might soon shut them down. The drivers and owners of the bullock carts and horse-drawn mail coaches often cursed the railway, which took over their business as long-distance carriers. But for every citizen who cursed, ten cheered. Most readers of Henry Lawson's poems agreed with his verse recalling that Progress and a new form of Civilisation reached the plains on the day the first steam train came puffing in: 'The mighty Bush with iron rails / Is tethered to the world.'

The writers and painters who in the 1890s were giving people a new sense of identity could not have preached their message but for the advance of the railways. Trains reduced the cost of travel in time, money and physical weariness. Henry Lawson knew that the train could travel maybe 350 miles on a winter's night, whereas the passengers who were jolting about in the cramped horse-drawn coach of Cobb & Co were lucky to travel 100 miles on the same evening. He put it in a nutshell: 'A hundred miles shall see to-night the lights of Cobb and Co!' He was able to describe the outback vividly to hundreds of thousands of eager readers, because the long railway conveyed him from Sydney to the River Darling and the town of Bourke, where he carried his swag into the dry country. 'Banjo' Paterson of Sydney and Christina Macpherson of Melbourne would not have combined to produce the song 'Waltzing Matilda' (he providing the words and she the melody) except for the steamship and steam locomotive which had separately conveyed them most of the way towards the Queensland sheep town of Winton and the outback homestead of 'Dagworth' where they first met. Tom Roberts would never have painted his evocative scenes in the shearing sheds but for the railways that carried him far from the capital city. Indeed most open-air paintings of the Heidelberg School that began to fire the imagination were painted within a short walk, horse-ride or coach-ride of the new railway stations.

3

In the United States, handsome inland cities arose at transport junctions, but they did not arise here. Not even a shadow of a Pittsburgh arose in the interior of South Australia, nor did a Cincinnati or St Louis emerge at some railway junction in Queensland. By 1900, Australia had only four inland towns with more than 30,000 people, three of which were founded on gold (Ballarat, Bendigo and Kalgoorlie) while the fourth (Broken Hill) was founded on silver. Unlike North America, the dry inland of Australia to this day has not one large inland city worthy of the name city, and not even one landlocked state sitting out in the interior.

Capital cities – already the seats of the bureaucracy, the big banks and most factories – used the new railways to siphon commerce to their wharves and piers. The swift rise of these capital cities was said in 1891 to have 'no parallel among the cities of the old world'. Timothy Coghlan, official statistician for New South Wales, slightly overstated the case in his enthusiasm: 'In these Colonies, perhaps for the first time in history, is presented the spectacle of magnificent cities growing with marvellous rapidity', and embracing about one-third of the people of the colony of which they were capital. Melbourne, which held about 25,000 people before gold was found in 1851, now held nearly 500,000. Sydney held nearly 400,000, Adelaide 133,000 and Brisbane 94,000. Then came two big provincial cities, Newcastle with 51,000 and Ballarat with 46,000, followed closely by Bendigo.

Melbourne and Sydney were amongst the world's top fifty cities. Even Beijing and Tokyo, the largest cities outside the North Atlantic region, were less than three times the size of Melbourne. In Melbourne's Elizabeth Street one office block of thirteen storeys was taller than any in Europe.

The big city was the showcase of prosperity. Immigrants were quick to notice the high wages, the ample leisure, the size of the typical house with its fenced garden and watered lawn. They were surprised to see the quality of the meat and other foods, the standard of clothing, the efficiency of suburban transport, the solidity of schools, public buildings and churches, the ring of parklands and sports fields around the inner cities, the virtual feast of public holidays and the scarcity of beggars. A Tyneside visitor in the late 1880s marvelled that during five weeks in Melbourne he did not once see a child without shoes or stockings and did not even see shabbily dressed people, except four blind men. Clothing was dear but people could afford it.

In fact there was poverty and distress, far more than he saw, but it was less common than in Vienna and Naples, Berlin and Dublin. The rate of unemployment was low but those who had no work or suddenly lost a breadwinner were hit hard. Those living in hopeless poverty had to think of entering a military-like institution like the Perth Poor House, where the paupers had to arise in summer at 5.30 am in readiness for the first rollcall at 7.30 am. No inmate could leave the house without permission. In the larger cities, inattention to the public's health was another flaw. Except in Adelaide, sewerage was a municipal afterthought. Not until 1897 was the first street in Melbourne, scene of serious outbreaks of typhoid, connected to the new sewerage tunnels.

Most Australians who longed for social security thought, at some stage, of becoming farmers. To own a small farm was a dream as intense as the later dream to own one's house. It was widely hoped that one day the horizon could be dotted with farms where diligent families supplied all their own needs, including social security when sickness and old age descended. In the 1860s the typical farm, perhaps of thirty to sixty hectares, seemed enormous to farmers from Europe but it proved to be too small. The soil, lacking phosphate, was weary after a few crops. One poor season was enough to inflict misery on a farmer and his wife, in debt to their ears. Ned Kelly, the last notorious bushranger, hanged in 1880, came from a struggling little farm near the highway from Melbourne to the Beechworth goldfield. Stealing horses, sheep and cattle was a hobby of some small farmers on moonlit nights.

A multitude of farmers, after erecting a hut to live in, sinking a well for water, building a shingle-roofed shed for the poultry, fencing a yard for the horses and a paddock for dairy cows, and after burning the stumps of tall trees and planting grain in the cleared land – after all that labour – made little money. Even with success, more land was soon needed to feed and give work to all those sons and daughters, and so the family set out for their promised land with cows and dogs walking alongside their wagon or dray. Camping beside the road each night, they finally reached the vast spaces where they could buy a bigger farm on time payment.

It is fair to suggest that less than half of the new farmers flourished on their first farm. Even South Australia, the granary of the continent, lamented that its disappointed farmers flocked to the Wimmera and Mallee of Victoria, even reaching the eastern Riverina of New South Wales. A line of wagons carrying families in search of untilled soil was one of the rural sights of the 1870s.

Amidst the failure were successes – the breeding of wheat suited to Australian seasons, the ingenuity in designing the stump-jump plough that could till ground littered with half-buried tree roots, and such other rural machines as James Morrow's and H. V. McKay's mechanical harvesters which collected the grain with remarkable speed in the burning summer.

In these years of confidence even the climate, it was thought, could be modified. In the 1880s artesian water was found beneath the sheep country of the far interior of eastern Australia, and hundreds of deep bores were sunk. Victoria began to experiment with irrigating its dry northern plains. Alfred Deakin, the young orator who later became prime minister, was inspired by India's irrigation of parched plains with water from the Ganges and Indus. In the orange groves of Los Angeles and Pasadena, Deakin admired the Californian irrigators, depicting them as upright and independent men wearing wide-brimmed hats, Garibaldi shirts and high boots, all masters of the long-handled spade. Some of these Californians came to Mildura and Renmark to build their costly oases on the banks of the slow-flowing Murray.

4

In most of the country the seasons were unreliable, but the coastal plain of tropical Queensland received heavy summer rains. Many who went in poky coastal steamships to Queensland were inclined to forecast that here lay the future paradise of the continent. Formed into a separate colony in 1859, Queensland soon set the pace. It poured money into paying the fares of immigrants from Britain, and borrowed millions to build railways across the dividing range and so to the hot plains. Gold rushes along the dividing range – from Gympie to Charters Towers and the Palmer River – attracted thousands of Victorian diggers. The drovers and stockmen arrived and Queensland by 1890 owned more beef cattle than any other colony.

Pale-skinned British families stepped ashore in Brisbane, wiping the sweat from their foreheads, and went by train, horse-drawn coach or bullock dray to the virgin farms they had dreamed of. The promise of cheap land attracted the kind of European who tended to prefer North

America. Queensland was the new home for thousands of Danes. It vied with South Australia as a home for German settlers. Second only to Victoria in the proportion of Scots in its population, it also attracted the Irish and that minor English sect, the Baptists.

Queensland's tropical zone was a magnet. The sugar planters cleared the jungle beside the wide rivers flowing slowly towards the Pacific and imported Melanesians, virtually kidnapping many of them in the New Hebrides and other Pacific Islands. There was one mental barrier. The belief was strong that in the tropics a white man could do hard manual work and his wife could work busily in the house only by endangering their health. The fear now seems odd but was valid in an era when so many in the population had to do hard manual work under the midday sun, when hours of work were long, when women had to cook on hot wood stoves, when air-conditioning and antibiotics were unknown, and the causes of malaria remained a mystery. People settling in the hot parts of Australia were wary, knowing of the high death-rate of British colonists in India and the West Indies and knowing that Africa was known as 'the white man's grave'. This was the era when a cool changeable climate was seen as most likely to lead to a nation's economic success.

In the 1870s Rockhampton, just inside the tropics, was one of those experimental towns where Europeans tried to live a leisurely life that coped with the heat. Many people slept on the verandahs, a mosquito net protecting them in the rainy weather. The barber might have his shirt open at the neck and his sleeves rolled up, and the bank clerk wore white clothes. It was said to be no place for women, most of whom agreed with that verdict.

Already the architecture of these northern ports was distinct. A typical house stood on stilts or tall wooden blocks. Verandahs were wide, the doors kept open to catch the breezes, and corrugated iron was used for roofing partly because imported slates cracked in the heat. The tropical settlers imitated India, and in dining and sitting rooms of the best hotels the punkahs made of cloth were suspended from the ceiling, like small oblong sails, and pulled back and forward to stir the sluggish air. They were manual forerunners of the electric fan.

It almost seemed that Queensland's centre of gravity would move north into the tropics, turning the ports of Mackay and Townsville, Cairns and Cooktown into baby cities. Queensland might become the most populous of the six colonies, if only it could prevent its tropical north from breaking away and becoming a seventh colony. Queensland's vast territory, four times as large as California, would surely support millions of people. Holding only 30,000 white people in 1860, it held 400,000 in 1891, by which time it had overtaken South Australia to become the third-most important colony. A sign of its vitality was its three home-grown banks, one of them the mighty Queensland National Bank, which operated scores of branches from its ornate banking temple in Brisbane.

The Queensland government showed its independence by subsidising mail steamers to run regularly from Brisbane to London, a service which shunned Sydney and instead called one by one at the balmy ports along the Queensland coast. Even at Cooktown it was possible once a month to catch a first-class steamer of the Queensland Royal Mail Line and make the seven-week voyage to London by way of Thursday Island, Jakarta and Aden and the Mediterranean. Queensland saw Torres Strait as its own lifeline to European markets. To protect that lifeline it effectively placed pressure on Britain to annex the other side of Torres Strait, the territory of Papua.

Queensland had some success in developing tropical regions but Western Australia had mainly failures, except the pearling fleet that anchored in Broome and other ports. The Northern Territory, governed from distant Adelaide, had glimmers of success after Port Darwin, first called Palmerston, was settled in 1869. At the top end, it welcomed a gold rush and a cattle rush. Its population, Aborigines not counted, jumped to 4,500 males and 100 females in 1881 and then declined during the next thirty years. The short railway built from Darwin towards Pine Creek by Chinese navvies failed to develop what was optimistically termed this new Africa.

5

The settling of so many regions in so many climates, in the face of so many difficulties, was seen by proud Australians as a marvel of a marvellous age. The conquest of physical obstacles was matched by an assault on the mental obstacles. A strenuous effort went into providing schools and teachers for young Australians living outside the cities.

At the time of the first gold rush in 1851, about four of every ten white children in eastern Australia were enrolled in a school, though how often they attended was another matter. The teachers were a motley crew. Many were apprentices who were quickly placed in charge of a class, with a stick or cane in their hand to provide the authority that their knowledge could not provide. All that was asked of these novice teachers in Victoria was to read a simple Irish school book. Then they had 'to write out neatly, in small hand, with correct spelling' any passage dictated to them from that one reading book, to understand the 'parts of speech in a simple sentence', to know a little geography and the map of the world, and to do simple sums and recite the table of weights and measures. The ability to teach girls how to knit and sew was an advantage.

Many small towns had at least two primary schools, a 'national' or government school and a church school subsidised by the government. South Australia was the first to remove the subsidy from 'denominational schools', and Western Australia in the 1890s was the last. After the government subsidy was cut off, only the Catholics insisted on financing large-scale education for children. Between 1870 and 1900, bit by bit, free and secular compulsory education had become normal.

Australia was one of the world's leaders in proclaiming that all children must attend primary school, but it was easier said than done. Children were called on by parents to help with the harvest, watch the cows, chop firewood and mind the babies in the house: the phrase 'compulsory education' was loose. In New South Wales on any given school-day in 1889, four of every ten students were marked 'absent' on the roll. Probably illness accounted for only a fraction of the absentees.

Despite their faults, the improved schools achieved much. An army of dedicated teachers slowly reshaped society and the popular culture. In 1861, one in four Australians on their wedding day signed the marriage register with only a cross or a squiggle, but three decades later very few adults were illiterate. By then the bride was as literate as the bridegroom. Before the era of radio, cassettes, films and television, so much entertainment and information was conveyed by the printed word. To be illiterate was to live in a cultural prison.

Over much of Australia, soon after seven in the morning, the straggling procession of children set out for school. There were fettlers' children walking parallel to the railway line, children tramping through the mallee scrub, children riding little ponies if their parents were wealthier. Hundreds of thousands of children set out, many barefoot, the girls often in pinafores, their tin or box of lunch with them, their books in a satchel or bag on their shoulder, fearing or looking forward to the day.

Little Enid, aged six, was a member of the little army of rural Tasmanian pupils. As she wore leather lace-up boots that did not fit, her toes had painful corns. She usually spent three-quarters of an hour walking to the one-teacher school, and along the way were events to be reported to the teacher: new-born lambs, snakes on the side of the road, and the seagulls flying in from Bass Strait when a storm was brewing. If she reached the school with wet clothes, her black stockings and boots and topcoat – along with those of twenty-four other pupils – had to be dried in front of the fire which the teacher lit in the schoolroom's fireplace.

Decades later, as the wife of the only Tasmanian to become prime minister, Enid Lyons recalled the weary walk home and then, at the last bend of the road, a burned-out tree stump coming into view: 'never were harbour lights more welcome to a storm-tossed mariner than the old dead tree to me'. Many rural children, after they reached home in the afternoon, were soon milking cows, weeding the garden, picking fruit, gathering kindling, setting the table for the evening meal, or fetching the bucket of water from the well or from the big iron tank beside the house. The standard of living of most families partly depended on the maxim that no hands should be idle.

At the age of fourteen the overwhelming majority had left school, while a small number went to the private or church schools that provided a secondary education. In 1890 three government-owned universities catered for those who aimed high. A trickle of high talent was always going overseas to Cambridge and Oxford, never to return. Samuel Alexander, a Jewish boy who lived in bayside Melbourne with his widowed mother, was to become Britain's most famous philosopher in the 1930s, at the very time when its most famous scholar in classical Greek was Gilbert Murray, once a Catholic boy living with his widowed mother in Sydney.

As the country had done well with little education, what might it do if every teenager could read, write and have a capacity to learn to handle the machines that seemed to be the formula for the future? Those who spoke about Australia's future were inclined to see it as a second United States. Nothing could halt Australia's rise, they said. Statisticians pointed to the multiplication table of population. Henry

The age of the marvellous

• • • • • • • • • •

Hayter, the Victorian statistician, calculated that if Australia continued to grow on the basis of the percentage gain of the decade 1871 to 1881 it would have – New Zealand included – 133 million people in the year 1991. That was six times the population actually achieved.

Hayter was throwing dry straw onto the bonfire of optimism. That fire was described in 1887 by a visiting Congregational clergyman from Birmingham, Dr R. W. Dale, who summed up the hopes he heard on all sides:

> With a population of a hundred millions, having in their veins the
> best and most vigorous blood of these islands, blending in themselves
> all the best qualities of the English, Scotch, and Irish people,
> inheriting the material, intellectual, and moral triumphs of European
> civilization, living in a country the resources of which are boundless,
> and under skies such as poets in their dreams have seen bending
> over the isles of the blessed, Australia, a hundred years hence, will
> be one of the greatest, most powerful, and most splendid of nations.
> These are the prophecies and hopes on which the more ardent and
> generous of the young Australians delight to dwell.

Beneath the optimism were new fractures and divisions. The period from 1860 to 1890 was marked by the forming of impersonal and opposing groups of owners and of employees. Banks, coastal ships, gasworks and most mines and many factories were now controlled by companies with shares traded on the stock exchange. Many pastoral runs, in debt, were bought by public companies. The proportion of the self-employed had been much higher in the gold rushes. Industrial relations tended to deteriorate in industries ruled by big public companies.

The trade unions became important. Initially they were vigorous amongst the carpenters. stonemasons, printers, the mechanics who minded the new steam engines, and the other town tradesmen who, seeing themselves as superior to the unskilled labourers, were determined to maintain their substantial margin in wages. Many unions showed a preference for winning shorter hours. As the pay of their members was already high by world standards and as many of their members were single men who, with no family to support, lived on their wages with ease, the demand for higher wages could often take second place. The decision to seek shorter hours was also influenced by the instinct that the climate, even in Melbourne, was too hot for long hours of work, especially for people working under the midday sun.

In 1855 in Sydney a few stonemasons won the eight-hour day or forty-eight-hour week. In Melbourne a year later a big group of stonemasons won the same privilege, a victory which was soon celebrated by an annual holiday in which workers marched through street displaying banners extolling the virtue of eight hours' labour, eight hours' recreation and eight hours' rest. Melbourne saw itself as the world's leader of the movement for shorter hours of work. Its annual procession, however, signified hope more than reality because in 1900 most Australians still worked more than forty-eight hours a week, and big numbers worked sixty and even seventy hours a week. Nonetheless the emphasis on leisure became a hallmark of unionism and social life. Without it, sport could not have become a cult.

William Guthrie Spence, a Scot who first worked in Australia as a boy shepherd, did more than anyone to create the mass union movement that embraced the less skilled workers. He did not found the first miners' union but he revived it in the late 1870s, spreading it far and wide until twelve years later it had about 23,000 members on both sides of the Tasman Sea, the biggest union in Australasia.

Spence initially favoured capitalism as a way of producing wealth. He believed in incentives, and when later he organised the thousands of men who sheared the sheep at isolated woolsheds around the continent, he accepted that the fast workers were entitled to earn much more than the slow. Though many union leaders came to be seen as saboteurs of the work ethic, it was hardly true of Spence. One of his supporters was the immortal Jacky Howe, the fastest shearer the world had seen.

Spence had one foot in the old way of life and one foot in the new. On Sundays in his hometown of Creswick, near Ballarat, he led the singing in the Presbyterian Sunday School. Those who heard him talk of gentle Jesus did not fully realise that Spence himself was not entirely meek and mild. Though he was law-abiding, he must have known the value of the punching fist. His shearers would not have become the world's most powerful union of rural workers but for the tactics of some muscular henchmen who insisted that every shearer should join the union or lose his job. On distant plains where only one policeman lived within 150 kilometres of a shearing shed, it was easy for the unions to take the law into their own hands. Later known as the Australian Workers Union, this union became the strongest in the land.

An idealism in trade unionism caught the imagination of many Australians around 1890. Cardinal Moran of Sydney said he could see no reason why labour should not unite so long as it did not replace one tyranny with another. 'The present labour organisations', he said, 'are really the old Catholic guilds under another name'. Spence said his unions opposed those who turned money into a god, and he regretted that the 'preachers of Christianity have wandered from the teachings of the lowly Nazarene'. In a more secular vein the Brisbane *Worker* in October 1890 predicted that unionism would create 'one great industrial Brotherhood, in which employer and employed shall join hands', eventually banishing vice and crime and poverty from the land.

A new aggression was also seen in unionism. By 1890 the falling prices of wool and nearly all other exports meant that the national cake was smaller, but both sides were reluctant to accept a smaller slice. Capital and labour were about to enter the boxing ring. In 1890 there was a maritime strike and a halt to coastal ships, in 1891 the first of the fierce shearers' strikes in Queensland, and in 1892 a major strike at the silver-lead field of Broken Hill, a high-wages city where 30,000 people lived in poor conditions. The relatively smooth relations between capital and labour had ended. The unions, though defeated, were ready to bounce back from the ringside ropes when prosperity returned.

6

People would look back with wonder on the wide prosperity in the forty years following the first gold rushes. They had enjoyed a very high standard of living because they were developing the minerals, soils, grasslands and other untapped resources of a vast continent. They were using machines to make the most of opportunities. Steam engines were at the core of the new technology but a host of other ideas and devices were adopted. The simple Scandinavian separator, turned by hand, separated cream from milk in the new dairy farms hacked from forest; and the new refrigerating machine enabled frozen meat, cold butter and apples to reach England. Mines were aided by the heavy jackhammer, the Nobel dynamite, and new crushing and separating techniques in the noisy mills. The growing of wool was aided by new breeds of sheep, the size of the average fleece nearly doubling in the space of forty years. That fact alone placed more money in the pay packets, even of those who had never sniffed the aroma of greasy unwashed wool.

Business decisions were now influenced by knowledge of the latest commodity prices and interest rates, telegraphed from London. The telegraph was another marvel of the age, enabling daily newspapers and colonial governments to receive quick messages – from London in 1872 and from New Zealand in 1876. A telegram, however, was too expensive for most colonists to think about. For the price of a short telegram to London, a Sydney clerk could travel steerage in the coastal steamship to Melbourne, spend four days there and then return with a few pence left over.

The latest ideas could not be introduced without money. England, the world's money lender, financed railways and telegraph lines by the thousands of kilometres. Australia's progress seemed easy in the forty years from 1850 to 1890, because the combination of hard work and natural wealth, bright technical ideas and sober English capital, worked wonders. Yet another mainspring of prosperity was not appreciated at the time. The climate in the rural heartland, the south-east corner, had smiled from perhaps the 1840s to the late 1880s: soon the smile would vanish.

There was coming to an end a rare time when Australians' qualities and skills seemed to have found a pleasing balance. Towards most strangers except the Chinese migrants was accorded a deep generosity, a quality that would survive. The energy level was higher than in the British Isles, though it would slip. Most people worked hard, and many worked themselves to exhaustion, though there were signs of a less energetic attitude to work. People respected success but not so much that they despised failure. Admittedly some feared that a growing instinct for equality would lower incentives for the people on middle incomes as well as those struggling on the bottom.

Here was the first full generation of Australians to show the advantages of material plenty. They were also showing, in the opinion of many, the advantages of the long-standing infusion of free migrants instead of convicts. The Rev. Dr R. W. Dale thought, after travelling around Australian cities, that the typical woman and man were superior to those in the British Isles 'in physical vigour, in general force of character, in fearlessness and self-reliance'. Walking along the streets he saw the relative tallness of young people. When he entered a schoolroom he noticed how well fed, bright and well clad were most of the children. In manner the children were easy and free without being 'free and easy'. The richer and poorer mixed without much sign of the class chasms of Britain. A chasm, however, was about to appear.

Eyes

One crucial change was so slow that it was almost invisible: most people were feeling a little more at home in Australia. The old strange feeling did not go away, but retreated a step. Even migrants who came prepared were still surprised by the strangeness of Australia. Those who were born in Australia and knew no other land must have felt more at home but were constantly told of their homeland's strangeness by the flood of newcomers who dominated the newspapers and wrote most of the poems, novels and descriptive books about Australia.

From the days of the First Fleet some observers – how many we do not know – found beauty as well as strangeness in the new land. They admired the harbours and the scent and delicacy of the wildflowers; the crimson colours of the waratah tree were a joy. Grassy plains, especially for those who owned cattle, gave an aesthetic as well as commercial pleasure, the more so if they were green and reminiscent of home. Commanding views gave delight, and John Lhotsky, climbing the Razorback beyond Camden in 1834, gloried in the majestic panorama as he halted with his horse. George Bennett, a surgeon making his second visit to Australia in 1832, gave the common view when he rejoiced in some of the picturesque views and the English-like farms but lamented how 'very dull' were Australian forests and bemoaned the 'utter want of variety' of scenery on the inland road to Yass. He knew that the free migrant who came knowing he would 'lay his bones in a distant soil' was bound to feel despondent when he 'compares with regret the arid land before him with the fertile country he has forsaken'.

Even in the 1860s and 1870s most native-born white Australians did not feel fully at home in their land. New migrants, mostly from the British cities, thought rural Australia strange and even hostile at first. Above all, in the long European see-saw of ideas and taste, the wilderness and untamed nature were falling somewhat from favour, to be revived late in the century. Attitudes to Australian landscape reflected the swing of this see-saw.

2

So much was strange to the newcomers. Thus migrants to Melbourne and Adelaide complained of the summer: their descendants a century later would complain with equal zest about the winter. When the hot wind blew from the north and sprinkled red dust on the streets most people who were indoors pulled down the blinds and acted as if their town was about to be besieged. On those furnace-like days the governor and his entourage longed for some cooler place; and obligingly the parliaments voted money for a summer residence to be built in the hills. So the Victorian governor retreated to Mount Macedon and the New South Wales governor escaped to the coolness of a hilltop in the highlands near Moss Vale, and the documents to be signed by the vice-regal hand were sent by train to these colonial Simlas. The governor of South Australia, not to be outdone, retreated to the Adelaide hills to await the cool change.

Some mothers who lived on the coast of northern New South Wales took their young children at the height of summer to the tablelands of New England, maybe 100 or 200 kilometres away. 'In summertime the Grafton climate was too humid to be healthy', G. F. Young recalled. In the late 1870s he spent several of his childhood summers on a Hereford cattle station at Texas, on the border of Queensland, where the heat was dry and lazy house guests – English remittance men – sat on the verandah in spotless suits of white duck. Anywhere north of Brisbane those who performed clerical work dressed in white in summer. In their eyes Queensland was a southern India. Melbourne, in contrast, was seen as a southern England, and bankers, clergymen and successful merchants were likely to wear, on the hottest day, a heavy black suit with waistcoat.

A heart-warming sight to a new British migrant was snow. It was a rare sight even in the cooler parts of Australia. At the end of April 1849 Bishop Charles Perry, new to Melbourne, was travelling up-country on what became the Hume Highway. He ascended a range of hills, just off the road, and to his astonishment saw in the distance the snow-capped mountains of what were called the Australian Alps. 'It was a deeply interesting sight', he wrote, 'reminding us of other and far distant lands to which our thoughts love to revert'. Pure white was one nostalgic colour: green was another. Ernest Giles, an Englishman, was exploring in the dry centre of Australia in October 1872, with the search for water foremost in his mind, when he came across a small plain and a waterhole large enough to keep 100 or 200 horses alive for weeks. The sight of the green grassy plain was even more emotive than the water: 'How beautiful is the colour of green!' He decided that emerald green was the loveliest colour that nature could devise.

In the towns and sheep stations the experience of spending Christmas in the heat and glaring sunlight was startling to newcomers. The young writer Marcus Clarke, fresh from England, saw people eating hot greasy roast beef with the hot wind raging and the temperature reaching over 40 degrees Celsius in the shade – he cribbed a degree or two. He decided that it was a 'gigantic mistake' to transplant Christmas to summertime. For many of those living on the hot brown plains, Christmas Day was like any other. There were no Christmas greetings, and the shepherd, with only his cabbage-tree hat for shade, sat alone and ate his mutton and stale bread while his sheep lay panting nearby. Except for the huge size of the Australian flocks, it was almost like a scene from the Holy Land in the time of Christ, but so many generations of English painters and hymn-writers had converted the climate and landscape of Palestine into that of the British Isles – 'There is a green hill far away' – that few Australians realised the biblical nature of their own land.

To make themselves feel more at home the newcomers planted the trees and shrubs of home, and the roses and the lavender wherever they might flourish. They brought out the yellow-flowered gorse and the hawthorn for the farmland hedges they planted in the cool south-east and in Tasmania. They imported starlings, thrushes and other British birds, and rabbits, hares and foxes. Most Australians now are slightly puzzled by the nostalgia and obstinate ways of their ancestors.

Many migrants, while slowly adapting their ways to a new climate and landscape, put even more emphasis on old pastimes and rituals, whether it was the hot Christmas dinner or regular attendance at church or membership of one of those friendly societies – Druids, OddFellows, Freemasons, Foresters and a galaxy of others – which gloried in regalia and ritual, reminded them of Galway or Bristol, and provided them with social security for a shilling a week. At the same time they eagerly entered into new pastimes, including the picnic in the open air and the crying aloud of the word 'cooee', which was almost the Australian password for much of the nineteenth century.

All the time the new land was being observed, digested, inhaled. Decade by decade the unfamiliar became a trifle more familiar as poets chose the symbols and artists found the scenes with which to soothe the sensation of strangeness or hostility. In the 1860s two poets led this slow process of adaptation. Henry Kendall, a native of Ulladulla on the coast south of Sydney, hearing the tinkling sounds of the bellbirds in the coastal gullies, began to convince thousands of young Australians that the strange metallic song of the bellbird was 'softer than slumber and sweeter than singing'. A more popular poet, Adam Lindsay Gordon, praised the golden blossom of the wattle trees. In the early 1900s this symbol of Australia was to reach a popularity it has since lost.

Curiously, the charming song of the Australian magpie was not initially praised by poets. Perhaps magpies had been less plentiful in 1850 but multiplied as the vegetation and their supply of food was changed by the grazing of sheep and the sowing of crops and the coming of rabbits. Frank Williamson, a schoolmaster and bush-walker writing in Melbourne at the turn of the century, was one of the first Australian poets to praise the magpie 'and its warble in the blue-gums on the hill'. It was in the 1890s that the new football club of Collingwood, not yet famous, adopted the magpie as its emblem.

3

Very small bands of Australians living in the cities began to seek out the bush, visiting it for picnics in summer, tramping in the mountains, and learning the names of wildflowers or giving catchy names to those that were nameless. In the 1880s the spread of railways and the growth of leisure fostered the bush picnic. The first national parks were set aside: the sandstone coast just south of Sydney in 1879, the Fern Tree Gully near Melbourne in 1882, and the Russell Falls near Hobart in 1885. In this part of the globe Tasmania and New Zealand led the way in setting aside forest and coastline to form a national park. Those islands possessed the kind of landscapes that were pleasing to European eyes. The idea of fencing off a desert as a national park was almost unimaginable, for a desert was seen as hostile.

The few wealthy patrons of the arts preferred to buy or commission Australian landscapes that showed ponds and rivers, waterfalls and bays, dark forests and wooded mountains, and lush green pastures where cows and sheep grazed behind crooked post-and-rail fences. Even in the 1880s the outback was rarely visited by a painter: it was too remote. If a typical scene of the outback had been painted in oils, it would have attracted no buyer except at a bargain sale. Who would wish to display on the walls of a dining room or club a parched landscape when more homely or fertile scenes could be framed and hung as reminders of that nostalgic other world?

A red gum or a wattle tree in flower, a ghost gum or another such tree, now seen as distinctively Australian, were rarely painted. The parched grasslands were also shunned, though the watery blue ranges in the distance already had an attraction. Then in the late 1880s the Heidelberg School of painters began to annex and paint part of that Australian wasteland that had repelled most of the earlier painters and patrons. Tom Roberts, Arthur Streeton, Fred McCubbin and other young painters went in the suburban steam train to the Yarra Valley at Heidelberg and painted the fierce light, the white grass and red river gums of the valley and the haunting blue of the timbered ranges in the near distance. They rarely painted the valleys when they were green after rain or floods, or when they were white with hawthorn blossoms in the springtime. While earlier painters had positively preferred winter to summer, Streeton exulted in the hot north winds. When he went to Sydney and painted one of his best known works, 'The Purple Noon's Transparent Might', he was content to stand with his paintbrush in the open air though the temperature exceeded 41 degrees Celsius in the shade on successive days. These artists captured chosen corners of the landscape with new eyes. In due time their eyes would be multiplied a million-fold and transplanted into the heads of most Australians.

Dorothea Mackellar, living mostly in the green Hunter Valley not far from Newcastle, praised similar scenery in her poetry. Early in the twentieth century she announced in what became one of Australia's most recited verses, 'I love a sunburnt country'. In contrast, most Australians did not love a sunburnt country. Farmers certainly did not; most city people preferred green lawns to brown. Even Henry Lawson and 'Banjo' Paterson, young Australian-born poets now seen as heroic nationalists, did not fall in love with the sunbrowned plains. Paterson's most popular poem was about a dashing horseman, the 'Man from Snowy River', who rode in the cool coastal mountains rather than on the scorched plains out west. Lawson, a master of the short story, described the outback scenery a thousand times but wrote few sentences that would have inspired a burning desire to emigrate if read aloud to children in a Glasgow school. He wrote that Australia was 'the land I love above all others' but his love did not really reach the dry outback.

It was becoming more than just a land to which people came, hoping to find here a worthier version of the way of life they had left behind. It was becoming a people, a spirit and often a fellowship. Some migrants disliked, to their dying day, the landscape, glaring light and heat, but still did not wish to return to their first homeland. Others rejoiced in almost everything Australian and began in the 1890s to nourish the idea that it was the Australian climate, environment and especially the bush which made Australians a different people in attitude and even in physique.

Meanwhile, most of the native-born Australians were increasingly nationalist in their sympathies. The powerful lodge and friendly society, the Australian Natives' Association, was formed in the 1870s to cater for and promote those who saw themselves as different because they were born in Australia or on the voyage out. The ANA provided a back door into the house of politics, especially for Victorians. In the 1890s it was to be one of the strongest promoters of the idea of one nation instead of a cluster of colonies. The birth of the ANA reflected the simple fact that Australians were becoming slightly different: they tended to be taller, their accent sounded slightly nasal, and they were more equalitarian and less respectful than newly arrived British families.

4

Australians of that generation are sometimes depicted as isolationist, turning their backs on any culture except the British. In part it is true of them. But they were not exceptional in their attitudes. In 1890 almost all the peoples of the world, and probably the Chinese even more than the Australians, were suspicious of alien cultures.

At the same time many Australians helped foreigners in distress. They could be called occasional citizens of the world at a time when few people saw themselves as such. Thus, during the Irish and Scottish famines of 1846, meetings were held in towns of New South Wales to raise money for those in need in their old homelands. Eight years later, when the Chief Rabbi of Britain appealed for money to provide farms and workshops for the Jews living under Turkish rule in Palestine, the Australian Jews sent him donations equalling almost half the sum he raised in wealthy England. In the early 1860s, when the mill workers of Lancashire were in poverty as a result of the curtailing of their cotton supplies by the American Civil War, they received help from hundreds of lodges in the Australian friendly societies.

When India and China suffered from famines, many ordinary Australians were generous. In 1877 all the gate receipts from a big football match, Carlton versus Melbourne, were given to the Indian Famine Relief Fund. The money sent to ease that famine in India was equivalent to the donation of about one day's full pay by one in every four people in the workforce. In 1890 in London the long strike of the dock workers depended heavily on money from Australians.

Enthusiasm for helping foreign lands was reflected in the exodus of missionaries. Hundreds of Australians worked in missions in foreign lands – from New Guinea, the New Hebrides and Fiji to Africa and China – in the belief not only that their own Christian culture was superior but that people in 'benighted lands' were worthy recipients of that culture. The Aborigines were also a renewed target, and those in central and tropical Australia were found to be more receptive than those in the cool south had been to the missionaries and to the teachers and nurses who arrived with them.

There were now several main groups of Aborigines, often very different in culture. Inside the closer-settled districts was a fast-increasing group of mixed parentage, mostly with some European or Chinese ancestry as well as Aboriginal ancestry. They usually lived in huts and shanties on the edges of outback towns. Few in this mixed Aboriginal group lived in cities. Most were near the bottom of the economic ladder. They did seasonal work on farms and enjoyed the periods of leisure that came with it, or worked on cattle runs where their horsemanship was respected. Smaller numbers worked on farms all year round. Many were classified by the local civic authorities as Aboriginal, but most were probably counted in the national census as part of the general population. Many did not call themselves Aborigines. There were social and economic gains in such an attitude.

Another group consisted of 'full bloods' who lived far from the capital cities. Most were fully Aboriginal in ancestry and culture. They were widely viewed as an inferior race – more so in 1900 than in 1840 – but that view was far from general amongst those whites with first-hand knowledge. Simpson Newland, a pastoralist on the Upper Darling, recalled in his *Memoirs* that an Aboriginal girl, Miola, was 'brightly intelligent'. A valuable nurse for the children on his remote sheep station in the 1870s, she learned to read and became capable at sewing, housework and cooking. With her curly black hair, brown eyes, brilliantly white teeth, 'velvety' skin of a copper tint and musical voice, she was highly respected by her white employers and guardians. She seemed to wish to follow a European way of life and asked for her own neat, roofed hut to live in. Unexpectedly she returned to the Aborigines' camp and to an arranged marriage, and Newland lamented that she 'died the early death that seems the fate of the best of her people'. This was the tragedy: young people torn between two incompatible ways of life. Even if she had refused to return to the old way of life, her future in a white society would have been challenged by many.

Ever since the arrival of the British in 1788 it had been rare for a person of total Aboriginal ancestry and reared in their traditional culture to take fully to the new way of life. If they took to it, they eventually abandoned it. They had no wish to be self-employed farmers and no wish to be manual labourers. Even when swift to learn, they had no wish to persist in their studies after a few years. Possessions and property rarely interested them: money was only a temporary lure. If they worked as housemaids or farmhands, they were eventually tempted to return to their families and old ways.

Their traditional way of life, its unusual mixture of leisure and work and travel, its deep family ties, its rituals and ceremonies, had an intense appeal. Admittedly certain European tasks excited them. One West Australian observer in the early 1900s explained that they were 'valuable as messengers, pearl-divers, shepherds, horse-breakers, stock-drivers, hunters or any employment requiring only light manual labour.' In searching for lost livestock or lost children or escaped criminals, their ability to find traces of their footprints or their stumbling tracks was uncanny. By then it was the trend to segregate the people of total Aboriginal ancestry. Most governments set up special boards to 'protect' them. Increasingly they lived in reserves on their traditional lands, remote from the big cities. Freedom to move outside the reserve was restricted. Inside the reserves in Western Australia especially, alcohol was usually banned. More Christian churches, using mainly money collected from their own worshippers, set up mission stations, often with a school and a hospital.

The Aborigines in the mission stations lost most of their freedoms, but there were compensations. They rarely starved. In effect they lived in a welfare state at a time when such a benefit was not available to able-bodied Australians of other ancestries. Moreover, most learned to read and write. The penalty for learning the British culture and religion was that the young lost much of their own cultural inheritance. They belonged neither to their own shattered world nor to the one which had shattered it.

By 1900 probably only a few thousand Aborigines were living their own traditional but systematic way of life. Most inhabited the arid lands that were deemed to be unfit for sheep or cattle and lay almost beyond the reach of men who were searching for minerals. Many had not seen a white person.

The rise of the sporting hero

The first famous sportsman in Australia was The Flying Pieman. An athlete and minor stuntsman, he decided in 1848 to race the Brisbane to Ipswich coach. As a handicap he carried a long carriage pole. He beat the coach by one hour. Twice he raced the crack mail coach from Sydney to the town of Windsor. If he were alive today he would probably embarrass the post office and its delivery of letters. Sometimes in his record-breaking runs he wore a top hat and carried a live goat – just to show his contempt for his competitors.

2

The gold rushes of the 1850s dramatically increased the popularity of spectator sports. With the trebling of Australia's population in that one decade, the spectators at big sporting events grew. With more leisure, people had the time to attend sporting contests and with more prosperity they had money with which to bet. Gambling was a vital part of many of the popular sports.

Australia became probably the first country in the world to give a high emphasis to spectator sports. British sports such as horse-racing, football, cricket, boxing, rowing – and later golf and lawn tennis – migrated with ease to Australia. Migrants who stepped ashore were astonished that in a land of so few people such huge crowds could be found at racecourses and football grounds. Even in the bush, sport seemed to fascinate people. Villages with fifty people might have a racecourse. Further out, the hunting of kangaroos and the shooting of ducks were popular pastimes, and in a few districts the squatters would sometimes dress up in English hunting costume and ride with their pack of dogs in pursuit of anything that could be pursued. The English fox, rabbit and hare were imported as targets.

In a land where grass was virtually free, tens of thousands of people owned horses and often rode them. Horse-racing was a natural sport for Australia: even in Sydney as early as October 1810 three days were devoted to horse races organised in Hyde Park. The nation's most famous race, the Melbourne Cup, was first run in 1861 before a mere 4,000 people, but the annual race soon attracted so many fast horses from distant towns that the crowds multiplied. By 1865 the banks and government offices in Melbourne gave their employees a half-holiday so that they could be free to attend the race meeting held on the floodplain a few kilometres from the city. Three years later the running of the Cup was seen by 25,000 people. In 1883 it was reportedly seen by 100,000, equivalent to one in every three of Melbourne's population. The Tuesday when the race was run became a holiday for a big part of Melbourne's population.

On each Melbourne Cup Day the pastors of many Protestant congregations arranged picnics at the beaches or hills to deter their adherents from succumbing to the temptation of gambling at the racecourse. Curiously, for many years the home of the spectacular betting on the Melbourne Cup was the rival city of Sydney, and there the Tattersall's Sweep (short for sweepstake) offered huge prizes for the individual or syndicate lucky enough to draw the name of the horse that won the Cup. When ten men living on Thursday Island in tropical Queensland won the sweepstake in 1890, they received enough money to live in idleness for the rest of their life.

The horse permeated the nation's life. Many of Adam Lindsay Gordon's verses celebrated the fast horse. A man of action, a far cry from Browning and Tennyson and the sit-about poets of England, Gordon was a champion rider when the steeplechase was at the height of its popularity. Though his eyesight was defective he guided his horse over the series of high fences built across the grass track. His racing skills and his love of horses added to his popularity as a poet. His galloping poem 'How We Beat the Favourite' was familiar to tens of thousands who themselves loved a day at the races and the sight of the jockeys' silk colours, the green and crimson and red, and what Gordon described as the 'hum of hoarse cheering, a dense crowd careering'. Even after Gordon committed suicide in the tea-tree scrub beside the seashore at the Melbourne suburb of Brighton in 1870 his fame grew and grew. Eventually a sculpture of his head and shoulders was to be placed, amongst the great poets, on a wall of Westminster Abbey.

'Banjo' Paterson, another poet of the horse, wrote the words of Australia's most popular song, 'Waltzing Matilda'; and the matching of words and melody reflected the national passion for sport. The tune was first heard by Paterson when he was visiting outback Queensland, but how did it reach Queensland? It had been played by the brass band during an interval between the horse-races at the Victorian port of Warrnambool, well known for its steeplechases, and there a young woman named Christina Macpherson heard the band playing and later carried the catchy tune in her memory to the family sheep station in outback Queensland. She chanced to play it when Paterson was visiting the homestead in 1895, and he fitted his words to her tune.

Cricket became a rival to horse-racing in Australian cities. The size of the crowds watching cricket matches was a surprise to visiting English teams, the first of which arrived in 1861. A few years later, Aborigines formed the first Australian cricket team to visit England, and they must have noticed that in England fewer women attended the game. The enthusiasm of many Australian women for sports extended to football where they boosted the size of crowds.

In Melbourne excited crowds gathered at the main football grounds each Saturday afternoon in winter. Whereas in England about 6,000 people saw the FA Cup final in 1880, in Melbourne that year a big match between teams from neighbouring suburbs might draw 'an immense concourse of people' numbering at least 15,000 on a fine winter's day. In 1886 South Melbourne and Geelong played a match before 34,000 people assembled at an embanked arena by the Albert Park Lake, possibly the largest football crowd in the world up to that time.

One unusual fact explains why such crowds could watch a football match even when the grounds had no grandstands and no raised embankments to provide watchers with a clearer view. Australian football is still played on an arena much larger than that used for soccer, rugby or American football, and so more people can stand along the sidelines. The Australian code of football and its vast playing arena was an invention of a city rich in public parks and open spaces. Indeed the first permanent ground for football was in Yarra Park, just outside the Melbourne Cricket Ground, and for years a few big gum trees stood on the playing pitch. By 1880 the game was being moved to the cricket grounds, partly so that the large crowds could be controlled by the outer fence enclosing the ground and the inner fence around the boundary of the arena. In a climate favourable to the growth of grass, the same arena could be used for winter and summer sports, and so big grandstands and sloped embankments could be afforded. Soon the main Australian cricket grounds held crowds larger than could be crammed into Lords, The Oval and most of the other English grounds.

As most Australian institutions are young by the standards of Europe, it is normal to think that the famous sporting clubs are young, but this is not so. The football clubs of Melbourne (1858) and Geelong (1859) are older than any club in the four divisions of the English Football League, for long the world's most famous football competition. Other senior clubs such as Carlton, Essendon and North Melbourne are much older than the oldest clubs in such famous footballing nations as Germany, Italy and Argentina.

Sydney, smaller than Melbourne in these decades when sport took root, had a different tradition. It adopted rugby rather than the Melbourne game of football. It loved rowing and sailing, and great crowds lined the headlands and banks of the Parramatta River, at the western end of Sydney Harbour, to watch the races between individual oarsmen. The strongest New South Wales rowers paid their fare to travel to London to compete on the Thames where the world sculling championships had been staged. In 1876 big Edmund Trickett of Sydney won the race. When he returned to Sydney with his world title, at least 25,000 people waited at the waterfront to hail this first national sporting hero. A succession of young Australians challenged Trickett, and the world's sculling championships were staged for a time in Sydney. He was emerging as a star, and in hundreds of households his portrait in black and white was cut with scissors or knife from the illustrated weeklies and pinned or pasted to walls and doors. By 1880 the champion sportsman who refused to bask in the publicity was becoming an oddity. Thus Elias Laycock, a fine sculler, defeated Trickett but dismayed the journalists when he 'withdrew at once and lived for some time in seclusion in a solitary island'.

The rise of the sporting hero

• • • • • • • • • •

Professional sculling had an international appeal rivalled only by boxing. In New York the public was more interested in sculling than in the America's Cup. Australians became fans of sculling, partly because their countrymen were capable of defeating the best in the world. In the 1880s the fastest message sent along the telegraph wires all the way from England to Australia was the jubilant news, received on 10 September 1889, that another young Australian had won the world championship on the Thames.

Henry Searle was the new sculling hero. A Grafton lad, brought up on the Lower Clarence River when the wide mouths of the rivers of northern New South Wales were not yet crossed by bridges, Searle used to row his brothers and sisters five kilometres to school and back. Becoming a professional sculler, he went to London where, at 22, he defeated an American for the world's championship and a prize of 1,000 pounds – a sum equal to ten years' wages, free of tax. Alas, on his return voyage to Australia, Searle caught typhoid and died soon after the ship berthed in Melbourne. In Sydney, 170,000 people packed the streets for the funeral of their hero. A little steamship conveyed Searle's coffin to his own northern river where another 2,500 mourners stood, one hot day, at his final burial place at Maclean.

In the nineteenth century, Australia's largest funerals were those of sportsmen. Tommy Corrigan, a small Irish-born jockey with a huge moustache, had won the Grand National steeplechase in Victoria seven times. He was respected for his honesty, and many punters reaching the racetrack would say, 'What's Tommy riding today?' On 11 August 1894 at Caulfield racecourse he was riding a horse called Waiter. The horse stumbled and fell, and Corrigan was fatally injured. The day of his funeral was long remembered in Melbourne. In the heart of the city all traffic was halted for two hours. When the coffin, crowned by Corrigan's green and white colours and his riding boots, reached the cemetery near the Carlton football ground, the rear of the procession was still marching along St Kilda Road, maybe three kilometres away.

3

The mania for spectator sport increased in the quarter-century before World War I. A host of young Australian boys had a burning desire to be champions of the world. In cycling and tennis and almost every other new sport that gained the public's interest, Australians became prominent in world contests. From the three to four million people of Australia came an astonishing proportion of the world's champions.

When the first of the modern Olympics was held in Athens in 1896, Australia sent no team – the events were too far away – but a 22-year-old Australian decided to attend. Edwin Flack was tall and fair-haired, the founder of a running club called the Melbourne Hare and Hounds, and twice the winner of the Australian mile championship. He was working for a firm of accountants in London in the year of the first Olympics and, permitted a brief period of leave by his employer, he went by trains and ferry to Athens, arriving just in time for the opening of the Games on Easter Monday. For most events almost anyone could enter, virtually without notice, and Flack won the races over 800 and 1,500 metres and even led the field at a late stage of the marathon before falling down in exhaustion.

Admirers of athletics who wished to watch the fastest foot-runners in the world did not have to go to the Olympic Games. Their wisest choice was probably to follow the professional running circuit that extended from Melbourne and Stawell in Victoria to Kalgoorlie and other Western Australian gold towns and on to Durban and Johannesburg in South Africa. In 1906 a crowd of 15,000 – some say 20,000 – saw the running of the world's sprint championships in remote Kalgoorlie. At one time in that decade, two Australian sprinters, Jack Donaldson and Arthur Postle, held almost half the world's sprint records.

An impression of the talent active in sport at the start of this century can be gained from very different events staged in three successive years. On Easter Monday in 1906, perhaps the fastest sprint run in the world up to that time was run over the classic professional distance of 130 yards at the Western Australian outback town of Menzies, now almost deserted. Alas, a slight hitch occurred: the earthen running track had a fall of three feet six inches, and the record was rightly disallowed. In 1907 in London the winner of the Wimbledon championship in lawn tennis – usually called the world championship – was for the very first time not a Briton. The winner was Norman Brookes, a left-handed player from Melbourne. In the same year the team called Australasia, consisting of Norman Brookes of Melbourne and Anthony Wilding of Christchurch, New Zealand, won the Davis Cup and were to hold it for five years.

In 1908 in Melbourne and Sydney the world heavyweight championship in boxing was contested several times, though at first a doubt was expressed in America about whether Australian promoters could possibly raise the huge prize-money required. It was at the new wooden stadium at Rushcutters Bay, on Sydney Harbour, that for the first time the major world boxing championship passed to a black man, Jack Johnson from Galveston, Texas, USA.

Women did attend big sporting occasions in Australia more than in Britain but they were allowed only the smallest role as players of the spectator sports. Their first champion was a swimmer, Fanny Durack. She learned to swim in the Coogee baths, and showed such skill at breaststroke that money was raised publicly to enable her to visit Stockholm for the Olympic Games in 1912. The only individual event for female swimmers was the 100 metres, which she won in record time by using a stroke called the 'Australian crawl'. She died in 1956, just a few months before the Olympic Games were staged in her homeland.

• • • • • • • • • •

4

It is not hard to find reasons why, from the gold rushes until the eve of World War I, sport pervaded Australian life more extensively than the life of perhaps any other land. Australia then had ingredients of the sporting life which other nations would later foster, often artificially. Cheap or free land was plentiful for sports such as horse-racing, football and cricket that required wide spaces lying not far from the heart of a city, while long arms of sheltered water – uninterrupted by steam vessels – were available for professional sculling in Sydney. In most towns the climate favoured outdoor activities. As an exceptionally high proportion of the people lived in the two large cities of Melbourne and Sydney, they each could muster large crowds for sporting events.

A high standard of living made it possible to offer attractive prize-money and to finance fine facilities for sports. The rather masculine culture, with a high proportion of single men in the population, also favoured sport. Above all, spectator sports depended on abundant leisure time; and it so happened that Australia now provided a short working week for most city people and for miners, though not for those who worked the soil. As organised sport was illegal on a Sunday, and as night sport in the open air was rare before the era of powerful electric lighting, the free Saturday afternoon was vital. Melbourne and Sydney were probably the first large cities in the world where a majority of the wage-earners ceased their working week by two o'clock on the Saturday afternoon and were thus free to play or watch games. The power of the sporting tradition in Australia owes much to the liberating of Saturday afternoon.

For much of the nineteenth century the sports culture in Australia was not far apart from the work culture. People's attitudes to daily work and to weekend sport were alike. In both arenas, the typical Australian prized determination, stamina, courage and the will to succeed, and relished competition and the incentives that are part of competition. The work ethic normally prevailed in work and play. Indeed some of the Australian sports were really work-sports. Professional sculling was in many ways a work-sport, for some scullers made their weekday living as ferrymen and rowboat men. In the countryside some of the popular sports were simply extensions of work: the ploughing matches that aroused so much excitement, the hammer and tap contests between miners, the tossing of the sheaf. One of the noblest work-sports, competitive woodchopping, was a local invention and flourished in the heavily timbered country of north-west Tasmania by the 1880s. Even shearing almost became a work-sport. The daily tallies of the fastest shearers were kept permanently in the record books, and when the celebrated Jacky Howe was shearing sheep in outback sheds a few spectators would ask permission to watch him at work. At one time most young men in the outback could rattle off the fact that in less than eight hours Jacky Howe sheared 321 sheep, ewes to be exact, at the Alice Downs shearing shed in Queensland in 1892.

A rising young painter managed to capture that special time in Australian history when so many people found satisfaction or pleasure in hard physical work. Tom Roberts went three times in the train from Melbourne to visit a shearing shed at Brocklesby, just across the Murray in New South Wales, and there he observed the men shearing with hand shears. He rejoiced to hear the click of the shears and 'the subdued hum' of the men at work, 'the whole lit warm with the reflection of Australian sunlight'. In 1890 he completed what was to become an icon of Australian art. His 'Shearing The Rams' shows energy and contentment, with smiling boys lending a hand, the shearers busy, and an old bearded spectator smoking his short pipe and surveying the blend of individualism and teamwork. The painting remains a celebration of work and the bush and what Roberts enthusiastically called 'the great pastoral life and work'.

Tom Roberts painted his energetic picture just when some of the energy and competitiveness were starting to sag in many workplaces. There was to be more and more regulating of the pace of work and the hours of work. Australia's two cultures, sport and work, were beginning to go their separate ways, and increasingly the competitiveness was seen more often on the sporting field than in workplaces. It was almost as if Australia developed a sports culture that demanded the first-rate and a work culture that often accepted the second-rate: the one revelling in competition while the other was wary of it. Certain events in the 1890s would help to sharpen this contrast.

• • • • • • • • • •

Riding the disaster

A time of wonderful but brittle optimism was coming to a close. Ever since the finding of gold in 1851, Australia was one of the small but rising stars of the economic world. There were recessions but they were short and were often followed by a mineral boom, a drive to build more railways, a surge of immigration, the opening of vast tracts of ploughable land, building booms in the suburbs, and an ever-rising standard of living.

By 1891 the forty years of fat were almost over. The danger signals were multiplying but were ignored. The price of wool, most other rural exports and the base-metals had been falling; the inflow of British loans which had financed so many railways and rural and urban projects began to falter. The country had incurred enormous overseas debts but could no longer pay the annual interest and repay the loans that fell due, without experiencing pain.

Many Australian banks and companies which had lent heavily found their profits slipping. The bad debts now bred like the rabbit. In the autumn of 1893, financial panic set in. Customers with deposits in banks demanded them back, fearing that the banks would fall; and their actions actually precipitated the failures they feared. At the start of the year there had been twenty-two banks of sufficient status to issue their own banknotes for general circulation – there were no government banknotes. Thirteen of these banks were forced to close while they raised more capital and made internal repairs. In 1893 half of all the deposits in the banking system were frozen for terms ranging from five weeks to nearly five months. Australia's credit slumped in London. No nation in Europe had suffered such a banking disaster in the previous half-century, perhaps in the whole century.

2

By sheer hard work, by dint of cost-pinching and frugality, the country began to crawl out of the depression. Then drought set in. In 1895 the drought covered much of Australia. In a continent so large, no drought is universal, but this was the most widespread arid period so far recorded. Fortunately most of Tasmania, the Gulf country of north Queensland, the top end of the Northern Territory and the safer districts of Western Australia largely escaped from a drought which elsewhere burned up a vast area of cropland and grassland and scrubland. Rain occasionally fell, merely settling the dust for a day.

In some districts the drought persisted for eight to ten years. In the far inland the wide roads were jammed with slow-moving flocks and herds searching for new pastures. Edward Quin, a pastoralist on the western plains near Wilcannia in New South Wales, gave a vivid account of his parched lands where 100,000 sheep had declined to almost 40,000. His hardiest tree was the mulga but, he said in 1900, 'I can show you thousands and thousands of trees of mulga dead'. He pointed to miles of his fences in which the lowest strand of wire was far above the ground. The earth underneath had turned to dust and been swept away by wind and the rare rainstorm. He knew huge paddocks where the loose sand was exposed to the wind, 'and a fence was covered in one year, and a buggy could drive over it'. Quin admitted, as an old grazier, that the country had suffered through overstocking in the good years. It was too late to regret it.

In less than a decade the total number of sheep had halved. In many areas the worst year was 1902. The wheatlands of the Victorian Mallee were so dry that special trains arrived carrying as their only freight the oblong iron tanks filled with water. Many farmers spent two days of each week carting the water to their farms in order to keep alive their horses and other livestock grazing in bare paddocks. Often the grass became scarcer than water. Even the dry grass vanished. The wind whipped up storms of dust, forming a black cloud that blocked the sun. Women who were shopping in the main street of country towns had to feel their way along the dark streets, sometimes groping for the verandah poles. In Melbourne the day was switched into night by several gales of dust descending from the interior.

About a quarter of the country's workforce was rural, and so the many years of drought pummelled the economy. The harvest of 1902 was so poor that Australia, instead of exporting wheat, was forced to import wheat and flour by the shipload from the USA and Argentina. Ships even arrived with wheat from India. In much of South Australia and New South Wales in 1903 the drought was in its ninth year when the welcome rains fell, making the bare earth emit that strangely sweet aroma that often marks the end of the parched time. In parts of outback Queensland the drought went on. Many Chinese market gardeners supplying the towns ceased work: the nearby river was dry. Camels were brought in to haul supplies, for the horse teams could not cope with the long stretches of road without water or feed.

The depression and drought discouraged immigrants. In some years more people left Australia than arrived. In the years from 1891 to 1906, Australia gained a miserable 8,000 people through net immigration, or fewer people in fifteen years than it gained in one busy month of the 'golden fifties'. Australia was almost a despised name in the British Isles, especially in financial circles.

The main sufferer from the depression, Victoria, was also one of the main victims of drought. People left cities and country towns in their tens of thousands. The glut of suburban houses and city offices persisted for years. Melbourne lost to Sydney its title of Australia's largest city.

3

Western Australia was the popular magnet for fleeing Victorians. Often the cripple of the colonies, the West had usually been ignored in discussions of the country's future. In the 1870s its white population grew by a mere 400 a year, mostly the excess of births over deaths. Slumbering in isolation, its capital city, little Perth, was not connected to the telegraph system of eastern Australia until 1877. Year after year the vast colony did not grow enough wheat for its own humble needs. Its chief port was not Fremantle but Albany, and there the mail steamships plying the Sydney-to-England route called for coal and stayed in port not a minute longer than was needed. Even in the mid-1880s Perth held only 5,000 people, and those newcomers who saw St Georges Terrace and its handsome Cape Lilac trees felt they were in a country town or even a feudal town, for the governor of Western Australia exercised so much power.

In that vast area the only railway went from Perth to Fremantle, an unsafe port with a hospital for decrepit convicts, a prison and asylum, and a coating of white dust on its rooftops on the windy days. It called for a journey of many weeks by sea and land to visit some of the outlying sheep and cattle stations where pitiful groups of Aborigines camped. Perth had poor contact with the pearling ports in the tropical north-west, for the telegraph line was blown down in the cyclones that buffeted the exposed harbours where the little pearling vessels and their Malay crew took shelter. A total of sixty-nine men were drowned in one cyclone that hit Exmouth Gulf, just north of the tropic.

In the faraway tropics, gold was found in 1886, and rush followed rush. The colony was now ripe for self-government. It was given its own parliament in 1890 with the same law-making powers that had long been held by the five other colonies, except that it was not immediately given control over its Aborigines. The first premier was John Forrest, a son of the colony, a big bluff man with back and shoulders as strong as an ox. He had proved himself at the age of 23 to be one of the greatest explorers by finding a way from the western coast to the overland telegraph line that ran across the centre of the continent from Darwin to Adelaide.

When his horses were exhausted he walked beside or behind them, thinking nothing of travelling in the one day through thirty-odd kilometres of barren country or prickly spinifex. 'He was a cool customer, with an old head on an active young body', wrote the historian Kathleen Fitzpatrick. The same shrewd head was useful for a politician. Forrest was to be premier of Western Australia for ten continuous years. Australian voters had never given a leader such trust but he did possess one unusual advantage. The voters active in the colony when he first won power numbered a mere 6,000, and he probably knew half of them by name.

As an explorer he had discovered no gold but as a politician he was the main beneficiary of the gold now found close to the land he had once travelled over. In 1892 the finding of gold on the surface of the soil at arid Coolgardie, and a year later at Kalgoorlie, attracted a stampede of young men to the last grand gold rush of the nineteenth century. Soon Western Australia passed Victoria to become the big annual producer of gold, and remains so to this day. Kalgoorlie was the king of the goldfields, and by 1907 the Great Boulder, Golden Horseshoe, Oroya Brownhill and three other mines, all controlled from London, had each paid more than one million pounds in dividends. In contrast Victoria had only one such mine in its long history of gold.

At Fremantle, near Perth, the building of an artificial harbour and the blasting away of the shallow rockbar allowed the English mail steamers to call on their way to Melbourne and Sydney. For the following six decades the first sight of Australia for nearly every migrant was the low-lying sandy coast and then, coming closer, the pale stone buildings of Fremantle, bathed in sunlight. When the wind was favourable the incoming migrants might smell a slight fragrance that blew offshore from eucalypts or sand or soil. Fremantle became one of the world's busiest gold ports, while in Perth the new mint coined glittering sovereigns and half-sovereigns for Australian pockets in an era when paper money was not always trusted.

Big John Forrest presided over the miracles: the building of long inland railways, the opening of the far-spreading wheat belt, and the export of jarrah from long jetties to London to pave the streets with blocks of wood. He took pride in financing what was perhaps the longest water pipeline in the world and the erection of a succession of steam engine-houses to pump the fresh water from a new coastal reservoir to far-off Kalgoorlie, lying on the inland plateau. He also introduced compulsory schooling: 'Did they want', he asked his fellow politicians, 'these children in the bush to grow up as if they were only kangaroos?' A fox of a politician he even posed in 1898, to the astonishment of old friends, as a champion of women. He initiated a law granting them the vote, for he realised that most women lived in Perth and in that coastal fringe where he gained most of his electoral support. By giving the vote to women he weakened the power of his opponents in the populous goldfields where women were few.

Blunt, honest, far-sighted, and at times opinionated, this bulldozer of a man presided over the fastest transformation any colony had experienced since the 1850s, when Victoria was galvanised by gold. The Nothing Colony had become a somebody. By 1901 Perth and Kalgoorlie had entered the ranks of the ten top cities of Australia. In population Western Australia even ran past Tasmania. More than eighty years were to pass before another alteration took place in the ranking of the six states, with Western Australia passing South Australia in population.

4

Political life was moulded afresh by the depression of the 1890s. Two reformist strands became powerful, a radical-liberal strand that was most influential in South Australia and Victoria, and the Labor Party itself which was most influential in Queensland and New South Wales. Victoria and South Australia were distinctive in their politics before they were thumped by economic depression, and they became more radical when bad times arrived. South Australia led the way, for it experienced an economic setback in the mid-1880s. It imposed a tax based on Henry George's idea that the increase in the value of private land in a prosperous economy – especially when state railways served that land – partly belonged to the state and should be collected as a land tax. South Australia was also the first colony in Australia to impose an orthodox income tax, though it taxed only the higher incomes. In the early 1890s it went further by emulating liberal New Zealand and granting the vote to women, and by pioneering the method of arbitrating industrial disputes that became the practice in Australia. Victoria had a radical burst, creating wages boards that fixed a minimum wage in bakehouses and many other workplaces. It also awarded an old-age pension to long-time residents.

The Labor Party was propelled to prominence by the adversity of that decade, and ultimately it snatched the initiative from the Liberal reformers. The rise of the Labor Party was made possible partly by the recent laws which decreased the electoral power of those owning money. Thus the payment of politicians enabled poorer people to give up their job and sit in parliament; and the abolition of plural voting ended the tradition whereby a person owning property in five electorates could exercise five votes if he travelled hard on polling day. American as well as English thinkers sowed the seeds from which the Labor Party germinated. Several of the new Labor Party's policies clearly echoed Henry George. They were also influenced by the strong wave of British immigration in the 1880s to Queensland and New South Wales, where Labor was to enjoy early success. Two of those British migrants of the 1880s, Andrew Fisher and Billy Hughes, were to be the most successful Labor men in the first forty years of federal politics.

There was no socialism in these Labor parties, which won nearly 100 seats in the five main parliaments in the early 1890s. The members included owners of property as well as miners, printers and tradesmen. In New South Wales most of the thirty-five Labor members who won seats in the election of 1893 were under the age of 40 and most were products of a simple schooling. Most were unionists, but a pastoralist and a mine-owner were not refused membership. Labor called for laws that would not only increase the bargaining position of trade unions but also help small farmers, self-employed miners and those workshops which were threatened by the cheap furniture made in local Chinese-owned workshops.

Labor promised to make mines, factories and engine houses safer for their workers, to restrict work to eight hours in a day, and to enforce compulsory education: many children were sent to work rather than school by their empoverished parents. Eventually, nearly all the policies enunciated by the first Labor Party in New South Wales became law.

The notable exception was the American idea that magistrates should be elected by the people.

The Labor Party had something for all citizens, so long as they were not too rich. Its rise was swift. It was the first Labor Party in the world to win power, both in a provincial and a national parliament, though at first its grip was shaky, for it depended on the short-lived support of other parties. Andrew Dawson was the first politican to head a Labor or social democratic government. As a baby he had been placed in a Queensland orphanage; he left school at twelve and worked at manual trades in the gold town of Charters Towers in northern Queensland, before briefly joining in the rush of 1886 to the Kimberleys on the far side of the continent. He married a young widow in Charters Towers, learned to speak and write emphatically as editor of the *Eagle*, and was one of the two Labor members elected by that goldfield in 1893.

Six years later, when he was only 36, his election as the Labor premier of Queensland must have been reported in nearly every daily newspaper in Europe. Many people wondered what the world was coming to. They were relieved when six days later he was forced to resign. Dawson was to die in 1910 of over-drinking, by which time his party was triumphing almost everywhere.

The success of the Labor Party was a sign of the egalitarian, levelling spirit that was growing stronger and would prevail during the first half of the twentieth century. It was widely agreed that there was a strong role for government in regulating work, industry and social life. The idea spread that tall poppies, or too-tall poppies, should be cut down. In the United States on the other hand the belief was strong that a certain ideological and religious soil was desirable because it allowed tall poppies to flourish. There the tall poppy, especially if it was self-sown, was hailed as a sign of national energy: individual achievement was a hallmark of American nationalism. In Australia in contrast the mateship and egalitarianism were seen by many, though not all, as the

• • • • • • • • • •

hallmarks of nationalism. Courage in the face of defeat often earned more prestige than courage leading to triumph.

It is unwise to venture too far in contrasting two nations which had much in common, being democratic and prosperous and European in their institutions. Sometimes the contrast is exaggerated. Sometimes, as we have seen, a quality or attitude which seems to be weak in one country is really present but disporting itself in an unexpected arena of national life. Much of Australia's competitiveness was seen in sport rather than work. It was also seen in the intense rivalry between regions and colonies, a rivalry fiercer than in the United States. How to tackle and tame that rivalry was a dilemma of the 1890s.

The flush of violet

The six colonies gloried in being separate. They ran their own post offices and issued their own postage stamps, lit their own lighthouses, built their own railways, and conducted their own immigration programmes in good years. Each colony, until 1895, set its clocks to a different time. At the inland borders, customs officers collected import duties; and so a Wodonga hotel-keeper who wished to import Sydney beer from the other side of the Murray River paid an import duty of twopence a bottle, the same duty as he paid on a bottle from Germany. A bank manager who moved from one colony to another might have to pay duty on some of his own furniture.

2

Each colony controlled its own defence forces. South Australia had its gunboats with Gatling guns, and New South Wales had torpedo boats. Tasmania had its volunteers wearing magnificent uniforms, and two dozen permanent artillerymen manned the forts guarding the sea approaches to Hobart and Launceston. In 1889 the seven colonies of

• • • • • • • • • •

Australia and New Zealand could call on 30,000 part-time soldiers in an emergency but barely 1,000 full-time servicemen. Here was a sign of how peaceful was this corner of the world: Australasia supported nearly as many politicians as full-time soldiers and sailors.

In the event of war the colonies, each a law to itself, would be unlikely to run a cohesive campaign. So long as they relied on Britain's naval strength their disunity did not matter. By the early 1880s they were not sure whether they should rely so much on Britain. Moreover their overseas interests were not always the same as Britain's but they rarely spoke with one voice when those interests were challenged. Many Australians rightly feared that Germany would annex part of New Guinea and nearby islands and that France would annex the New Hebrides. These events came to pass. Great European powers were entrenched not far from Australia. In a major war their presence would be dangerous. In 1885, when Russia and Britain were at loggerheads over central Asia, there were rumours that Russian cruisers were about to attack Australian ports. Eventually the Australian colonies agreed to defray part of the cost of the British naval squadron which had long been based in Sydney. Subsidising the British navy gave Australians more say in matters of foreign policy.

In 1889 Major-General J. B. Edwards, a veteran of the Crimean War and Indian Mutiny, arrived to inspect the various little armies. The task did not take long. He was not impressed by what he saw. If Australia were invaded the armies could hardly help each other quickly because of their divided command, their medley of armaments, and the various railway gauges that might prevent the quick movement of troops and arms. His report was too strongly influenced by the speed with which the Germans in 1870 used their railways to bring to the French border a huge invading army. He failed to realise that ships – not the coastal railways – would be Australia's main way of moving troops to a likely point of attack. Edwards was sensible, however, in calling for 'a federation of the forces of the different colonies'.

His report was influential. The premier of New South Wales, Sir Henry Parkes, who imagined himself the patriarch of Australian politics, used the Edwards report to preach the case for a wider federation. In October 1889, at a banquet at the inland town of Tenterfield, this fine orator with his high-pitched voice and his habit of dropping an aitch or two, argued that Australia was an infant United States, holding as many people as that land held when in the 1770s it became an independent nation. Surely – the words rolled from Sir 'Enry's long white beard – 'surely what the Americans had done by war, the Australians could bring about by peace'.

Parkes knew how to elevate political questions far above the sordid jangle of pounds, shillings and pence. In his oration he recited the somewhat stilted but strangely moving verse by the Queensland poet, Brunton Stephens, who saw a united Australia about to rise like a sun entering the flushed morning sky: 'Not yet her day. How long "not yet"? There comes the flush of violet!'

Parkes invited the colonies to send delegates to a convention in Sydney in 1891 in order to draw up a constitution for a federal government. The Commonwealth of Australia was the name he proposed. Curiously, New Zealanders also took part in drawing up the proposed constitution but later went their own way. If the federal movement had gathered momentum a decade earlier and all the colonies had achieved federation in 1891 instead of 1901, New Zealand would probably have been a founding member. In economic trouble in the 1880s, it had incentives to join what was to become a common market, but in the following decade it was more prosperous than Australia and saw no powerful reason to join. Nonetheless, section six of the Australian constitution still begins with the hopeful words that the potential states of the Commonwealth are New South Wales, New Zealand, and so on down the list.

Defence had carried the idea of federation one step. Now in the 1890s the economic hopes began to carry it to the next. The fierce depression and the collapse of so many banks in 1893 made Victorians especially see economic advantages in forming a common market covering the whole continent. Victoria, unlike New South Wales, was protectionist. It envisaged a united Australia guarded by a high tariff wall that would restrict foreign and British imports, abolish the customs houses on the internal Australian borders, and thereby foster local factories and workshops. A few of these federal enthusiasts met at the border town of Corowa, New South Wales, in the winter of 1893. Corowa stood on the Murray, a river whose quietness was broken by the chugging sound of the passing paddle steamers and the throb of the steam engines at the two flour mills. The town was about 400 kilometres from Sydney and only half as far from Melbourne, its natural port, but every bag of flour and cask of wine it sent by railway to Melbourne had to pay a Victorian import duty. Corowa therefore had a vested interest in demolishing the customs houses scattered along the banks of the river.

Fortunately, John Quick of Bendigo was a delegate at the Corowa conference. He had emigrated from Cornwall as a child, and had worked when very young in the noisy crushing mills and foundries at Bendigo – a fatherless boy making his way in the world. Studying after work, eventually becoming a lawyer, his career consisted of doggedly walking through obstacles. He viewed the six obstinate and proud colonies as just another obstacle to be overcome. He devised a scheme for reviving the federal movement and enlisting the enthusiasm or interest of every colony.

The Quick formula was ultra-democratic: no nation had ever been created on the basis of such a formula. His idea was that the voters of each colony would, at a special poll, elect delegates who would then come together to devise a federal constitution. The constitution would be approved by the colonial parliaments and then go to the people for their decision in a special referendum. Finally it would go to the British parliament for its approval. It was in keeping with the Quick formula that, after the federation was created, a change to any part of the final constitution had to be approved at a referendum, in which a majority of voters in a majority of colonies (now called states) said 'yes'.

Quick's idea was endorsed. The constitution that was finally set in place in 1901 has not often been amended; and decade after decade, most of the proposed changes to the constitution have been defeated by popular vote, prompting many commentators to say that the Australian people are innately conservative. This diagnosis is overstated. Since 1901 no national leader seeking to change the constitution has ever tried a version of the Quick formula. Instead he has preferred to hand-pick a team of his supporters and sympathisers to draft major changes to the constitution, and then has expressed indignation or astonishment when the people voting at a referendum said an emphatic 'no'.

At Parliament House in Adelaide in March 1897 the fifty elected delegates – ten from each participating colony – devoted long days and evenings to debating and altering that constitution which had been quickly written down in 1891. The absentees were especially noticed: Sir Henry Parkes was dead, no New Zealand delegate arrived, and even the Queenslanders were absent. Of the fifty delegates, half had been born in Australia and almost half in the British Isles. The only exception was Canadian-born Simon Fraser, grandfather of that prime minister who in 1975 was to be a commanding figure in the first grave dispute about the interpreting of the constitution.

None of the delegates who drew up the constitution was a woman and only one was a trade unionist – the Victorian politician William Trenwith who had been a bootmaker. Jews were well represented, Catholics not, in the delegates who met under the name of the Federal Convention. They took to their task with eagerness. After leaving

Adelaide they had a long recess and then assembled in Sydney in September. They met again in Melbourne, in the fiery heat of the early weeks of 1898.

One key question was easily asked but not easily answered: which responsibilities should remain with the colonies or states and which powers besides defence and tariffs should belong to the new federal government? Another vital question was how to distribute the electoral power. Could the popular method of one vote for each person be reconciled with the fact that smaller colonies would enter the federation only if they were given the iron assurance that they would receive more political power than their population merited? Tasmanians demanded that in the senate or upper house a colony with few people would have the same number of senators as the populous Victoria and New South Wales. In the final decision the senate was weighted in favour of the smaller states, while the lower house was weighted in favour of the populous states. Victoria and New South Wales had the large populations and so they received most seats in the House of Representatives, but in the Senate each state was entitled to the same number of senators.

The new constitution was to consist of 118 sections or clauses, most of which contained just one sentence. It began by affirming that 'the people' of the Australian colonies, 'humbly relying on the blessing of Almighty God', agree to unite in 'one indissoluble Federal Commonwealth'. But would the people agree? In June 1898 the voters in the three strong federalist colonies – Victoria, Tasmania and South Australia – went to the polling booths and voted decisively for the new constitution. In the gold city of Ballarat and the hilly farms of north-western Tasmania they were in favour by a margin of more than twenty to one. New South Wales, however, was not convinced: there was partly a fear that Victoria would dominate the new parliament. In Sydney most electorates voted against the federation. In the colony as a whole the yes vote was 71,600 and the no vote was 66,200. As the New South Wales government had decreed that the referendum would only be regarded as decisive if at least 80,000 voted for federation, the result was really a defeat.

At this time, New South Wales and especially Sydney were passing through a phase that mingled confidence and fear. The original ruler of Tasmania, Victoria and Queensland, Sydney had lost prestige after Melbourne passed it in population in the 1850s, and was only now regaining its full self-esteem. New South Wales was now the dynamic economy. Its seams of black coal and its sweeping expanse of grazing and ploughed land generated economic success. New South Wales was so breezily confident that it would actually pass Victoria in population that in 1888 it actually proposed to alter its name to Australia, an audacious plan shelved only after loud protests rolled across the borders. Nonetheless it remained nervous of Victoria; and numerous Sydney politicians and merchants were inclined to see federation as a Victorian conspiracy.

Olive branches had to be offered to woo the voters of New South Wales. Now they were to be awarded the site of the new federal capital city, so long as it was not near Sydney: in actual outcome the present Canberra was to be the bribe. A new referendum was needed to endorse this proposal. In 1899 the modified constitution was again voted for decisively in the three pro-federalist colonies. It was also endorsed by a safe margin in New South Wales and a narrow one in Queensland. If 4,000 Queenslanders had changed their minds on polling day, their colony would not have joined. A year later Western Australia, largely through the votes of the new goldfields, agreed to join. Probably the two reluctant entrants, Queensland and Western Australia, saw themselves as the lands of the future. They believed they might survive and prosper, even if they stayed outside the federation.

3

The Commonwealth of Australia, proclaimed on the first day of 1901, came into existence before the first election was fought. Edmund Barton, a native-born lawyer who had been Sydney's strongest advocate for federation, was nominated as prime minister; and after he won his seat in the March election he formed his ministry and won the support of the lower house. Melbourne was to be the federal capital until the new capital city in New South Wales was selected and built. So Barton presided in Victoria's noble Parliament House on the hill at the top of Bourke Street, while the new governor-general, Lord Hopetoun, occupied the Victorian governor's former mansion, perhaps the most imposing vice-regal palace in the British Empire.

The six states remained powerful. The laws they passed, even more than federal laws, changed and shaped daily life. Their combined budget dwarfed the first federal budgets, for in the early years they were entitled to keep three-quarters of the customs revenue they collected. For years the states were the only collectors of income tax. In Melbourne, the capital both of Australia and Victoria, far more civil servants were employed by the state of Victoria than by the new Commonwealth, for the states retained control of railways, prisons and police, education, lands and mines, social welfare and many other matters.

In the first parliaments three parties competed for power. The conservative Free Traders, led by George Reid of Sydney, held office briefly in 1904–05. Later they fused with Alfred Deakin's Liberals, who were middle-road, protectionist and politically successful in most years until 1910. Labor enjoyed its time of triumph under Andrew Fisher, a Scottish migrant who once drove an engine in a Gympie gold mine. His first Labor ministry consisted largely of British migrants, whereas the Liberals tended to be led by native Australians.

The flush of violet

· · · · · · · · · ·

One of the first federal laws, passed in 1901, restricted Asian immigration. The policy was inevitable: the difficulty was how to express it and enforce it. While many politicians, especially on the Labor benches, thought that the Chinese were an economic, moral and political menace, other politicians passed no slur on Asians as human beings. Alfred Deakin, who was three times prime minister in the first decade, eloquently expressed a widely held opinion: 'It is not the bad qualities, but the good qualities of these alien races that make them dangerous to us'. The Japanese even more than the Chinese impressed Deakin: 'It is their inexhaustible energy, their power of applying themselves to new tasks, their endurance, and low standard of living that make them such competitors'.

While the Chinese already in Australia were allowed to remain, new Asian migrants were discouraged. Those who arrived had to pass a dictation test, a device borrowed from Natal in South Africa. The test was primarily designed to prevent the entry of any Asians who wished to be permanent migrants. At the ports a Commonwealth official, choosing any European language, could dictate aloud several sentences totalling no more than fifty words and instruct the would-be migrant to write down the words. Failure to write them correctly meant that the migrant could not land. In the first year, eight Japanese, six Hindus and four Assyrians were amongst those who passed the dictation test but 459 Chinese failed and so were forced to stay in their ship. In 1905, few Asians arrived, and nobody who was actually given the dictation test recorded a pass. The new immigration law and its intricacies could also be used to exclude unwanted Englishmen. Six migrants, hat-makers by trade, were detained on arrival in 1902 but eventually allowed to land.

Of the 40,000 or so Asians living in Australia, many felt humiliated by the policy. Most, however, were allowed to remain. The Chinese were content to be market gardeners, laundrymen, shopkeepers and furniture-makers, but prayed that their bones might finally be carried back to their ancestral home. Between 1905 and 1912 entry was permitted for specific Japanese, Indian and Chinese businessmen, students and other newcomers who carried a passport; and many lived here for long periods.

This so-called White Australia Policy ultimately harmed Australia's reputation. It was too rigid, persisted for too long, and was often defended with derogatory and unfair rhetoric. Modern Australian and Asian critics, however, have exaggerated the policy and removed it from its historical context. They forget that the world was then more insular: foreign travel was less common. Most nations then displayed stronger views about religion, race, kinship and culture, and their leaders rightly thought a high level of national unity was an asset in the event of war. Moreover the ways of life of Europeans and Asians were then so far apart that misunderstandings easily arose.

The White Australia Policy was far from unique. Canada, the United States and New Zealand – three other democratic nations which faced an inrush of Chinese – had built their own walls against Asian immigration by the 1880s. China and Japan usually gave no welcome to foreigners; and even today it is difficult for a foreigner to become a citizen of either nation. Indeed, late in the nineteenth century it was much safer to be a Chinese living in Australia than an Australian in China: six Australian missionaries, young women and men of compassion, were murdered in various anti-foreigner episodes in China. Of course the Chinese suffered when they migrated to other countries fronting the Pacific Ocean, but in a typical year they probably suffered less in Australia than in other lands they entered. When the Emperor of China sent commissioners to other lands in 1887 to see whether Chinese residents were ill-treated, he was informed that the numerous Chinese living in Java and the Philippines were treated rather worse than those living in Australia.

Australia sometimes expressed its official policy with arrogance and utter contempt for other races. At the same time it seemed more willing than most other nations to admit people who seemed different. Between 1901 and 1914 many Italians, Greeks, Maltese and Jewish Russians arrived, and in some years they must have formed a considerable minority of the migrants who stayed. Italians had long ago formed small colonies in Australia, with active pockets on the Victorian diggings in the 1850s and later on the north Queensland cane-fields. At first few Greeks arrived. The new shipping route through the Suez Canal made migration to Australia easier for Greeks. Many arrived as seamen and stayed. By 1914 at least three times as many Greeks lived here as in 1890, and cafes and fish shops were their special occupation. In recent years some critics have claimed that Australia actually excluded Mediterranean people, but in the twelve years to 1914 a total of 4,775 Greeks arrived, and only one was excluded, and he had spent time in gaol.

Pacific Islanders and the Chinese were the main targets of the new immigration policy. The Islanders had worked on the sugar-cane fields dotted along the river estuaries of Queensland. They must leave Australia, decreed the first parliament. No more could be recruited after March 1904. As their labour had been vital for the success of the sugar industry, a large subsidy was voted for all the sugar-cane which henceforth would be grown and cut and carted by white labour. In the summer of 1906–7, about 4,400 Melanesians prepared to go home with all their new possessions including kerosene lamps and the occasional sewing machine. The Solomon Islanders sailed from Cairns, the New Hebrideans sailed from Brisbane. About 1,500 were allowed to remain on the basis of the sympathetic argument that they had long lived here, or owned freehold land, or were married to a woman of another race.

In politics nearly every solution to a problem begins to germinate a new problem. The economic growth in northern Australia had depended on cheap labour, and that slowly vanished. The sugar-growers on the hot Queensland coast received a federal subsidy as compensation but no subsidy was given to west Queensland and the Kimberleys where the Afghan camelmen were the main carriers, no subsidy to the Northern Territory and far north Queensland where the Chinese were amongst the main miners, market gardeners, shopkeepers, tailors and other tradesmen, nor to the scattered northern waters where Asians were the main divers in the pearling fleets.

If tropical Australia had been open to cheap labour its population would have continued to advance. Instead – apart from the sugar fields – it tended to stagnate. It was the economic casualty of the White Australia Policy. Possessing few railways and depending heavily on the small ships that plied along the coast, it suffered when the federal government insisted that all coastal ships should be owned and manned by white Australians. The policy was understandable, but it led to dear transport and it retarded economic development. So the tropics of Australia, embracing two-fifths of the land and even more of the coastline, were placed in economic quarantine for the following half century.

The new federal government also had to devise a policy for the coastline lying opposite tropical Australia. The mountainous forest-clad island of New Guinea and its chains of islands had been subdivided into three colonies, the Dutch, German and British. From 1906 British New Guinea, including the territory facing the Queensland coast, was governed by the Australian parliament under the formal name of the Territory of Papua. How many people then lived in this land which was the size of Victoria? Nobody knew, for many of the mountains and swamplands had not even been explored. Most people were illiterate, but their tenure of land – unlike that of the Aborigines in Australia – was respected because it was understood. The Papuans, as a gardening people, fitted into the global economy with far greater ease than the nomadic Aborigines had initially fitted. Their eagerness for the Christian religion likewise delighted the missionaries.

The Australian who did most to influence Papua was Sir Hubert Murray, a Catholic lawyer who had fought in the Boer War. He was chastened by his first view of the capital, Port Moresby, in September 1904. Protected from the ocean by a coral reef and from the interior by ramparts of steep hills, the town was a straggle of white-painted, iron-roofed buildings, some standing on stilts alongside roads that were muddy after rain. The town's fifty European men and women lived largely on tinned and bottled foods bought at several stores and a hotel. It was no wonder that Murray's wife, Sybil, returned to Sydney after one week. Her husband was to administer Papua for one-third of a century.

4

There was now an actual Australian flag that flew in these foreign outposts. A competition to design the nation's flag – prizes were offered by a popular magazine and by the Havelock Tobacco Company – had attracted 33,000 entries from Australia and New Zealand; and the flag was first flown from the dome of the Exhibition Building in Melbourne in September 1901. The southern cross and Union Jack's three crosses dominated the flag, and public opinion admired this combination of Australian and British symbols. In the eyes of most Australians the southern cross was more important then than it is now. It pointed to Australia's geographical place in the world and it reflected the intense interest people took in the night sky which, in the era before electricity, was a brilliant sight in the big, dimly lit suburbs where Australians increasingly lived. The flag's crosses were seen proudly as Christian symbols in a nation where church-going was as customary as in the British Isles. The new flag was slightly altered after Papua was taken over, and a seventh point was added to the large Commonwealth star.

Banknotes and coins curiously were not amongst the new symbols of nationhood. Since the 1850s Australia had minted most of its gold sovereigns and half sovereigns, even exporting them, but these gold coins – and the silver and copper coins imported from England – had no distinctive Australian emblems. The new nation continued to use the familiar English currency until the crowning of George the Fifth in London in 1910, when it was resolved to design Australia's own coins, from the copper halfpenny upwards. The banknotes rather than the coins circulating in Australia had long been distinctive, though they were usually issued by Australia's numerous private trading banks and not by the colonial governments. In 1911 the creation of the Commonwealth Bank of Australia by the federal government led to the first official banknotes two years later. The visiting English novelist Rider Haggard stood at the special colour-printing press in Melbourne and formally printed note number 4, after the governor-general and his family had had their turn.

The first banknote to find its way into the purses of most Australians was the ten-shilling note. Of deep blue with dashes of other colours, it showed water spilling over the Goulburn Weir, the country's first big irrigation scheme. The pound note showed miners working deep underground, the fiver showed a placid scene on the Hawkesbury River, the tenner depicted teams of horses carting wagons loaded with wheat bags, and the twenty-pound showed men chopping down a tall tree in Queensland. In essence, the hero on most of the new banknotes in circulation was the Australian workman. For many years the reigning English monarch did not appear on Australian notes. The first Commonwealth postage stamp appeared in 1912, replacing stamps issued by each state. The popular penny stamp, which paid for a letter to be sent all the way to London, depicted a red kangaroo standing on a map of Australia.

The spirit and political mood of the country had changed since the bank crashes, depression and drought. In 1890 most Australians had believed that all people should work hard, should save for their old age – if they should chance to live that long – and should not ask the government for too much help; but twenty years later those ideas were shrinking. The dream of paying a deposit on a small farm and setting to work with an axe and a plough was still alive. The old dream influenced perhaps half of the population but certainly no more.

Most people in the cities turned to the trade unions and to the governments to improve their lot. The unions were possibly more powerful than in any other land, and unionists increasingly received a preference when applying for certain jobs. Left-wing Liberals and mainstream Labor tried to outbid each other. Election became an auction day. Election promises came to be seen, mistakenly, as vital determinants of the average Australian's standard of living.

Between 1895 and 1910 the average family entered a seemingly more secure world, protected by an umbrella of benevolent laws. For the average child, primary schooling had long been free but now in bigger towns a high school was built. The workplace was increasingly regulated. In most city jobs, whether in shops or factories or railways, a minimum wage and shorter hours of work were stipulated by government authorities, but the same privilege did not reach the rural workforce, which provided perhaps a quarter of all jobs. Major industrial disputes were increasingly settled by judges or by specialist panels with strong powers. Many of those who lived to be 65 were entitled to an old-age pension equal to just over one-quarter of a labourer's wage. From 1910 the mother of a newborn baby received a maternity allowance. In contrast there was no free housing, no free health service, and no relief for the unemployed, who were becoming far more numerous.

The new umbrella tried to protect Australia from foreign competition, a difficult task. Government activities like the railways and post office were already protected: there the unions were so successful in lobbying for high pay that in 1903 the state of Victoria experimented by segregating railwaymen into two special electorates and public servants into another, thereby hoping to stem their influence on election day. A rising Australia-wide tariff against imports now protected the multiplying factories. The federal government began to insist that protected factories, in return, should pay a higher wage to employees. A landmark was the decision in 1907 by Mr Justice Higgins of the new Commonwealth Court of Conciliation and Arbitration that McKay's big factory at Sunshine, Victoria, an efficient maker and exporter of mechanical horse-drawn harvesters, should pay its unskilled workmen what was called the basic wage of two pounds and two shillings a week.

State and federal governments intervened in more industries. Australia set out to protect local seamen and ships on the busy coastal trade by banning foreign ships and crew. State governments began to set up more business activities, Victoria opening a big state coal mine in the new town of Wonthaggi, and Queensland even opening a chain of state butcher shops. As electricity became important several of the private powerhouses were nationalised. Big pastoral estates were compulsorily acquired and broken into small farms, or singled out for a federal land tax in 1910. Social issues were tackled by busy governments. The sale of alcohol was more and more regulated, and in Victoria about half the hotels were compulsorily closed in the space of thirty years. The strong Women's Christian Temperance Union, rejoicing that the federal vote was granted to all women in 1902, predicted that their vote would shake the 'political power of the Drink Traffic'. Now the average adult was drinking less than twenty years previously.

Australia and New Zealand led the world in this phase of the social experiment. What they did was eagerly reported upon in Europe, sometimes with dewy-eyed exclamations, or sighs of dismay. Most Australians gained strong satisfaction from the feeling that their society was fairer and that a strong protective arm was stretching everywhere. The arm was sometimes frail and concealed by a long sleeve. While part of the welfare payment came from the redistribution of wealth, especially through the new income tax that richer people paid, much of the new welfare payment, whether higher money or shorter hours, came from an incredibly complicated series of government regulations and payments that quietly penalised one group of wage-earners so that another could be publicly rewarded. The rising umbrella of social security, soothing as it was to people who had battled all their life, reduced incentives all around.

In the years 1900 to 1925 the United States indirectly did more than Australia to aid the welfare of people in its control; it passed fewer protective laws but allowed incentives and unrestrained energy to increase the standard of living. Steadily the USA overtook and passed Australia's standard of living. There is a delicate balance between shielding people and encouraging them, and the USA perhaps went too far in one direction and Australia in the other. The Soviet Union, born in 1917 and influenced by the exciting Australian and New Zealand experiments, would eventually show how the umbrella, if too big and cumbersome, exposed people far more than it protected them. The price of the umbrella was a loss of personal liberty.

The rate of income tax paid by a millionaire was not yet punitive. Huge fortunes were still won from old and new industries. In cities and sometimes the sheep country could be seen the mansions of magnates whose money came from wool, beef, property dealing, import warehouses, and especially the later mines as distinct from the earlier diggings. To travel overseas in style was still the dream of Australia's rich. Archibald Marshall of the London *Daily Mail*, writing of his tour of Australia in 1909, was entertained in many of the big houses in the pastoral country: 'I cannot recall one where some member of the family was not either in England, or recently returned, or talking of going "home" shortly'.

5

Cars were on the roads – just a few of them. In 1896, Henry Ford in Detroit in the USA made the first of his celebrated cars. It had a petrol engine and was propelled by a chain drive rather like a bicycle. The driver steered with a tiller, not a steering wheel and, as a warning to horses and pedestrians, a man usually walked in front of the car. In the same year in Melbourne an inventor named Herbert Austin began to make a car. Later he moved to England where he made the cars that carried his own surname: his Baby Austin was a celebrity.

Near the river bank at Mannum in South Australia a steam-driven car was built by a manufacturer of ploughs, John Shearer. Another was built in Melbourne by a maker of steam engines and boilers named Herbert Thomson. He used a flame of kerosene to boil the water in a small rectangular boiler in the car. Equipped with the new pneumatic bicycle tyres, Thomson's front wheels were smaller than the back wheels. The body of the car, resembling a fine horse-drawn carriage, was made of fiddle-back ash and silky oak. In 1900 the Thomson safely travelled the 800 kilometres from Bathurst to its home in Melbourne. It was, for some tradesmen, an easy transition from the making of horse-drawn vehicles to making cars. Edward Holden, after whom the popular Australian brand of car was named, was originally a coach-builder in Adelaide.

In 1900 the main demand for petroleum products was kerosene rather than petrol, but petrol sales were growing. For several decades the imported petrol was distributed around Australia in four-gallon tins packed in pinewood boxes: the petrol bowser had not yet been invented. Motorists filled up a car by pouring in petrol from the tin. The pinewood petrol box was one of the common items in the Australian backyard. Women put their washing in the box and carried it to the clothesline.

Most cars on Australian roads were imported, and all were noisy. In the busy streets the horses drawing carts, cabs and buggies were often frightened by rowdy cars. In 1901, after a young racehorse led along a road took fright and charged a slow-moving car with fatal results, an Australian court ruled that the driver of the car should have halted before reaching the horse. He was ordered to pay heavy damages.

A new car was expensive and prone to frequent punctures and other breakdowns. The roads, except in the cities, were rough. The whole country was on the brink of a revolution in transportation and in sources of energy. The age of coal and steam was about to be challenged by the age of oil. No nation was to gain more from the motor engine than Australia, with its vast distances. But in another sense the new engine weakened the whole economy. It demanded oil, and Australia had to import it at massive cost for more than sixty years.

Before 1900 the country produced virtually all its own fuel, its own artificial energy. It mined all the coal it needed for railways and steamships, and the port of Newcastle even exported black coal in a fleet of sailing ships to Shanghai and Chile and other ports. Similarly the country cut all the firewood it needed – it was perhaps the most widely used fuel, whether in houses or bakehouses or even locomotives. And of course the grass and hay and chaff was a form of petrol, for it fed several million bullocks and draught horses. Wind too was a vital source of energy, and it drove the windmills and the deep-sea sailing ships. And then along came the motor car, truck, motor bike and soon the simple aircraft. They needed petrol but Australia produced virtually none. A local source of oil was therefore crucial.

In the interior of Queensland, Roma township and its 2000 people wanted more water, and on Hospital Hill they began the slow process of sinking an artesian bore. The first bore found water but not enough. In the darkness of the morning of 16 October 1900, a second well was down one kilometre when suddenly water mixed with mud shot to a height of nearly twenty metres. The gushing was not steady and sometimes retreated. Nobody at first could be quite sure what caused it. In fact it was the first discovery of natural gas in the continent.

Gas was pouring into the air and an optimist claimed that its quality was '50 per cent better than London gas' produced from black coal. In 1906 on Hospital Hill a gasometer was built to store the gas, and the mains were laid to the main streets, and on 9 June the first of eleven shops in Roma were illuminated with the fruits of this chance discovery of six years before. In the excitement a street lamp was also lit. The gas, however, soon ran low. After fourteen days it ceased to flow. A lot of fiddling took place with the disobedient bore before it was abandoned. Many geologists of that era did not think payable oil and gas would ever be found in Australia.

Another Queenslander thought he knew the appropriate rocks. A little-known giant in the world's history, William Knox D'Arcy had migrated as a 16 year old from London to the river port of Rockhampton where he became a solicitor and president of the local rowing club. After the discovery of a rich gold lode in nearby hills in 1882, he became the major shareholder in Mount Morgan, the first Australian company to pay one million pounds of dividends in the space of a year. With his wife, three daughters and two sons he returned to England where he lived like a shah. For the dining room of his towered mansion, Stanmore Hall in Middlesex, he commissioned Edward Burne-Jones to design the tapestry based on the Legend of the Holy Grail, now displayed in the Glasgow Art Gallery. He entertained in his private grandstand and dining room at Epsom racecourse and usually hired a special train to escort his guests to the Derby. With his round cheerful face, drooping moustache and bald head, he and his bejewelled wife were fixtures at the London opera and the European spas.

In 1901, using the fortune won from Mount Morgan, he began the costly search for oil in Iran. Seven years later, his money almost gone, he found the first oilfield in the Middle East. The long-term effects of his discovery on world trade, on war and technology, were not visible before he died, in 1917. But he was to be the most influential man – since Mohammed – in the history of the Middle East.

6

In the decade after the bank crashes, those Australians living in the interior had picked themselves up from the hard ground and had set to work with a will. A chain of goldfields was opened across the continent, in west and east, and for nine successive years their gold exceeded that mined in the rich years of the mid-1850s. A wheat belt was pioneered in the south-west of the continent, many of the farmers coming from the wheatlands of South Australia. In Victoria the mallee scrub was rolled down and burned in bonfires, and wheat planted in the dry, light-red soil. Never had so many people gone onto the land. In moist parts of Australia the forests were felled, and post-and-rail fences enclosed herds of Ayrshires, Jerseys, Guernseys, Shorthorns, Kerrys and other breeds that were milked twice a day, and the cream was extracted by the Danish separators and sent to the local butter factory. By the early 1900s, England's main outside supplies of factory-made butter came from Denmark, France and Australia.

From the northern rivers of New South Wales to Port Douglas, some 1500 kilometres to the north, little narrow railways conveyed piles of new-cut cane to the sugar mills. For dried fruits the north-west of Victoria was the centre and for wine it was South Australia: the Commonwealth's official *Year Book* observed that 'Australians are not a wine-drinking people', an observation that was dramatically reversed in the 1960s and 1970s. From the apple orchards of Tasmania the St Germain pears. Sturmer and York pippins, and Scarlet pearmains were sent in wooden cases to the wharves for shipment to India, the Malay Peninsula, South Africa and Egypt. Many of the apples and berries were boiled in big vats in Hobart whose tinned jam had won fame in 1885 when British officers wounded in the Sudan had spread it on their biscuits.

There was a dramatic increase in the output of the farmlands, especially after the drought was over. The flocks, halved to some fifty million by the drought and low wool prices, rose rapidly in the next ten years though the old peak was not passed until after World War I. All other kinds of livestock increased, acreage in crop soared, and most produce was carried away by railway, for this was the last great era of railway-building. After dark in tens of thousands of farmhouses, by the light of a kerosene or tallow lamp, people had the satisfaction of eating their own meat and eggs, and perhaps their own bacon, potatoes, cabbages, carrots, onions or maize in season.

The nation's exports were leaping. In every year but one in the long period from 1876 to 1891, Australia's imports had exceeded the exports, but in each of the following twenty-one years the value of exports exceeded the imports. Wool and gold were dominant, and a diversity of other products brought up the rear. In producing the nation's primary wealth the small and medium-sized farms as a group were becoming as important as the big sheep stations.

The small farmer was the butt of countless jokes. It was Arthur Hoey Davis, writing in Queensland under the name of Steele Rudd, who in 1899 produced the first of his best-selling books about Dad, who was all obstinacy and long whiskers, and Mum and the children. Davis's humorous book, called *On Our Selection*, told of everyday life on the farmlands of the Darling Downs where he himself had grown up. Dad's first crop of grain, harvested from a mere four acres, didn't even pay for the months of provisions he had bought at the general store on credit. The money owed to the local storekeeper was the one sum which most farmers carried in their head. Perhaps until the 1940s, the most common jokes told in city pubs were centred on Dad and Dave and his girl friend Mabel.

In the cities the factory was the busy hirer of workers. Old factories grew, new ones sprang up in their thousands, and in 1910 it was easy to find factories that employed more than 700 hands to serve the market once dominated by importers. C. J. Dennis, a popular poet, had written caustically for his own little paper the *Gadfly* about the days when Australia imported so much: 'This country was created, as full everybody knows, / For the foreign manufacturer of cheap and shoddy clothes.'

Now the clothes and hats and boots were made in Australia, along with countless other items previously imported. Steam locomotives and railway carriages were made on a large scale at such works as James Martin's of Gawler, Clyde Engineering of Sydney and the big government workshops at Newport, Victoria, and Redfern, New South Wales. Australia had several dozen woollen mills, scores of boot and shoe factories (the Melbourne suburb of Collingwood smelled of fresh leather), numerous breweries and tobacco factories, and big workshops that made farm machinery. By 1912 iron and steel, which were the hard core of an industrialised nation, were made on a small scale by Hoskins brothers at Lithgow in New South Wales, while a far larger steelworks was about to be built by Broken Hill Proprietary Company on the riverfront at Newcastle. But the typical workshop was still small: a bicycle-maker or printer working in a city lane, or a saddler stitching in a main street of a country town, or two female dress-makers working at home and filling orders for a city emporium.

The nation, while seen as unsophisticated, had bold problem-solvers in science and industry: A. G. M. Michell, the quiet Melbourne engineer who invented the thrust bearing that made possible the huge warships of World War I and the long oil-tankers of today; F. J. Lyster, who as a humble foreman at Broken Hill devised the selective flotation process which, used throughout the world, is one of the notable innovations in the history of metallurgy; and the Braggs of Adelaide, father and son, who pioneered crystallography and together won the Nobel Prize in 1915.

Optimism had returned to the nation. The humiliation of the 1890s was half-forgotten by the old and unknown to the young, except by hearsay. Australia again was attractive to migrants. In the fifteen years to 1906 it had gained virtually nothing from migration, because those disillusioned workers going overseas – young men seeking work, old people returning to their motherland – almost equalled those new migrants who were arriving. Now immigrants poured in. During 1911, 1912 and 1913 the scene at the wharves as the British migrants walked down the gangways was reminiscent of the boom years of the previous century.

The optimism did not last. Drought intervened, and war.

. . . .

part three

From Gallipoli
to Uluru

. . . .

The war to end war

On the eve of World War I, Britain was close to the peak of its power. Australians bathed in the warmth of the British sun. In many ways the two nations were one. Between them the flow of migrants, commodities and ideas was usually smooth. In 1914 most of the high official posts in Australia were still occupied by people born and educated in the British Isles. Australia's governor-general and the six state governors came from the British Isles. The prime minister, Joseph Cook, an English migrant, was succeeded at the start of the war by Andrew Fisher, a Scottish migrant. It almost seemed a backsliding, for the first four prime ministers had spent their childhood in the southern hemisphere, and, of those four, the two most prominent – Barton and Deakin – had been born in Australia. In many fields of life, especially the higher rungs of big business, the migrants were not so dominant.

The accents of the British Isles could be heard in pulpits and newspaper offices. Probably not one of the Anglican and Catholic bishops scattered across the land was a native of Australia. The Methodists, alone of the big four churches, were essentially Australian, having few links with their English mother church. In private grammar schools the British link was strong. British scholars held at least half the university chairs in Australia and sent on their brightest students who wished to do further study to Oxford and Cambridge or, if they were musicians, to Germany. Most of the popular songs and gramophone cylinders sold in the music shops came by ship from England. News from the British Isles studded the daily newspapers. The only influential newspaper to sneer regularly at Britain and royalty was the weekly Sydney *Bulletin*, and it was quietening down.

In schools the geography of Britain as well as Australia was learned. Clever schoolgirls knew by heart the names of all the rivers and mountains of Britain. On Sunday they sang hymns that had converted the dry Australian-like landscape of the Holy Land into the green hills and fast streams of England. In the bookshops – and Australians were probably more avid readers of books than the British – most best-sellers came from London.

Most ships in the ports were British, though Germany and France ran their own passenger liners to Australia. British companies owned the telegraph cables that snaked under the sea to link with the major cable-transmitting stations on Australia's coast. Britain was the main market for Australia's wool, gold, butter, beef and other exports, though more and more products, especially the base metals, went to Germany, Belgium and France. That threesome actually bought 31 per cent of Australia's exports compared with 44 per cent bought by Britain, and shrewd businessmen forecast a decline in Britain's commercial role.

Of the adults born in Australia or for long resident here, most were proud to belong to the British Empire but saw themselves as different to Britons. They believed that they had a fuller dose of what they saw as the stoutest British qualities – courage, self-reliance, and the appropriate blend of independence and loyalty. The typical Australians of 14 were more advanced physically than their English-born cousins.

2

Australian manners, whether of miners in a pub or bankers in a club, were not the same as English manners. English visitors could no longer safely make the remarks that would have passed unnoticed a few decades earlier. Rudyard Kipling, a favourite poet of the 1890s, wrote a verse which he put into Sydney's mouth, a verse referring favourably to the city's convict origins: 'Greeting! My birth-stain have I turned to good'. Kipling, a respected individualist, could say what he liked. But when in 1899 Lord Beauchamp arrived in Sydney as the new governor, a mere lad of 27, he thoughtlessly invoked Kipling's verse, slightly altering it to read 'your birth-stain have you turned to good', and was swamped by a wave of indignation. In Melbourne and Adelaide of course there must have been as much merriment as indignation but in Sydney the convict past was still unmentionable or, when mentioned, a family secret. To his credit Beauchamp learned to read the new radical and nationalist currents in Australian minds and he became a financial patron of the young radical writer, Henry Lawson.

Bishop H. H. Montgomery, popular as the Bishop of Tasmania but known today as the father of the famous soldier, Field Marshal Montgomery, decided on his return to England that he should instruct young clergymen heading for the colonies. In a small book of 1910 he advised them to clean their own boots when in Australia and to learn how to fit an iron horseshoe to a horse. Beware, he wrote, of 'the affected voice manner'. Never speak, he warned, about 'the lower classes' because in democratic Australia most people did not see themselves as belonging to lower classes. He knew that Australians were becoming touchier.

The fast flow of British migration just before World War I provoked a burst of anti-British feeling. It was becoming easy to identify the new British migrants because Australian accents and even clothes were now different. To describe British migrants, a slightly derogatory word came into use. For decades a migrant had been called a 'new chum', a phrase which sounds harmless but could be pronounced with a touch of derision. The latest word for migrants was cheeky and maybe derisory. The word was 'Pommy', and it came into use from about 1912. Pommy stemmed from the rhyming slang then common in Cockney London and especially in Australia. In rhyming slang the practice was to alter playfully the name of common nouns; and so a snake became a Joe Blake, and pomegranate in turn was the slang word for immigrant. So this, it seems, was how the word Pommy was devised.

Some cultural ties with the British Isles were slightly frayed. Certain Australian institutions – including trade unions and friendly societies – now had only a faint contact with British organisations which had once been their mothers or sisters. Similarly many Australian authors and painters were finding a wide and avid audience by appealing to local interests and prejudices. In the shops the distinctive and even assertive Australian brand names were gaining popularity. A famous brand of tea was Billy Tea, Donaghy's ropes adopted the Kangaroo brand, and there was a Dingo brand of eucalyptus oil – that national medicine and cure-all. Boomerang was the name of a tyre and brandy, and Cooee was the brand name for items ranging from galvanised iron to tomato sauce.

Other products carried such Australian names as Platypus, Possum, Kingfisher, Rosella, Wattle, Waratah, Kurrajong, Eureka, Nugget and Swan – black of course. Nationalism was more visible in shops than in schoolrooms. In the shops Australian manufacturers competed directly with English products and increasingly, with the aid of import duties, outsold them.

Even in finance, nationalism asserted itself. The big English-owned banks were losing business to the Australian-owned banks. They lost not merely to the nation-wide giants like the Bank of New South Wales and the National and new Commonwealth but also to small regional banks like the Bank of Adelaide and the Bank of North Queensland. Amidst all the rhetoric about the close ties between Britain and Australia there was intense competition. Nationalism was even stronger in commerce than in the arts.

In defence and foreign policy, where the speechmaking was most fervent, a sense of imperial unity still reigned. In line with that unity, Australia sent 16,000 horsemen and even more horses across the Indian Ocean to fight with Britain against the Boers in the war of 1899–1902. The economic and strategic interests of Britain and Australia, however, were not always the same. The crushing defeat inflicted by the Japanese navy against the Russians in east Asian waters in 1905 was seen by many Australians as a warning that one day Japan might come south. As Britain and Japan were now naval allies, where did Australia fit in that global triangle?

The military rise of Japan, as well as the growing naval might of Germany in the Pacific Ocean, worried many Australians. Labor as well as Liberal politicians believed that Australia should learn to defend herself as well as help to defend the British Empire. In 1911 the federal government introduced compulsory military training for boys and young men. At Duntroon, near the village of Canberra, a college began to train military officers and at Jervis Bay a naval college was opened. The new Royal Australian Navy had already ordered expensive cruisers and destroyers from British shipyards. The first, HMAS *Sydney*, was one of the most advanced fighting ships in the world when she reached Australia in 1913. Australia's vigorous spending on navy and army, in the five years before World War I, was becoming a burden for a small nation.

Some historians now express their puzzlement that Australia, once the war began in Europe, should almost unthinkingly see herself as bound to go to war. Why did Australia not hesitate, they ask, before

• • • • • • • • • •

making this momentous decision to fight vigorously on the far side of the world? Australians did not need to pause. The decision to fight on Britain's side, come what may, was unconsciously made years earlier, and made with massive support from public opinion. Australia was emotionally and culturally tied to Britain. Her trade was largely with Britain. Her naval defences depended on Britain. She even entrusted, in most matters, her foreign policy to Britain. Without doubt, self-interest as well as emotion knotted her to Britain. Australia relied on Britain to keep Japan at bay and to prevent France and Germany from intruding into Australia's sphere of influence in the south-west Pacific.

3

Today, World War I is often seen as an Australian adventure far from home, entered with blind loyalty to British interests. On the contrary the early battles were close to home and fought partly to protect Australia's precious lines of communication. It has long been forgotten that the two major Australian engagements in the first eight months of the war centred on radio and telegraph stations at a time when radio, invented by the Italian Marconi, seemed likely to become a crucial factor in warfare at sea.

Early in the war, Australia sent a naval force to German New Guinea and captured the port of Rabaul and its powerful wireless station – possibly a stronger transmitter than any in Australia. Australians captured the German isle of Nauru and its wireless station. The Germans now were about to retaliate. On the Cocos Islands, a British cable and wireless station stood alongside the vital sea lane between Australia and Colombo and Suez, and on 9 November 1914 it reported that the German raider *Emden* was steaming into sight. The Australian light cruiser *Sydney* chanced to be not far away. In a quick battle the

Sydney outgunned the *Emden* and drove her into shallow water. Although the first part of the war, for Australia, was largely naval, thereafter it was the army's war.

Australians thought the proudest day in their history was 25 April 1915. On that Sunday, while families in Australia were going to church or eating their Sunday roast, the British, French, Australian and New Zealand troops were landing on cramped Turkish beaches in the darkness of early morning. The attack on the narrow peninsula at the mouth of the Dardanelles was an attempt to crush Germany's ally, Turkey, and so open a route whereby munitions could be shipped to help Russia and its huge but ill-equipped army.

The Australian casualty-lists were long. Hundreds were killed as they tried to advance a short way inland. A grandson of Peter Lalor, the hero of the miners' fight at the Eureka Stockade, was one of those killed. The commander of the Australians, General Bridges, was wounded by a sniper's bullet and died in a hospital ship that stood a few kilometres from the shore. In the fighting, respect grew for the brave uncomplaining peasant soldiers of Turkey – collectively called Jacko, Abdul and more colourful names by Australian soldiers.

Thirteen days after the landing the first detailed account of the Australians' exploits was printed in nearly every daily newspaper. The London journalist, Ellis Ashmead-Bartlett, a correspondent at two earlier wars, insisted that there 'has been no finer feat in this war than this sudden landing in the dark'. For a nation with centuries of military tradition, such praise would have been stirring. But for a nation whose troops had previously fought in no major war, the landing at Gallipoli was seen as a glorious entry on to the world's stage. Warfare was viewed as the sportsfield where the nation with the heroic qualities was victorious. Australian soldiers filled their homefolk with pride for another reason. The nation, reluctant to accept its convict past, greeted Gallipoli as the sign that it had redeemed its beginnings and had come of age.

The doctors and nurses did not feel the glamour and the glory. Their hospital ships anchored for a day or two and treated the wounded who came from the shore in lighters and trawlers. Sister Elsie Gibson, fresh from Hobart, described the stretcher cases coming aboard, and the men walking though, their faces streaming with blood, and those whose clothes were sodden with seawater. Occasionally she nursed a bleeding Turk or a Gurkha. At times the incoming wounded were 'nearly all smiling'; but during other nights hundreds of soldiers arrived who, having been in the trenches for a week, were now in 'a most horrible dirty, bloody condition'. A few days later, the ship would berth in 'smelly fly infested noisy Alexandria', where a convoy of Red Cross vehicles was waiting.

In the first months half a million Allied troops landed on the Gallipoli peninsula, though most of the men were not there at the same time. They won footholds on the narrow beaches, captured steep foothills and dry gullies but could penetrate no further. The fighting was now deadlocked. No armies could break through the enemy's line of trenches, and all suffered heavy losses when they tried.

After eight months the Allied forces quietly abandoned Gallipoli. The last Australians left during the winter darkness, six days before Christmas of 1915. They left behind thousands of graves. Of the Allies' death toll, 21,000 were British, 9,900 were French, 8,700 were Australian, 7,500 Indian and 2,700 New Zealanders. All these deaths were far outnumbered by the tally of Turkish deaths.

The anniversary of their landing was to become a national day in two faraway lands. Anzac Day – ANZAC was the code word for the Australian and New Zealand Army Corps – was to be holier than Sunday. It was a day of patriotic marches and solemn sermon-like speeches, the wearing of old digger's hats and war medals and the flying of flags at half-mast with the buglers sounding the last post at thousands of dawn or daylight ceremonies all the way from Coolgardie to Dunedin. Some military observers would classify Gallipoli as a defeat but many Australians cherished it as a drawn game gallantly played on the enemy's tricky homeground.

Most of the Australian soldiers were henceforth to serve in France and Belgium, the seat of the heaviest fighting. There the veterans from Gallipoli were joined by recruits. The death toll soon passed that of Gallipoli. As the fighting became deadlocked and as Allied casualties on the French battlefields passed the million, the call for more Australian soldiers grew louder. Late in 1916 the Labor prime minister, W. M. 'Billy' Hughes, decided that the reliance on volunteers should be replaced by the compulsory calling up of young men for service in foreign lands. In retrospect he would have been able to persuade his own party, the Labor Party, to adopt the policy of conscription in the first enthusiastic months of the war; but two years later enthusiasm for the war was slipping. The war, in lives and pounds, was far costlier than expected. Moreover the fighting was far from home, and Australia no longer seemed in danger after the capture of the nearby German colonies and the bottling up of the German navy in distant ports.

The trade unions which backed the Labor Party began to complain that workers more than employers were the economic victims of the war; real wages were falling in the face of wartime inflation. The punitive British policy towards Ireland also made many Irish-Australians lukewarm towards the war. Hughes himself had the knack of multiplying his enemies. He provoked fire-eating speeches from Coadjutor Archbishop Daniel Mannix of Melbourne, who had come from Ireland only four years previously. The swing of Catholic opinion virtually turned Victoria from a supporter to an opponent of Hughes's conscription plans.

Hughes, having alienated many supporters, tried to divert the heat by holding a national referendum on the question of whether young men should be forced to join the forces and fight overseas. Even before the referendum was narrowly defeated in 1916, Hughes was facing defeat within his own party. The Labor Party was torn apart. In November 1916 Hughes and twenty-four of his colleagues left the party, began to form an alliance with the conservatives, and so were able to cling to power even while losing the fight over conscription. In federal politics Labor henceforth was to wander in the wilderness, holding office for only ten of the next fifty-six years. Labor's hostility towards the conscripting of soldiers for overseas campaigns was to remain vigorous even during World War II when Australia itself was in peril.

4

The four years of fighting reshaped the economic life at home to a degree that nobody had predicted, partly because the war was longer and more expensive than foreseen. Prices of food and rent went up faster than wages; and the wartime year of 1917 was the worst so far experienced for strikes and industrial disputes. The fight over wartime conscription was partly an extension of the fight between capital and labour in the workplace where the wage-earners' standard of living was falling.

The war dislocated workplaces. Inflation of working costs crippled gold mines because the price at which they sold their gold bars remained the same. Maybe a hundred gold towns and villages suffered, and in the dry country of Western Australia a few gold towns were almost dead when their soldiers returned from the war. Likewise those base metals which, before the war, had been sold to German and Belgian smelters were now deprived of a market; and to treat the lead the smelters at Port Pirie had to be enlarged until eventually they became the biggest in the world. Wool, the most important export, had to be stockpiled. The scarcity of ships, after the German submarines won command of sea lanes in the North Atlantic, impeded the flow of manufactured goods from Europe. At least this gave some stimulus to Australian factories. Thus the shortage of imported steel boosted the steelworks just opened by Broken Hill Proprietary at Newcastle. The making of local munitions, copper cables and carbide was boosted by the scarcity of imports.

The war also increased Australians' self-respect. In the final phase of the fighting most of the high military posts were held not by permanent pre-war officers but by amateur soldiers: by engineers, bankers, businessmen and even politicians who were originally part-time militiamen when the war began. Sir John Monash, of Jewish background, was one of those all-rounders. He had shown his versatility as a young married man in Melbourne by using his spare time after the day's work to skip through a degree in law and complete a degree in arts, all in the space of two years. A civil engineer who used the new reinforced concrete to build bridges, he took up soldiering as a peacetime hobby. In 1918, in command of some 200,000 soldiers, including Americans, he was foremost in the advance that broke through the German lines and helped force Germany to the point of surrender.

The typical Australian soldier, it was said, displayed more vitality and nerve than the typical British soldiers of the same rank. It was observed that many Australian soldiers, on leave in Cairo or London, mimicked the formality of English officers or ran amok in the streets. An Australian was more likely than a British soldier to be a deserter or be absent without leave. C. E. Montague of the *Manchester Guardian* observed in the trenches of the western front that soldiers from the far side of the world 'had learned already to look at our men with the curious, half-pitying look of a higher, happier caste at a lower'. Not all Australians were taller than the British soldiers. After all, a big group of Australian soldiers had migrated from England as boys or young men in the decade before the war.

The Australian soldiers were self-selected; they were volunteers, and they proved brave fighters. Their casualty rate was higher than that of the New Zealanders and much higher than that of the British and Canadians. For every 100 men sent overseas or preparing to go, Australia suffered sixty-three casualties. General Monash privately noted at Gallipoli that his troops were admirable in their willingness to volunteer for dangerous tasks. 'Our wounded are most amazing', he added, 'they sing, they cheer, they smoke their cigarettes'. On the other hand Australia as a whole did not make wartime sacrifices that were as high as those in the nations that actually conscripted soldiers. Counting simply the men of enlistable age in each country, a higher proportion enlisted in Britain and New Zealand than in Australia or Canada.

Of more than 300,000 Australians who went overseas to fight, most served in Gallipoli and France but thousands were on other fronts. Allenby's forces, which captured Jerusalem from the Turks in 1917, included light horsemen from Western Australia. Many of the small planes that flew low over the western front or Mesopotamia were piloted by Australians. An Australian won the Victoria Cross in 1919 while fighting in an Allied army intervening in the civil war that raged in the new Soviet Union. Australian army nurses worked in hospital ships which anchored near Gallipoli each night, their white lights ablaze.

In all, 59,258 Australians were killed, or died of wounds. The United States, which entered the war in 1917, did not suffer so many deaths. Perhaps the most drastic effect of the war would never be enumerated: it was the loss of all those talented Australians who would have become prime ministers and premiers, judges, divines, engineers, teachers, doctors, poets, inventors and farmers, the mayors of towns and leaders of trade unions, and the fathers of another generation of Australians. It was a war in which those with the gift of leadership, the spark of courage, and the willingness to make sacrifices often took the highest risks. A young nation could not afford to lose such men.

A loss of such proportions must have affected perhaps half of all the marriages and half of all the births taking place in Australia in the following thirty years. If there had been no war, the list of marriages after 1918 would have been rewritten; and many of those reading such books as this, and even writing them, would not have been born, their mothers having married other men.

W. M. Hughes and Sir Joseph Cook represented Australia at the peace conference in Paris. It was a sign of the new status of Australia and the main British dominions that each was given seats at the conference which drew up the new boundaries of Europe. Hughes was aggressive – he could afford to be, he said, because he spoke for 60,000 dead. In the peace treaty Australia was granted a mandate over German New Guinea, including the island of Bougainville, where the huge copper mine was to be opened in the 1960s. Australia acquired an interest in another German colony, a one-third share in the Pacific island of Nauru, which was rich in the phosphate rock used in the fertilisers increasingly spread on the inland wheatlands. Australia in fact received even more territory than Italy, whose sacrifices in the war had been huge and whose hunger for colonies was intense. In June 1919, Australia signed the peace treaty as if it were a completely independent nation. Hughes, who remained the prime minister for four years after the war, wanted his say in any British policy that might affect his nation's interests: he insisted that Australia must independently sign the Washington Treaty which limited the navies of the major powers.

The war had made Australia a nation, and none of the statutes and agreements which later set out the formal relations with Britain could have a comparable impact. When the assembly of the League of

Nations met for the first time at Geneva in November 1920, Australia was one of the forty-two nations represented as full members. The Statute of Westminster, passed by the British parliament in 1931, was formally to give Australia an independence it already possessed.

The idealists thought that this was the war to end all wars, but in hidden ways it perhaps helped to make another war more likely. The war served to increase the power of Japan, which had suffered only tiny losses in the fighting. By the 1920s Japan as a naval power was ranked third or fourth in the world. The war also hastened the little-noticed economic decline of Britain. Even in 1900 Britain had lagged behind Germany and the United States in the production of steel, then the barometer of industrial strength. And yet most Australians still believed the prayer, popularised in 'Land of Hope and Glory' by Edward Elgar's new tune, that 'God who made thee mighty, make thee mightier yet'. In Australia few observed that Britain was no longer so mighty. Its economy and its navy were probably not capable of defending a far-flung empire on which the Japanese looked with envy.

What an
'unlimited future'!

Plans to build thousands of war memorials, yes thousands, were under way. Every town, suburb and crossroads village, and most churches and schools, set out to erect a stone memorial or a gold-lettered honour roll to 'the honoured dead', 'the glorious dead', 'the sons of this church', 'men of this district' and 'our fallen heroes'. Working bees were organised to plant avenues of honour, and in the wide roads approaching cool-climate towns the lines of elms, oaks and other European trees were planted on each side of the road in memory of every local resident who died or enlisted: many avenues ran for kilometres, a metal plaque alongside each tree. No nation in Europe showed such a visible desire to remember, to honour.

The costly task of caring for the wounded and disabled, the war widows and their children, had to be faced. Tens of thousands of farms were needed so that returned soldiers could try their hand at farming. The sheer cost of these projects called a financial halt to Australia's rapid march towards the welfare state. New welfare schemes mostly had to be deferred, except by those governments that thumbed their nose at the normal rules of finance. In New South Wales and Queensland, where radical governments won elections, new pensions and other innovations in social security were to be a hallmark of the post-war period.

Soon after the war was over, economic activity sagged. Unemployment was unexpectedly high, perhaps rising to 13 per cent in 1921. The new steelworks at Newcastle were closed for nine successive months. The industrial tension of wartime persisted with bitter strikes in coal mines, the waterfront and even a section of the Victorian police force. More days were lost through industrial disputes in 1919 and 1920 than in all but two other years in the period 1900 to 1939. At the biggest metal-mining field, Broken Hill, where fine dust made the deep mines unhealthy, a bitter strike lasted for eighteen months, ending with underground men winning shorter hours. At a time when forty-eight or fifty-two hours was the normal working week for most wage-earners in Australia, the underground men at Broken Hill won the remarkable privilege of a 35-hour week.

In a hall in Sydney, close to the docks of Darling Harbour, a meeting was to send slow shock waves around the nation. On Saturday 30 October 1920 in this socialist hall, twenty-six delegates met to form the Communist Party of Australia. Jock Garden, a Scot who had first worked as a Church of Christ pastor near Bendigo, came as the secretary of the powerful Trades Hall. Many small leftist groups and causes sent their representatives. Tom Walsh came as secretary of the Seamen's Union and one of the three women present was his wife, Adele Pankhurst-Walsh, a member of the Women's Peace Army and daughter of the well-known English suffragette. Most of those sitting in the hall believed that the Russian Revolution of 1917 was the greatest event in the history of the modern world. Calling for the 'complete annihilation' of the middle class, they set out on the mission of trying to capture all unions and ultimately achieving a 'proletarian republic' in Australia.

In cities and towns the daily life was much the same as thirty years previously, except that the breadwinner's hours of work were slightly fewer. In the countryside, however, people still worked long hours. In the dairying districts the cows had to be milked twice a day, and in winter maybe ten thousand children rose in the hours of darkness to sit beside the teats and squirt milk into the buckets, before they ate breakfast and began the walk to school. Almost everywhere the mother worked long hours. She had no outside job: her inside job embraced many tasks that have now devolved onto paid specialists. She made jam and chutney, biscuits and cakes and glass jars of preserved fruits that were arranged on shelves in the pantry: every self-respecting house had a pantry. There was little money for tinned or packaged foods, frozen foods were unknown and the take-away was only a squint in the Kentucky colonel's eye. Mother mended jumpers and darned the holes in socks, and did the washing and ironing – almost everything had to be ironed in the days before drip-dry clothes. She even knitted or sewed many of the clothes for her children, using the sewing machine which she worked manually. The kitchen was still a small factory.

A typical house in 1920 had few devices that we would call labour-saving. In the cities a gas stove was replacing the wood stove for the cooking of meals, but most of the household heating in winter came from firewood rather than gas. The electric jug and electric iron were still a novelty, a refrigerator was a rarity, and an electric vacuum cleaner and dishwashing and clothes-washing machines were dreams. As for means of communicating, the wireless came later in the 1920s while the telephone, being expensive, was more for offices than for homes. Households that owned a telephone – it had no dial – called the women working on the distant switchboard so that contact could be arranged with another phone number. In 1920 there were only four phones, business and private, for every 100 people. Even if a family owned a phone the idea of an interstate call was preposterous: Melbourne and Sydney had been linked since 1907 but the real cost of a short conversation was far higher than a Sydney to London call today. The mechanised, labour-saving house lay a generation ahead.

In many of the paid jobs the working week was long. Domestic servants – they were becoming fewer – might be allowed one free day a week. Nurses were almost a form of domestic servant, and they actually paid a sum of money so that they could be trained in the hospital in their first year. Dr Kingsley Norris became engaged to a Melbourne nurse but he spent little time with her because she worked seventy-two hours a week. Her free day began at 6 pm and ended the next evening at 10 pm when she resumed nursing duties. Equal pay for females and males lay far in the future.

For most wage-earners the Saturday afternoon was free for the playing of sport, and the evening for dances or the new cinema: the talkies had not yet replaced the movies. Sunday was for church and Sunday School. In the afternoon at least half the Protestant children went to Sunday School, and throughout the day hardly a shop was open and no place of amusement. People wore their best clothes on Sunday even to stroll in the streets; men wore brimmed hats and women wore more ornate hats. Monday to Friday were the days for work, and most people walked to work, rode a bike, or went in public transport. Monday was washing day, an arduous day for a housewife, and the wet clothes were hung on lines in the backyard, there to dry in the open air. If rain fell on Monday, the laments and curses could be heard along nearly every street.

Each country town had its own special shopping day, usually midweek, and farmers and wives arrived in the morning, tethered their horse or parked their Ford in the shade and shopped and gossiped, went to the livestock saleyards, and paid bills or explained why they could not pay them. In the cities, Friday night was a late shopping night, for the shop assistants had at last won freedom on Saturday afternoon.

Saturday was wedding day – Easter Saturday was the special bride's day. Shotgun marriages were fairly common, divorce was rare, and the man was the head of the house and sat at the head of the meal table, carved the roast and sliced the bread. Most men smoked, the roll-your-own cigarette was supplanting the pipe, and on windless days at the football or horse-races a discernible haze of tobacco smoke floated above the crowd. Few women smoked and most women and maybe half the men did not drink alcohol in a normal week. The question of whether Australia should prohibit alcohol was the subject of fierce-fought referendums; and in most states since the war the law decreed that all hotels should close at 6pm or soon after. Victoria and South Australia were to retain those laws until the 1960s.

In theory and usually in practice the home was the sanctuary, and it was more secure than it was to be seventy years later. It was in the 1920s that Mrs May Brahe composed the music for her song 'Bless this House', and a decade later that the tenor John McCormack made it famous in the United States. Melbourne residents were proud that the composer of such a song was born and educated in their city. Some were pleased to hear that she was the daughter of a manufacturer of lemonade and cordials, the alternatives to the strong drink that was condemned as the saboteur of home life. Australia seemed to epitomise home life because the song 'Home Sweet Home' was made famous by another Melbourne woman, Dame Nellie Melba, who was at the long-postponed end of her brilliant career in opera in Europe and the United States and spending more time at her new home in the Yarra Valley.

A woman's place was in the home. That was one of the accepted sayings of 1920, and the twenty years to follow. And yet a woman was poised to enter parliament and debate the decisions which affected every woman as much as every man. Australia had been the very first nation to give women both the right to vote and the right to stand for its national parliament; but many election days went by, and few women stood and none was elected. In 1921 in a state election in Western Australia a woman seemed likely to crack the ice. Edith Cowan was the daughter of a pastoralist, and when she was about 15 she anguished when he was hanged for murder. At the age of 18 she was married, eventually rearing four daughters and a son. While secretary of the Karrakatta Women's Club, which from 1894 became a forum for eager discussion, she educated herself for politics by reading the Englishman John Stuart Mill and the American Charlotte Perkins Gilman, and busied herself in the guilds and leagues that worked to protect mothers and children. In 1921, standing for the prosperous electorate of West Perth as a conservative, she won. In her only term in parliament she initiated the bill that opened the legal profession to women.

2

Bonds between Britain and most, but not all, Australians had been tightened by the war. In 1920 a disloyal and angry statement made about Britain by the member for Kalgoorlie, Hugh Mahon, led to his formal expulsion from the federal parliament and the calling of a by-election for his seat. He stood again, losing by 443 votes. Loyalty to Britain, however, was higher on emotional than on pragmatic issues. Billy Hughes had no hesitation in elbowing Britain aside if he thought Australia's interests so demanded.

Sport was capable of creating tensions. In the summer of 1932–33, the English cricket team touring Australia practised dangerous 'bodyline' bowling in the hope of curbing the genius of Donald Bradman, known as 'The Boy from Bowral'. The wide web of Anglo-Australian relations was suddenly strained.

British ships continued to dominate the ports. Eight of every ten incoming ships – measured by tonnage – were British. Half of the exports were sold to Britain, though already Japan was a busy customer. Japanese buyers came regularly to the wool sales in Sydney, Geelong and other ports. Before World War I, other Asian countries had surpassed Japan as buyers of Australian goods, but in 1920 Japan became the biggest. Of the seven foreign banks operating in Australia, a rising performer was the Yokohama Specie Bank.

The migrants arriving in the 1920s – and in some years they poured in – were predominantly British. Italians, Maltese, Greeks and others came, but not in large numbers. Immigration was encouraged partly because Australia's birth-rate was falling. In Sydney between 1886 and 1900 the birth-rate for every thousand people fell from forty-four to a mere twenty-five births, and every city followed the same path. The falling birth-rate was a shock to those citizens whose duty was to comment on human behaviour. 'No people', thundered the Sydney statistician Timothy Coghlan, 'had ever become great under such conditions'. The young couples who caused the falling birth-rate were influenced by the lean times of the 1890s when they postponed marriage until they possessed a secure job. They would have delayed marriage even longer except for unwanted pregnancies. In New South Wales in 1905 it was calculated that, of the first-born children in each marriage, one of every three had been conceived before marriage. Social pressures usually made a pregnant woman go to the altar without much delay.

More and more married couples preferred a smaller family, thus running the risk of being denounced from the pulpit and parliament house as seekers of luxury and pleasure rather than true citizens of a nation which needed a higher population. Most couples ignored the rebuke and went to those pharmacies or barbers' shops which sold condoms. The demand for contraceptives is reflected in the story of a backyard firm in the Melbourne suburb of Richmond. It was opened in 1905 by a migrant from London, Eric Ansell, who used the sap of the wild rubber tree to make condoms or – to use their popular name – 'French letters'. The firm became larger, moving overseas from the 1970s, and becoming the largest maker of condoms and surgical and industrial gloves in the world.

For a husband earning income in the middle range the family home was now smaller, and the big wooden table in the middle of the kitchen was on the way out. The Californian bungalow with a low fence and one ornate brick chimney on the front or main side-wall became common in new suburbs, and from the front gate two thin strips of concrete with lawn in the middle were laid along one side of the house – in readiness for the day when the family bought a car. The new house needed only three bedrooms, for the small family was becoming the norm except amongst the Catholics who formed a quarter of the population. The change had been fast. The Australian women who began to bear children in, say, the late 1850s averaged seven children in their married life but those who began their families not long before World War I were to average just over three children.

Fewer children were born into each family but more were likely to survive. The lower birth-rate was accompanied by a lower death-rate. Between 1900 and 1930 the death-rate of infants under the age of one was halved. It was in the inner cities, previously less healthy than the countryside, that health was most improved. Typhoid and tuberculosis were curbed. At the ports the medical inspections were more careful. Dairies were regulated and the fresh milk carried fewer germs. With the extension of sewerage, fewer houses needed the 'night-soil cart' to collect cans of raw sewage for market gardens or night-soil depots. The decline of city horse stables reduced the population of germs.

The population of horses passed its peak during World War I. There was a fast decline in light carriage horses and riding horses, but not yet in the heavy farm horses or the horses and carts that delivered meat, bread and milk to the back doors of houses. The tradesman of course belonged to the back door, according to custom.

Australians were taking to the car and truck with an enthusiasm shown by few other nations. The arrival of the T-model Ford, cheap and sturdy, won over many farmers. The motor bike wooed young men. By the 1920s the motor accident had replaced drowning as the main cause of violent death. By the early 1930s Australia had more than half a million cars, trucks and buses and was one of the most motorised nations. In the aggregate number of motor vehicles it probably ranked sixth in the world, being ahead of Italy but behind Germany. America led in manufacturing cars, and through Dodges, Fords, Oldsmobiles, Chevrolets and many other 'makes' it captured a dynamic part of the Australian economy. Car-assembling plants were built by Ford at Geelong in the 1920s and General Motors-Holden's at Port Melbourne in the 1930s: the firm of Holden had originally built vehicles for South Australian horses before building bodies for American cars.

The train was at the height of its importance, and to be a stationmaster with braid on the uniform and a peaked cap was to be a pillar of society. No other nation had Australia's combination of such a length of railways and such a small population to pay for the cost of those railways. The long railway across the dry treeless plains to Perth was completed in 1917, almost half a century after America built its first railway across the continent, but few Australians travelled in the new train across the Nullarbor Plain. At least it was now possible for wealthier British migrants who were sick of the sea to leave ship at Fremantle, board a train in nearby Perth and make the long journey through Adelaide, Melbourne and Sydney to Brisbane, changing trains at various stations along the way. Mothers with little children found the journey could be a nightmare, even if they booked a compartment in a sleeping car. Setting out from Perth at 10 o'clock on Monday evening they finally reached Brisbane on the following Sunday evening at 6.40 pm.

In 1911 the Northern Territory had been handed over by South Australia to the Commonwealth, and one of the promises – in this land of promises – was that in return a railway would be built right across the continent so that Adelaide would have quick access to Darwin, some 3,000 kilometres to the north. In 1929 the railway reached the 'wild-west' village of Alice Springs. It remained the terminus for three-quarters of a century.

A slow steam train, christened the Ghan, enabled journalists and artists to see the outback and its red and brown soils. Some thought central Australia was just waiting for the railway, irrigation, diamond drill and electricity to convert it into a land of plenty. The 1920s were full of bold predictions, and the far outback figured in many of them. The continent, it was predicted, could easily hold 100 million people, even 300 million. Stanley Melbourne Bruce shared the hopes. As he recalled, 'I did believe, in the first term of my career as Prime Minister, that Australia had an unlimited future'.

'Unlimited' was a pet word during Bruce's six years of office that ended in 1929. Popular author E. J. Brady wrote a book of 1,100 big pages and called it *Australia Unlimited*. He argued that Europe's 'landless millions' must be invited here to prevent the country from falling into the hands of Asians from the near north. In his eyes the Northern Territory with a mere 3,000 white people was as potentially productive, mile for mile, as Victoria. The new aviation industry was sympathetic to the idea, arguing that aircraft would conquer the previously unconquerable distance. The airline that became the national airline, QANTAS or Queensland and Northern Territory Aerial Services, was formed to serve this part of Australia unlimited.

One man who shouted 'no' to the optimists was Professor Griffith Taylor. He had gone to the Antarctic with Scott, studying the weather as well as the geology, and thought that much of Australia was just another Antarctica with burning sand in place of ice. In Sydney, where he was head of the first geography department in an Australian university, he ridiculed the optimists. Australia would do well, he replied, to support 20 million people by the end of the 1990s. Much of the soil was poor, and the tropics were hard on women and children and those men who worked with their muscles. He warned that it was unwise to judge Darwin by one visit there during the sparkling winter months when the mild south-easterly was blowing. Taylor was more right than wrong, and the voices of caution were weakened when he moved to Chicago in 1928.

It was still an age for exploring. People believed that the surface of Australia had just been skimmed. In 1929, Dr C. T. Madigan, with the aid of two air-force planes, began to explore the monotonous parallel sand ridges of the Simpson Desert. It is incredible that a major desert of about one-third the size of Victoria should have been named as recently as 1932. Alfred Simpson, who helped to finance Madigan's exploring, was an Adelaide manufacturer whose washing machines later became well known.

While patriotic Australians were wondering what could be done to develop vast tracts of the empty continent, another Adelaide geologist and explorer, Sir Douglas Mawson, was claiming even more territory. Now praised as one of the finest of all Antarctic explorers, Mawson made his final expedition between 1929 and 1931. Two years later Australia formally annexed a huge area of the Antarctic, both sea and land, which Mawson called MacRobertson Land after his main sponsor, the Melbourne maker of chocolates. Australia in its own eyes was now a great territorial power. With its vast homeland, its empire of ice, and its enlarged territories combining the old British and German colonies in New Guinea, it laid claim to an area exceeded only by the Soviet Union. It was the least populated empire the world had seen.

3

A new landmark rather than a new land fired the people's imagination. The Sydney Harbour Bridge was hailed as one of the seven wonders of the world by people who had seen none of the other wonders. Said to be the greatest single-arch bridge so far built, it was wide enough to carry four tracks of railway and six lanes of cars for the traffic of a city of 1,200,000 people: Sydney was then as big as Cairo and ranked about seventeenth in the world, a ranking far higher than it holds today. There was a pleasing symmetry in the arrangement of the steel forming the arch above the bridge itself. With its stone towers and the sheer enormity of its steelwork, it made the other buildings in the heart of Sydney seem fragile. The bridge was so high above the water that an ocean-liner could pass underneath with absurd ease.

It was a celebration as much as a bridge. Opened in March 1932, in the worst year of the depression, it was designed and supervised by John Job Bradfield, a Sydney railway engineer, and built by the English steel firm of Dorman Long & Co. of Middlesbrough. Bradfield symbolised the soaring thinking of the more buoyant of the inter-war years. The public's imagination was long attracted by another of his gigantic dreams – to divert the waters of his native Queensland from the big coastal rivers to the dry inland plains.

The six states built most of the monuments of the era. Their influence on national life was more pervasive than that of the Common-wealth government, which advanced cautiously. The Commonwealth did not send an ambassador overseas until 1910 when Sir George Reid went to London with the title of high commissioner. It did not raise a loan until 1912 when it borrowed half a million pounds partly to build a London showplace, Australia House on The Strand. It did not join the states in imposing an income tax until 1915, and for years it raised much less than did the combined states from their income taxes. And

• • • • • • • • • •

it continued to use Melbourne as the nation's capital rather than hurry on with its own city.

The choice of the permanent capital city had been delayed partly by the Melbourne–Sydney rivalry. The capital city had to be in rural New South Wales but exactly where was the question in dispute. Victorians wanted it to be as far from Sydney as possible. They almost had their way in 1903 when the House of Representatives voted for Tumut, a remote and pretty town which was two hours by train from Gundagai, itself a remote town in the railway era. In contrast, the Senate selected Bombala, a windswept village high in the mountains south of Cooma and Canberra. In 1904 the freezing little town of Dalgety was chosen by both houses. Standing seven hours by horse-coach from Cooma, it was more suited for a penitentiary than a seat of government. New South Wales intervened and, probably in defiance of the constitution, refused to release territory to the Commonwealth to enable Dalgety to be the capital.

In 1908 the district of Yass–Canberra became a favourite, narrowly winning the vote of members of the House of Representatives. In the Senate every New South Welshman voted for Yass–Canberra, which was not too far from Sydney, but Tumut was the Victorians' preferred site. It was much closer to Melbourne. The long deadlock was finally ended by another ballot in which the senators gave a narrow victory to the Canberra district.

So Sydney, the city which at one time had done the most to thwart the creation of the Commonwealth, was given the prize of a new capital city, to be built only 300 kilometres away. One Melbourne newspaper called the decision a 'national crime'. Many Australians from all states came to echo that view in the 1980s, when Canberra seemed – rightly or wrongly – to be unusually prosperous and insulated, a lobby in its own right. But many of those who visited the city for the first time and saw the blue-clad hills and the rising Australian War

Memorial and the other national institutions, of which they had often read, were pleasantly surprised and even proud.

Canberra, when chosen, held not much more than a post office, a school for the farmers' children who came along the gravel roads, a blacksmith's shop, and a stone Anglican church built in the 1840s. The countryside was charming, the timbered hills rose majestically, and in the distance rode the blue ranges. It was the kind of dreamy nostalgic landscape that the Heidelberg School would have painted had it been more accessible. In 1911, this small district was transferred from New South Wales to the Commonwealth, along with a pocket of land at Jervis Bay which was intended to be the Commonwealth's own port; but the railway to the port was never built.

The war delayed the building of the town designed by Walter Burley Griffin of Chicago. On the grassy slopes a white parliament house was erected, like a five-star hotel far from anywhere. It was formally opened on 9 May 1927 but the expected crowd did not come to see the ceremonies. Amongst those who were present was a black wavy-haired Aborigine from the nearby town of Queanbeyan, an entertainer who threw the boomerang in return for a coin or two. His name was Marvellous, and when he was presented to the Duchess of York he took the chance to plead, 'Give poor Marvellous sixpence'. After the ceremony he walked the ten kilometres to Queanbeyan where he went to sleep, without a blanket, on an earthen footpath in a back street. The night was frosty and in the morning he was found dead.

On the previous day Marvellous had heard the singing of the honourable members and guests who were sardined into the new parliament house: 'A thousand ages in Thy sight, / Are like an evening gone'.

He might not have understood each verse but perhaps he, a survivor of the generations of earlier Australians, sensed their meaning as much as any leader who was there on that momentous day.

4

Canberra was a baby of the chequered boom of the 1920s: the boom was chequered because unemployment in some years crept close to 10 per cent. Late in 1929 the boom was clearly over. Prices of shares on New York's stock exchange fell by about 40 per cent in the space of two months. Confidence sagged in much of the world. The prices of wool, butter, lead, meat, wheat and the main Australian exports were almost halved in the space of three years. The Australian governments, which recently had been heavy borrowers for public works, especially roads and railways, now faced a big interest bill and the prospect of raising no new loans.

The unemployed were everywhere: queueing in their hundreds for one advertised job in a factory, camping in the small-town grandstands and rural showgrounds before they roamed the roads for work. The building of houses and shops almost ceased. By 1932 the unemployment rate exceeded 30 per cent – one of the highest in the world. Those workers who vividly remembered the depression of forty years previously had one consolation. In the new depression only one large bank closed its doors, the Government Savings Bank of New South Wales, which was said to be the second biggest such bank in the British Empire.

The gains in social security of recent years began to seem hollow. On paper most Australian breadwinners had the benefit of a 44-hour week, a minimum weekly wage, relative safety in the workplace, payment for overtime, and courts and boards to adjudicate in industrial disputes. The only catch was that there was no work. Some of those out of work received the 'sustenance' wage – the 'susso' – but it was makeshift and small. Many families lived on hand-out food. Except in New South Wales there was no child endowment. Tens of thousands of girls and boys were under-nourished, and thinly clad in winter. The schoolboy without boots became a common sight in the summers of the early 1930s.

Australia had once been hailed as the emerging Garden of Eden. By the early 1930s the garden was rather unkempt and even sterile in patches. Australia had few pockets of prosperity. Towns such as Kalgoorlie and Boulder were actually more bustling than in the previous fifteen years because gold – alone of the commodities – went up in price. Significantly, in April 1933 the people of Western Australia voted to secede from the Commonwealth which, they believed, was a political device for subsidising the old south-eastern states at the expense of the big outer states. Of the fifty electorates in Western Australia, the six that voted against secession were all gold-mining electorates and therefore more prosperous. The secession movement was thwarted by the big cities in the east. The revival of prosperity across the continent, with unemployment falling to 10 per cent by 1937, stitched up the wound.

In the federal parliament the years between the wars were a wasteland for the Labor Party. Radicalism enjoyed its only victories in the states, and Ted Theodore in Queensland and Jack Lang in New South Wales strode like giants. In the federal sphere Labor still suffered from its wartime split which centred on the issue of conscription; and Labor politicians were divided over the question of whether their nation should be isolationist. The typical Labor politicians before World War I believed in providing guns and ships to defend Australia, but after the war they were not so sure.

The high goals of the new Soviet Union inspired many trade unionists in Australia. The shock of the months of severe unemployment in the western world soon after the end of the war made them look beyond the regulated capitalism which they once tolerated. In 1921 the Australian Labor Party adopted a socialist platform, affirming that 'the socialisation of industry, production, distribution, and exchange be the objective'. The spirit as distinct from the words of the party's manifesto was not so revolutionary. In fact Catholics with moderate views were becoming more influential in a party that was their stepladder to power. Between 1929 and 1949, in all but two years, Australians of Irish ancestry held the office of prime minister. Three of these national leaders were Catholics and one a lapsed Catholic. All rose to power in the Labor Party; but one, Joe Lyons, dramatically left that party and headed a new conservative government in 1932.

At that time, in Britain and the United States, it was not conceivable that Catholic politicians could enjoy such success. Perhaps in no other Protestant nation had Catholics won the political victories they achieved nationally in Australia from 1929 onwards.

Meanwhile the conservatives dominated federal politics, except during the one term shaded by the world depression. They were reinforced by a new party which began as an opponent of regulation but changed its mind. The Australian Country Party, later called the National Party, was formed at the end of World War I by farmers. Its early gains depended on the new method of preferential voting which from 1919 onwards was applied at federal elections. As the third strongest party in parliament it put pressure on the mainstream conservatives (successively called Fusionists, Nationalists, the United Australia Party, and the Liberal Party). From 1923 to 1929 its leader Dr Earle Page, deputy prime minister in what was called the Bruce–Page government, protected the unprotected farmers by setting up various schemes to promote such commodities as sugar, butter and dried fruits. The typical farmer did not win as much protection as the manufacturers and their city employees had won.

Henceforth nearly every major industry – except wool and silver-lead-zinc and frozen meat – relied on a political walking stick as much as on its own efficiency. So was accentuated the tendency to see countless new laws as the prime solution to those problems which might often have been solved by economic vigour and ingenuity in daily life. About sixty years later, in the era of the computer, a slight majority of Australians agreed to throw away the political walking stick but they did not find it easy. Like a boomerang it returned.

The nation was becoming obsessed with politics, almost viewing it as a branch of spectator sport. The elections at least once in every three years for both the federal and state parliaments meant that the merry-go-round of electioneering seldom came to a halt. The introduction in 1924 of compulsory voting, a rarity in the world, compelled every citizen to attend the voting booth on the day of a federal election or pay a fine. The compulsion was the idea of an obscure Tasmanian senator, Herbert Payne, who held the enthusiastic belief – since disproved – that it would quickly lead to a 'wonderful improvement in the political knowledge of the people'.

People of talent were still attracted in impressive numbers to a political career. The left side of politics had its bright young men who had little formal education but made up for it in natural talent and a thirst for the knowledge they could find in books. James Scullin, John Curtin and Ben Chifley, the three Labor leaders to become prime ministers in the years from 1920 to 1970, fitted this pattern. On the other hand, the conservative side of politics was attracting university-educated men of talent such as Stanley Melbourne Bruce, John Latham, Dr Earle Page and Robert Menzies, for whom other attractive careers were also open. It was still unusual for such a person to rise high in the Labor Party. A glamorous exception was Dr Herbert V Evatt, who resigned from the High Court to win a Sydney electorate for Labor in 1940. The day would come when nearly every member of a Labor ministry in Canberra held a degree.

In a normal decade much talent went overseas, and did not return. One in three of the Rhodes Scholars who left home to study at Oxford made their permanent careers in Britain. Of the Australian-born scientists of high distinction, at least half of them – the Floreys and Oliphants – worked overseas. So many skilled Australian-reared artists, ranging from musician Percy Grainger to novelists Martin Boyd and Henry Handel Richardson and the Hollywood actor Errol Flynn, worked overseas. Many writers who remained at home still had to send their manuscripts to London to find a publisher. It became the cry of certain critics that Australia was a cultural desert, and that talented artists were wise to go abroad. And yet one well-informed observer, writing from England in 1939, pointed to the high esteem in which Hans Heysen, Arthur Streeton, and Norman and Lionel Lindsay were held, though they sketched and painted mostly in their homeland. He could point to at least six stay-at-home Australian painters who were 'certainly better known to the public in Australia than any six living English artists are to the man-in-the-street in England'.

The nation's intellectual and cultural life began to simmer and bubble after a period when the national pond seemed still. The serious audience for the arts was growing with the aid of radio. The Australian Broadcasting Commission, formed in 1932, became a promoter of music, arranging for famous musicians to tour Australia. By 1937 it employed 320 musicians full-time. Ballet won a following, after the visits by Russian companies.

On the eve of World War II the arrival of refugees from the imperilled Jewish quarters of Vienna, Berlin and other German-speaking cities enlivened the audiences at symphony concerts and art exhibitions. In 1939 the Melbourne *Herald* and its editor, Sir Keith Murdoch, staged an exhibition of modern European art, with nine Picassos and eight Van Goghs and several hundred other works which enthralled many viewers, though others just stood and stared blankly. Soon a cluster of very young local painters – including Sidney Nolan and Arthur Boyd, Albert Tucker and Russell Drysdale – began to excite a few local critics. Not perhaps since the Heidelberg painters arose half a century previously had there been such a seedtime in the visual arts.

Education was again on the national agenda, and a quarter of all 16 year olds now attended secondary schools. To study at a university was beyond the hopes and wishes of most students at high school, though Western Australia could boast that its university was free. Scientific research, if skewed towards economic problems, flourished under the protective wing of Canberra, and a major success of what became the CSIRO was to prepare a virus which in the 1950s began to decimate the rabbits that swarmed over farmlands and grasslands.

For observant Australians, the years between the two wars were disappointing in most ways. The depression ruined or scarred several million lives. The 'land fit for heroes' had certainly not been created, and now another war was at hand, and the nation was not prepared.

A tidal wave from Japan

When Hitler invaded Poland in September 1939, so igniting a European war that flamed into a world war, Australia was not ready. It was less prepared than in 1914, when its navy was remarkably strong for such a small nation. Though air power was now challenging sea power, Australia was weak in the air. Its own air force possessed few of the latest aircraft. And yet it had been one of the few nations that initially grasped aviation with both hands, producing many of the world's path-finding aviators.

For years the public had disliked heavier spending on defence because that would mean higher taxes and fewer social services. The government led by Joseph Lyons was late in sensing that war was coming, and the Labor opposition held many isolationists. Labor's leader, John Curtin, saw the importance of air power but he was at one time almost surrounded by colleagues who were suspicious even of machine guns. Similarly, a powerful slice of opinion in Britain and other democratic nations was repelled by the tragedy of World War I, and sought relief in internationalism, disarmament and pacifism. This anti-war movement was noble but risky. The penalty, if it failed, was catastrophe. The vogue for disarmament and for 'peace' at any price played into the hands of Germany and Russia, who hated the terms of peace imposed on them in the previous war and were eager to renounce those terms. Likewise, Japan and Italy, though on the winning side in 1918, were dissatisfied with the meagre prizes awarded them as victors by the peace conference in 1919.

For Australia this new grouping of the disgruntled nations would be a calamity. In World War I, Italy and Japan had fought on the same side as Australia. A Japanese cruiser helped to escort, across the Indian Ocean, the long convoy carrying most of the men who later stormed Gallipoli. The presence of the Italian navy in the Mediterreanen from 1915 to 1918 helped keep that sea safely in the Allies' arms. By June 1940, however, Italy was an enemy and its navy was capable of disrupting the eastern Mediterranean and thereby the main sea-route passing through the Suez Canal to Australia. Japan was even more menacing. W. M. Hughes had often predicted a crisis if Japan changed sides. He pointed out that Japan had such an efficient navy that if it had fought on the enemy's side in 1914–18 it would have diverted many British ships from the North Sea, enabling the German navy to win victories there. By 1940 the Japanese navy and air force, as enemy rather than as ally, could pose a serious threat to an isolated Australia.

The defeat of France by Hitler in June 1940 was a further blow to Australia's defences. Before the outbreak of war it had been agreed that the British and French navies would share their duties in the event of a war with Germany or Japan. And if Japanese forces seemed likely to attack south-east Asia, the French navy would defend the Mediterranean, allowing the British to despatch a large part of its navy to its new naval base in Singapore where it could be a spear point against the Japanese navy. The collapse of France, so unexpected, meant that its navy was no longer on Britain's side. Moreover the collapse of France meant that her colony in Indochina, and the naval and air bases in what is now Vietnam, could be seized by Japan and used as a springboard for its attack on Singapore and the Philippines.

2

Australia's crucial preparations for what became World War II began perhaps two years too late. Essington Lewis, the engineer who was head of Broken Hill Proprietary, had come to the conclusion while inspecting Japan's shipyards and steelworks in 1934 that Japan would ultimately go to war. Two years later, with government support, Lewis formed a private syndicate that began to build an aircraft factory complete with aerodrome at Port Melbourne. Its first plane, the slow Wirraway trainer, flew in March 1939, a forerunner of faster planes that might just be ready in time.

During the first year of the war Australia sent airmen to Britain, warships to the northern hemisphere, and an army to the eastern Mediterranean where it was to fight mainly against Germans and Italians in the desert of North Africa. At home a successful drive to make a wide variety of munitions was launched under Essington Lewis. More could have been achieved but for the strikes in the New South Wales coalfields, the reluctance of public opinion to accept sacrifices, and a political deadlock in Canberra.

Robert Gordon Menzies had become prime minister in 1939, after the death of Joseph Lyons. In August 1940 a bomber carrying three of his twelve cabinet ministers and his chief of general staff crashed while landing in Canberra, and all were killed. A month later the federal election was held, and Menzies suffered from his decision to ration petrol, and from the aircraft accident, which transferred a safe Liberal seat to an independent. Menzies' power now depended on the support of two sympathetic independents. Their sympathy faded and tensions increased in his own ranks. During those crucial months when Australia, Canada and Britain were the main allies fighting Germany and Italy, Menzies often had to concentrate as much on party politics as on the war. In October 1941 the two independents crossed the floor of the house, and John Curtin commenced what became eight years of Labor rule. As an opponent of Australia's all-out participation in World War I, Curtin now had to galvanise the nation in the face of increasing peril. Two months later the Japanese suddenly attacked the American fleet in Pearl Harbor and invaded the Malay peninsula, where Australian soldiers and aircraft had arrived in anticipation of war.

Japan's attack was not a complete surprise. More surprising was its success. Japanese planes won command of the air with ease, and in Malay waters they sank the two mighty British warships, the *Prince of Wales* and *Repulse*. The new Wirraways, forming more than half of Australia's operational air force, had to be used as fighting planes. Though faster than many British aircraft based on Singapore, they were no match for the Japanese. On 15 February 1942 the island of Singapore fell to the Japanese.

Most of the Australian troops shipped from the fighting front in North Africa to fight against Japan arrived too late. Those who landed in the Dutch East Indies arrived just in time to be captured by the all-conquering Japanese. In south-east Asia, 22,000 Australians were taken as prisoners of war, and more than one of every three died as slave labourers.

The first months of the war in south-east Asia had been like Gallipoli without the glory. In tropical jungles, beaches and towns there was bravery, but that was not enough. Whereas at Gallipoli in 1915 the Australians could finally retreat with honour and safety because their weapons were superior and their ally, Britain, held command of the sea, here the Australians were superior in almost nothing. Above all, their ally, Britain, was hopelessly over-extended and so could not contribute as much as was hoped. Britain was trying to fight the German and Italian armies in North Africa, their submarines and warships in the Mediterranean and North Atlantic, and the German air force over Europe as well as giving what military aid it could spare to the ill-equipped Russians, who had been invaded by the Germans less than six months before the attack on Pearl Harbor.

Australia held only seven million people and they depended too much on their long-time ally, Britain. The events of 1941–2 affirmed the inescapable fact that every alliance has its weakness. Britain was too busy fighting Germany to give Australia the help hoped for. Australia was too busy to give Britain the help it expected. Half a century later, the prime minister, Paul Keating, would denounce Britain for not defending Singapore more vigorously. He did not realise that thousands of Australian soldiers were captured in Singapore by the Japanese partly because they had been inadequately equipped for war by their own nation. Britain actually had contributed far more than Australia to the defence of the shared bases and strategic posts in south-east Asia.

The Japanese came like a tidal wave. It was one of the most brilliant campaigns in the history of warfare. Dutch Java fell, and Sumatra, rich in oil. Burma, Timor and the Philippines were about to fall. Rabaul in the old German New Guinea fell to the Japanese as quickly as it had fallen to the Australians in 1914. The mainland of New Guinea was invaded and Australia itself was in danger of being cut off from outside help.

On 19 February 1942, just four days after the fall of Singapore, an Australian port was a target for the enemy. From four aircraft carriers the Japanese launched 188 bombers and fighters to attack Darwin, the main port and airbase on the coast of northern Australia. Darwin received a radio warning from an Aboriginal mission on Bathurst Island where a priest saw the squadrons of Japanese aircraft approaching from the north. His warning was ignored. The Japanese fighters and bombers seriously damaged the town, harbour and ships, and killed at least 243 people in that first of many air raids on Australian soil. The government, fearing that civilian morale would sag, at first announced a death toll of only seventeen people. In another Japanese raid, a mere nine Zero aircraft destroyed twenty-four flying boats moored at Broome in Western Australia. Many military observers thought the raids were a prelude to an invasion. Why, they asked, should the tidal wave suddenly halt? For a time the Japanese could have captured the few ports on the northern and north-west coast of Australia with ease.

3

General Douglas MacArthur was America's commander in the Philippines, and there the Japanese were on the verge of victory. He reached Australia, unannounced, in March 1942 after a perilous journey, having just been appointed the supreme commander of Allied forces in the huge war zone that embraced the south-west Pacific. Landing in bombed Darwin, he and his wife and young son travelled to Alice Springs where they boarded the slow steam train for Adelaide. At the small wheat town of Terowie, well known because its break of gauge compelled passengers to change trains, his arrival was awaited by reporters. There on 20 March he made one of the war's celebrated statements: it was slightly pompous in its long first sentence but pithy and memorable in its second. To those waiting patiently with pencil in hand, he said:

> The President of the United States ordered me to break through the Japanese lines and proceed from Corregidor to Australia for the purpose, as I understand it, of organising an American offensive against Japan, the primary purpose of which is the relief of the Philippines. I came through, and I shall return.

His words were momentous. Australia was acquiring a new, powerful ally. The British cargo and naval ships remained important to Australia for the remainder of the war but on air, land and sea the American forces were vital.

In the autumn of 1942 Sydney and Melbourne were nervous. All blinds were drawn at night, and car lights and street lamps were dimmed, so that cities would not be a visible target if Japanese bombers approached. Zigzag trenches were dug in parklands and school grounds so that children and adults could shelter if the Japanese aircraft arrived overhead. Thousands of children were briefly evacuated to country towns. The presence of American soldiers, who arrived by sea, was a comfort to morale but the big money they spent was often a source of envy.

Economic life was more strictly controlled than at any time since the convict era. Regulations specified where people could work, the rents they could pay, the money they could borrow, the wages they could earn, the goods that could be delivered to their home, and whether they could travel interstate by train. New cars were no longer for sale, and many spare parts could be bought only at the wreckers' yards. After the Japanese captured most of the world's rubber plantations in south-east Asia, rubber was so scarce – along with petrol – that thousands of cars sat in the garage for the remainder of the war. Housewives became beasts of burden, carrying home the goods which normally were delivered to houses before the rationing of petrol. The building of new houses virtually ceased, through a shortage of materials as well as labour. Full employment, not once achieved in the years 1919–39, arrived at last.

Beer, tobacco and cigarettes were scarce, and clothes and such foods as sugar, butter and tea were rationed. Everybody had to carry a ration book, and a shop would not supply certain goods unless the correct number of ration coupons was handed over. Some of the shelves of milk bars and lolly shops were bare. The privation of the typical Australian civilian was small compared to that of most Europeans. Indeed there was less poverty and therefore less hunger in 1942 than in the depression years.

It was still feared that the Japanese might invade Australia. Instead Japan's plan was virtually to isolate the continent by capturing not only the Indonesian archipelago and New Guinea but also Samoa, Fiji and New Caledonia, thus cutting the main supply route between the United States and the east coast of Australia. Soon the Japanese forces walking across the mountain spine of east New Guinea were only 60 kilometres from the main town of Port Moresby. There on the Kokoda Trail and at Milne Bay they were halted by Australians – the first defeats the Japanese had suffered on land after their run of amazing successes.

As the Japanese retreated they left behind strange debris: the frames of bicycles on which they had hoped to ride into Port Moresby, the corpse of a white horse ridden by the Japanese general, and all their dead soldiers. The Australians who came a day or two behind the advance forces, walking along a grey muddy pathway that fell and rose steeply, and crossing fast streams on footbridges made of strong vines, could only admire their countrymen who fought in such exhausting terrain and the native men who carried supplies.

The Japanese had sent a large naval force on a long roundabout sea route in the hope of capturing Port Moresby but it was thwarted in the Battle of the Coral Sea in May 1942. It was the first naval battle in history in which the fleets did not fire at each other. Instead they attacked from the air with planes launched either from aircraft carriers or from land bases. Part of the battle was fought in the sea less than 1,000 kilometres from the Great Barrier Reef and the port of Cairns. The Japanese were forced to turn back. Their dominance had depended on the aircraft carrier, which was really a mobile airfield, but they lost more of these floating airfields in the Battle of Midway in June 1942. The months of Japan's ascendancy had ended.

A tidal wave from Japan

• • • • • • • • • •

The hard, slow task of driving the Japanese from New Guinea, the Dutch East Indies and the Philippines was under way. Almost three years later, in the middle of 1945, more Australians were at or near the fighting front than in any previous phase of the war. The pushing back of the Japanese from the tropical islands was far from completed when the first atomic bombs were dropped on Japanese cities in August 1945, forcing a quick surrender.

After 1941, Australia contributed little to the fighting in Europe and the Mediterranean, except in the air. Many of the finest pilots and air crew in the Royal Air Force were Australians; and they flew in many of the dangerous raids, including the low-level raid conducted by Mosquito aircraft against the Gestapo's gaol at Amiens in France in 1944.

While air crew were more glamorous, Australia also depended heavily on seamen. Most of the naval battles were fought far from home but two large-scale tragedies occurred near the coast of Australia. In November 1941, nor far from Carnarvon in Western Australia, HMAS *Sydney* intercepted a strange ship flying the Dutch flag. The stranger was the German raider, the *Kormoran*, which had destroyed many Allied ships in the Atlantic and Indian oceans. The commander of the *Sydney* approached the *Kormoran*, unwisely creeping within range of its guns. A battle was begun at short range, and both ships caught fire and went down. Of the 645 officers and ratings in the *Sydney*, not one survived.

Eighteen months later, on the opposite side of the continent, the Australian hospital ship *Centaur* was steaming north towards New Guinea to bring home the wounded. On a moonless night, east of Stradbroke Island and not far from Brisbane, she was attacked by a Japanese submarine. As the ship was brilliantly lit, and as the red crosses painted on her sides could be seen by any submarine coming to the surface, her destruction was a violation of international law. The *Centaur* caught fire and sank, and 268 Australian men and women were lost.

Aborigines had a part in the war, some as soldiers, some as coast-watchers. Furthermore, one of their medicines was a valuable aid in the Allied invasion of France in June 1944. For generations the Aborigines in parts of inland Australia took the leaves of a corkwood tree, *Duboisia myoporoides*, and threw them into small waterholes to stupefy the fish and bring them to the surface. The leaves were gathered in huge numbers in Queensland in 1944 and processed on a large scale to yield the drugs hyoscine and atropine. These drugs formed one of the few cargoes actually flown to Britain in the middle of the war. The success of the British–American invasion of German-occupied France depended on the armada of troops being relatively free from sea-sickness. For many their palliative was this ancient Aboriginal medicine.

4

John Curtin, prime minister from 1941 to 1945, grew in stature as a leader. He handled with tact the factions that had ripped apart the Labor Party in New South Wales during the previous decade. After Russia entered the war in June 1941 the more militant of the coal miners usually supported rather than hindered the war effort; and Curtin gained from their change of heart. He welcomed into his team Essington Lewis and those industrialists who were already organising the making of munitions and aircraft. He persuaded the Labor Party to moderate its reluctance to allow conscripted soldiers to fight outside Australia and Papua, a hostility strong since 1917. From 1943 those troops who were conscripts rather than volunteers could be sent as far north as the equator, and at times even beyond it.

Curtin was able to impose a uniform system of taxation on the country, and the six states abandoned the collecting of their own income tax in 1942. He mostly handled with skill the relations with the two main allies, Britain and the United States. But perhaps he was too eager to accept MacArthur's advice or commands. Nor did he pursue Australia's own strategic interests – in defiance of Winston Churchill's global strategy – as resolutely as folklore now insists. How could he be so independent? He was captain of a minor team playing in a world league.

Curtin's broadcasts to the Australian people were sincere and dignified, and even memorable when he delivered one of his pale-purple passages of prose. His utter dedication to his task quietly won him admirers. In wartime a prime minister had to spend long periods in Melbourne, which was the headquarters of the army and most federal departments; and when Curtin was seen leaving his alcohol-free hotel in Little Collins Street he was sometimes clapped by those who recognised him, though it was more the clapping of deep respect than affection. An old-fashioned man, seeking no limelight, he had become a leader.

Three-quarters of a million Australians enlisted or were called up in the armed services: one in every ten was a woman. The death toll was just over half as large as in the previous war, partly because there was no repetition of the stalemated trench warfare that had persisted in France. Moreover in World War II, many lives were saved by medical advances, including penicillin and sulpha drugs and blood transfusions.

As an arsenal the nation made far more munitions than in the previous war. The arsenal sped up the industrialising of Australia, for 150,000 men and women were employed in making munitions, and several hundred thousand more were making other goods that were important for the war effort. By July 1944 a total of 44,000 people – and most had not previously worked in a factory – made military aircraft. The grand tally of 3,500 fighters, trainers and bombers was built during the war, and the later planes held their own against the Japanese. Overseas industrialists were surprised, after the war, to see the variety of weapons that had been made by Australians: they ranged from anti-aircraft guns, mortar bombs, Owen submachine guns, optical munitions, land mines and tanks all the way to warships and fast aircraft. The capacity to make an endless variety of machine tools for the manufacture of armaments and equipment was to prove vital in peacetime industries.

At the end of the war one fact was not easily grasped because most Australians did not want to believe it or found it inconceivable. Britain, while winning the war, was losing its high place in the world. In the period between the fall of France in the middle of 1940 and Hitler's invasion of Russia a year later, it shouldered almost alone the fight against Hitler. Those were the twelve months when Australia ranked second or third in the humble and depleted list of allies led by Britain and still waging war against Hitler. At the end of the war, however, Britain was far behind the United States and the Soviet Union as a military power, it was waning as a manufacturer, and it could not be confident that it would retain its world-wide empire: India for one was almost certain to cut the ties.

The United States emerged from the war as Australia's blood relation. Nobody at the start of the war could have predicted this change. Admittedly, all those Australians who in 1939 spent their Saturday nights at the cinema were seeing more films from Hollywood than from any other place. They were buying more American than British cars, and were whistling hit tunes straight from America. It was true that, before the war, a few 'Australians' were well known in the United States, including Helena Rubinstein, who had moved her cosmetics business from Melbourne, the actor Errol Flynn, who had spent his childhood in Hobart where his father was professor of biology, and Harry Bridges, who had studied at Catholic schools in inner Melbourne suburbs before carrying, as a seaman, his militancy to San Francisco where he organised strong unions of seamen and longshoremen. But before the war the political links between the two nations were slender. Few of the leading Australian politicians of 1939 had set foot in the United States. Unlike Canada and South Africa, Australia posted no ambassador to Washington until 1940 when a senior politician R. G. Casey accepted the office.

Contacts with Washington were quickened by Pearl Harbor. For three and a half years the forces from the two countries fought side by side on many islands in the Pacific, sometimes with bickering at the top and barracking at the bottom but usually with harmony. A mass of United States servicemen, including future president Lyndon B. Johnson, served in or near Australia. In the long term Washington would become more important than London in the defence of Australia.

Even less to be expected in 1939 was the rise of Indonesia. For decades Australia's only near-neighbours were lands governed from or peopled from Europe, the exceptions being the kingdom of Thailand far to the north-west and the kingdom of Tonga far to the east. In such a setting Indonesia was seen more as Dutch than as Indonesian – until the Japanese occupation between 1941 and 1945 undermined the authority of the Dutch. Try as they might, the Dutch could not regain their old power in Indonesia. A war of independence broke out in July 1947. The Australian government and the water-side workers, who banned Dutch ships from Australian ports, sympathised with the Indonesians. In 1950 an independent nation arose in the Indonesian archipelago. For the first time Australia was next door to a potential power that was neither European in origin nor Christian in religion.

Islam had been of faint interest to Australians in the age of Queen Victoria. Admittedly the fighting at Gallipoli was against Islamic soldiers but not against Islam. There was not yet a general or even a vague fear of Islam. Even in the Middle East, the Islamic leaders were not yet showing the crusading fervour which the rise of Israel on the one hand and the rise of Arabian oil on the other hand would help to provoke and sustain. In the twenty years after the end of World War II, the fear amongst many Australians was not that Indonesia was Islamic but that it would imitate China and become communist. The defeat of Japan, it seemed, had simply replaced one threat with another.

A car and a mountain

On 15 August 1945 at least half of those Australian people who worked near a radio must have heard the new prime minister, Ben Chifley, make a special broadcast. No message was more eagerly awaited. 'Fellow citizens', he said in his husky voice, 'the war is over'. Calling on them to 'offer thanks to God' for the victory, he paid his respects to the 'gallant, loved ones who will not come back'.

Already airmen were returning from the war against Hitler, which had ended three months previously. Soon the soldiers, nurses, sailors, merchant seamen and airmen, the sergeant majors, wing commanders, able seamen and hundreds of other ranks began to come home. Some servicemen from New Guinea and the islands were easily recognised because of their yellow skins, the result of the anti-malaria medicine they had taken. In civilian life on winter days the returned men were distinctive in their thick, brown army greatcoats or blue air force coats, their heavy collars turned up to keep out the wind.

Older people could not help noticing that, compared with World War I, the permanent wounds of the servicemen were fewer. Few of those returning had lost an arm or leg. Those who returned received from governments, federal and state, more privileges than their fathers knew. Thousands went to the universities to take up free courses complete with living allowances, and on some campuses long army huts had to be erected to teach the overflow. Again tracts of land were thrown open for soldier settlers, but in a more urbanised nation the yearning to become a farmer was not so intense.

2

The Australia to which they returned would seem like a foreign land for the young of today. Various goods were still rationed. Customers had to hand in a rationing coupon to buy meat and sugar, butter and tea. Beer, cigarettes and the ready-rubbed tobacco favoured by those countless smokers who rolled their own cigarettes were subject to weeks of scarcity. Rented houses, and even one rented room with the use of a common bathroom at the end of the corridor, were not easily found in some cities. Petrol was rationed until 1950. Some returning soldiers who were met at a country railway station noticed a tiny trailer behind the family car. This was the gas-producer which, filled with lumps of charcoal, generated the gas that drove the car. Occasionally, in summer, falling cinders accidentally set alight the dry grass along the road. A new car was a rarity, and it was not easy to buy even a second-hand Ford, Chevrolet, Dodge, Essex or Rugby. Nearly all forms of communication were still regulated. In 1942 the sending of congratulatory telegrams for Christmas, New Year's and Mother's Day had been banned, because a telegram was delivered to a home or office by a boy riding a government bicycle: bicycles and tyres were scarce. Celebratory telegrams did not appear again until the first Christmas after the war.

Canberra's wartime rules and regulations set down in print were so like an encyclopaedia that hardly a bureaucrat or politician knew them all. There were controls over rents, food prices, and the size and design of new houses. Regulations limited interstate travel and specified the workplace of dentists. BHP and other shares were not allowed to rise above a certain price on the stock exchanges.

At the end of the war, the countryside remained influential. Maybe eight of every ten rural regions held more farmers then than now, and at hundreds of crossroads stood a church, school, general store and post office that were to fade away in the next half century. In amenities, however, the country was far behind the city. More than half of the farmhouses possessed no electric light and no refrigerator. Drought crippled the south-eastern corner of the continent, and many towns were almost blinded by dust storms. In November 1944 several Victorian trains had been halted by sands drifting onto the track, and many miles of irrigation channels were filled by sand instead of water. All those rural bank managers who worried about their clients could not foresee that a rural boom – aided by a long period of favourable rains – lay just around the corner. The world wanted food and was willing to pay for it.

Nurses and servicemen back from the war were reassured to see familiar sights. Family mealtime prevailed as a formal occasion at least once a day with a tablecloth, cutlery neatly arranged, and a tall loaf of white bread resting on a breadboard, an ornate knife alongside: a packet of sliced bread was still unknown. The two-parent family was normal. 'Partner' was a term used mostly for the dance floor; unmarried people who lived together were frowned upon. If they finally decided to marry, they conformed by marrying in a church, on a Saturday afternoon. A typical marriage involved people of the same religion – most Methodists married Methodists and nearly all Catholics married Catholics. Divorce was frowned upon. Across the nation in a typical week there were no more than sixty divorces, though that seemed an alarming number to those old couples who recalled the era when every single divorce was newsworthy and spoken of publicly in whispers.

A honeymoon was usually spent at a nearby beach resort or city. To travel more than 200 kilometres was an adventure and a half. The idea of flying away for a honeymoon was inconceivable, airline tickets being expensive and scarce. When a newly married couple, perhaps through parental influence, did manage to buy a ticket they were likely to be off-loaded at the last moment if an important politician, general or bureaucrat decided to travel. To go overseas by aircraft was a source of envy. The country's best known scientist, Sir David Rivett, decided in 1946 to make his first overseas visit for nearly a decade. At Mascot he boarded a noisy Lancastrian with seats for nine, and was pleased when he reached London after only four days and three nights of acute discomfort. Most people who set out for Britain – and they travelled to work or to study – had to spend a month at sea. Global tourism, which was on a small scale before the war, was even smaller after the war.

International contests, abandoned during the war, were awaited eagerly by sport-starved fans. When would the English cricket team arrive? That burning topic was discussed even by prisoners of war as they returned from east Asia. At last, the English cricketers arrived by ocean-liner, playing their first Test match in the steamy atmosphere of Brisbane late in 1946. When Don Bradman walked to the wicket, every second pair of ears in the nation was close to a radio. Nothing else signified so strikingly the coming of peace.

Many who recall those first post-war years see mainly the clouds. Stern penalties were still enforced in many facets of life and death. The infliction of the death penalty and the flogging of male prisoners were not yet abolished. In 1946 in Tasmania and South Australia a prisoner was hanged. Homosexuality was taboo. Sunday sport on public grounds was mostly banned, except in outback towns. Many of the performing arts were confined to amateurs. Education changed slowly, and most girls and boys left school after year eight. And yet teachers possibly were held in higher esteem then than now, for the teaching profession and the banks often skimmed the cream of young talent in country towns.

There was still a premium on home-made fun and humour. It was an inventive time for words and nicknames. In 1945, Sidney J. Baker produced the best book so far written on Australia's own words and phrases, and he listed whole columns of words mostly coined during the war and now used widely. A lazy person was called a spine basher or a bludger. Chaos was called a balls-up; and an idiot or misfit was labelled a drongo, galah, nitwit or no-hoper. To talk too assertively was to shoot one's head off. A girlfriend was a Mabel, a sheila, sort, bit, bag, floosie or popsie. An attractive young woman was a tasty drop, while her boy friend, if too flamboyant, was a two-bob lair. Two-bob was the nickname for the two-shilling piece, which slowly became less glamorous with the inflation of the currency in two world wars.

To raise a laugh was a major occupation in 1945. The yarn-spinners and the tellers of jokes and tall stories must have numbered a million. New migrants were often taken aback to find themselves the target for jokes, but nearly everybody was a target for jokes and nicknames.

The morning for most city residents began by opening the newspaper – delivered by a newsboy to their front door – and turning to those cartoons where Ginger Meggs, Wally and the Major, Bill Bowyang, and those raggle-taggle soldiers Bluey and Curly exercised their simple humour:

'What', asks the new recruit, 'are the mosquitoes like up here, sport?' Bluey, his army hat askew, his cigarette dangling on his lip, eagerly explains that only the other night a 'mob of mozzies came over and, fair dinkum, they swooped down and carried off a tent and sewing machine'.

3

Politics was veering sharply to the left by the end of the war. Ben Chifley, the new prime minister, puffed at his pipe with pleasure when he heard the results of the by-election held for the late John Curtin's swinging seat of Fremantle in August 1945. The Liberals won a humiliating 33 per cent of the vote. The numerous ballot papers coming from the armed forces had been counted separately, and only one in every five went to the Liberal candidate.

Chifley and the reigning Labor Pary reshaped the nation during the four years after the war. He typified the old-time Labor leaders whose links were with the country as much as the city, and whose rough hands revealed their manual occupation. Born in Bathurst, just west of the Blue Mountains, and the son of a blacksmith, he was to be buried there in 1951 in the presence of thirty thousand people and his favourite band, Bathurst's own brass band. When steam was king, young Chifley had been one of the leading locomotive drivers and an ardent unionist who stuck to his principles even when the penalty was high. Educated more by books when older than by teachers when young, he had spent only a total of four years in parliament before he was made federal treasurer in 1941. In appearance he was more like a fine-looking dog, a Great Dane, and a pipe was perpetually in his mouth.

He loved economics and the national accounts. His face lit up if a voter discussed with him the price of greasy wool or petrol. He liked to regulate: raw capitalism worried him. He believed in big government. To nationalise all the private banks was his decision: only the High Court halted his plan. He was to toy with a scheme for nationalising all private radio stations and all private airlines.

The war had instilled a sense of purpose. Political divisions, while fierce, concealed a wide arena in which the major parties agreed. A fear of unemployment, the curse of that generation, was high; but most Australians now believed that with determination they could solve it. In the federal parliament in May 1945 the official Labor formula for full employment was introduced by J. J. Dedman, who held the revealing title of minister for post-war reconstruction. His mission was not to reconstruct damaged buildings, which were few, but to reconstruct the whole framework of society. Re-tinting the popular hymn by William Blake, he promised that he would not cease from mental fight: 'Till we have built Jerusalem / In "Australia's" pleasant land'.

All parties, following the shock of Japan's military thrust, agreed that the nation should be prepared to fight another war. Few observers expected that peace would enjoy a long reign. Whereas in 1919 most people expected a long peace and did not see it, in 1945 they expected an early crisis, perhaps even another war. It was widely feared that nuclear weapons – and Russia soon acquired them – would ensure that a major war would be more devastating than the one now ended. The knowledge that the world was perilous removed some of the solace of peace. The peace would have to be fought for, and Chifley pinned his hopes on the new United Nations Organisation which his colleague, Dr H. V. Evatt, had helped to create. He also pinned his hopes on defence, and for several years Australia kept a large occupation force in Japan.

The war memorials, proudly erected in every town and quarter-town after the previous war, were fewer. The old memorials had proclaimed that men had fought for God, King and Country; that their sacrifice was not in vain and they would 'grow not old, as we that are left grow old'. In 1945 it was not so easy to think of confident texts for the new war memorials. Most towns recycled the memorial of 1914–18, adding a column of new names.

Australia was determined that Japanese leaders and all those who had been brutal to prisoners of war should be punished. An Australian judge, Sir William Webb, presided over the international court that tried and convicted the main Japanese war criminals. In Tokyo an Australian philosopher, William Macmahon Ball, joined the Russian and the Chinese representatives who sat on the Allied Council that was set up to advise General MacArthur in the governing of Japan. In those first years of peace it was utterly inconceivable that Japan would eventually rise again and dominate much of Australia's economic life and, forty years after the war, send a daily procession of tourists to Canberra on the back of the all-powerful yen.

Social security became a priority in Canberra. The Commonwealth resumed its role, largely abandoned in 1914, as a provider of new welfare benefits. There were pensions for widows and invalids, the beginnings of a health scheme, subsidised funerals for old and invalid pensioners, a maternity allowance, and the family subsidy known as child endowment. In July 1945 the Commonwealth paid its first regular dole for the unemployed: previously a few state governments had often paid in food and clothes. The new welfare schemes were costly but Canberra's revenue was high because far more people paid income tax, and paid it at higher rates. Moreover the war itself had not generated the need for such massive aid for returning servicemen. If the casualties had been on the same scale as in World War I, the welfare schemes for the general public would probably have been cut short.

With only seven million people, Australia needed a larger population in order to defend itself. What proved to be the boldest immigration venture of the century was planned by Arthur Calwell, Chifley's new minister for immigration. He summed up his plan by pointing to the simple fact that Japan and its large fighting population had been able to threaten Australia: 'They were so many. We were so few'. He called on his fellow Australians to grasp the truth that one day, if the population remained small, 'this wide brown land' might be over-run by an enemy.

Originally Calwell hoped that ten migrants would be enticed from the British Isles for every one from other lands. Initially some refugees would be allowed to come from Europe but relatives already in Australia must house them and care for them – it was feared that they might be unemployed and a burden on the nation. He soon turned to the crowded refugee camps of continental Europe for large numbers of the migrants he needed annually. He recruited thousands of Baltic peoples – first known as 'Balts' or 'displaced persons' – and Ukrainians, Poles and Yugoslavs. He welcomed 2,000 Jewish survivors from the Nazi concentration camps, and more were to come. Melbourne was to be the home of so many survivors of the holocaust that eventually they set up a special museum and acted as guides to the school children who came.

In the British Isles, people did not show quite the eagerness to emigrate that Calwell had anticipated. In the whole decade from 1948 to 1957, three people were to come from continental Europe for every one from the British Isles. Here was the start of a profound change in the composition and culture of Australian people.

Perhaps no other nation had ever deliberately set out, at the public's expense, to bring such a large quota of people from different cultures. Unease was only to be expected. The crowds of 'foreigners', easily identified by accent or clothes, faces or names, were sometimes resented. In 1947 Calwell coined the friendly phrase 'New Australians' in the hope that they would be welcomed everywhere. Most did feel at home, after the first months of strangeness and nostalgia. They had more to eat than the people of any land in Europe and higher pay than they received at home. For those who came with high qualifications, the transition was difficult. Either they lacked the verbal skills to match their qualifications, or their foreign degrees were not seen as instantly entitling them to practise medicine, law, engineering and other professions. Those coming from famous universities in central Europe had some right to resent their temporary exclusion, but they did not always appreciate that medicine and various other Australian professions, though unpolished at the edges, had set such high standards.

Every migrant of working age was given a job, perhaps in a remote mining town or construction site, perhaps in the kitchen of a hotel, but more often in a factory. The factories multiplied, for it was official policy that everything which could be manufactured at a reasonable cost should be made in Australia. At first Europe offered little competition, for its cement and steel, machines and tools, were all needed to rebuild the flattened suburbs of Rotterdam, Hamburg and other bombed cities. In the five years after the war, thousands of Australian factories and workshops were built – tin sheds or handsome buildings, some at the end of rough dirt roads and some with their own railway siding. They manufactured cars, chemicals, plastics, glass, batteries, textiles, spare parts for trucks and aircraft, and hundreds of products not previously made here. The governments did not have to advertise that shoppers should buy Australian-made goods. Often there was little else to buy.

People had intense pride in what could be manufactured here. They were delighted when their train approached the steel city of Newcastle and they saw the columns of dense black and white smoke billowing from the enlarged steelworks or, approaching Geelong in the evening, they saw that the new oil refinery was brilliantly lit. Pollution was an active word in very few vocabularies.

At four or five in the afternoon from the gates of the large factories emerged a cavalcade of bicycles with a few buses, cars, utilities and vans crowded with passengers, including women with scarves around their heads. At least half the people in the nation still worked hard at jobs where they were likely to be grimy at the end of the shift. Most people stood while they worked. Few were noticeably overweight – until the era of the cheap car. Blue-collar workers were not outnumbered by white-collar workers until about 1970.

The war had spurred the engineering skills of Australians. The pistons, valves, radiator cores and hundreds of other parts for cars were already made in the cities. If fighter aircraft could be produced in Melbourne, surely a popular car, engine and all, could be made there too. The head of General Motors-Holden's was L. J. Hartnett, an English migrant, described as 'a ball of energy'. When he talked of making an Australian car his word had to be taken seriously. He found he could count on the support of Canberra. His tough task was to sell the idea to the heads of his company in America, for an Australian-made car would eat into the export sales of their own. At the vital meeting in New York in 1947, he was pleading his case when he was interrupted by his American chairman, the celebrated Alfred P. Sloan. 'I don't like this country, Australia', snapped Sloan. 'It's a socialist sort of place: the Government owns the railroads, doesn't it?' Hartnett seized the chance to point out that the government not only ran the railways but might even make cars if Sloan shunned the opportunity. So New York gave permission.

There were few more exciting days in Australian history than 29 November 1948, when the first Holden car was unveiled. On the streets hundreds of children who were mad about cars looked eagerly for the first Holden. With its distinctive bulging bonnet, it could not be mistaken. Indeed, a few wags called it a pregnant whale with false teeth. The whale's six-cylinder engine – its gear lever on the steering column, its top speed of '80 miles an hour' and its frugal use of petrol – wooed the car buyers. Holden dominated the roads for years. Long before Japanese-made cars were seen in Asian cities, the exported Holdens were on sale there.

Ben Chifley, as prime minister, was at heart still a locomotive driver: he kept his hand close to the brakes. His belief that the economy should be tightly controlled led him to continue the unpopular rationing of petrol, even four years after the war had ended. At the same time he would not yield to all the demands by Labor's left wing and the communists. Black coal was the main source of industrial energy, but the coal miners did not always provide it. In 1949 when they were on strike, Chifley courageously sent soldiers and airmen to work the open cuts, though not the more important underground mines.

4

At the federal election in 1949, Chifley was defeated by R. G. Menzies and his Liberal Party. Many of Chifley's policies – the stream of immigrants, the endless lines of smokestacks, and the social welfare – were continued. But the ideology of the nation was rewritten by Menzies in the course of his new and remarkable political innings. The merits and defects of his policies will always be debated. His towering role in Australian post-war life is beyond dispute.

Robert Gordon Menzies was born and reared in the small Victorian wheat town of Jeparit where his father ran a general store in the wide main street and his uncle ran the local newspaper. The boy's second name, Gordon, came indirectly from Africa, from General Gordon, who was the hero of the siege of Khartoum in northern Africa. In background he was a man of the people – his father had been a skilled tradesman in Ballarat and his maternal grandfather had led the gold miners' union. When Robert Menzies was about 11, a phrenologist announced, after feeling the contours of the boy's head, that he would one day become a barrister and public speaker. 'From that day on, my course was charted', Menzies recalled. From the country he went, a scholarship boy, to shine at a little Ballarat academy and then at Wesley College and the University of Melbourne. Brilliant as a young barrister, he carried his brilliance into state politics. Thinking he might serve as a politican only for six or seven years, he was to stay for thirty-seven, nearly all in federal politics. Prime minister when war broke out in 1939, he fell from power two years later, and seemed unlikely to win another chance. He did not suffer fools gladly; sometimes he felt that he was encircled by them.

In the political wilderness he stiffened his resolution and learned to be patient. He founded his own political party, the Liberals. That he called it Liberal – though the Liberals in England stood to the left of him – showed that he understood the post-war mood in the western world. He sensed that voters wanted a new social order, so long as the new zeal for order was not carried to extremes. He himself was innovative. He distanced his party from big business and its financial support. He welcomed women from suburban homes and the returned servicemen, hoping that his party would gain a huge membership that was a mirror of the post-war nation. In Victoria, the early stronghold of his party, a revolutionary rule allowed women half the votes at the meetings that chose Liberal candidates for parliament.

Meanwhile he found the common touch in dealing with ordinary people, though his tongue could be barbed and his wit sharp when he spoke in the packed public halls to which people flocked in order to hear him. A fine orator, speaking in slow resonant voice, he pointed to the merits of the middle path. In 1949 he captured power in Canberra and shared it with the smaller Country Party in a smooth coalition. He had digested another lesson after his earlier fall from power: a coalition is like a dry garden and quickly withers without constant attention.

He saw communism as the gravest threat. In his eyes it had even more power to wound than did wartime Japan, for communism fought with the aid of powerful ideas as well as other weapons. When China became communist in 1949, his anxiety was increased. When South Korea was invaded by communists from the north in 1950, he sent forces there: 359 Australians died in Korea. He sent soldiers and airmen to the Malay peninsula to fight communist insurgents. His willingness to allow the British to test nuclear weapons and rockets in the wide inland spaces of Australia reflected his belief that a strong Britain was in his own nation's interest.

Menzies knew that he could not maintain prosperity unless he gained more success than Chifley in curbing those trade unions in which communists reigned. Menzies tried – and failed – to make illegal the Australian Communist Party, which in proportion to its small membership was the most influential political party the nation had known. The debate about 'the reds' did not harm the pygmy Communist Party but eventually it undermined the strong Labor Party. It was about to suffer its third major split in the space of forty years. In 1955 a Catholic breakaway wing – inspired by the ideology of B. A. Santamaria – left the main Labor Party and formed its own Democratic Labor Party. For the next two decades the DLP normally won about 10 per cent of the nation's votes and its second preferences went usually to the Liberals, thus tipping the scales in their favour.

Several of the loves and hates of R. G. Menzies seemed to lie across the seas, with communism his first hate and the monarchy his first love. He valued Britain and the monarchy partly because, in his words, they gave much to 'that simple sense of continuity and endurance to which the world has owed so much in two great wars'. Much later his royalism was to be ridiculed but during the war the Labor government had also been royalist, appointing the King's stolid brother, the Duke of Gloucester, as governor-general. It was Menzies who in 1954 welcomed the first reigning British monarch to stand on Australian soil. Queen Elizabeth the Second had the mix of pageantry, dignity and humanity expected of a modern monarch; she was also young and attractive. Maybe two of every ten Australians were neutral rather than sympathetic towards the monarch, but even this minority paused to look at her pass by in a train or black car, and found themselves more excited than they had anticipated. More hand-held flags, especially British flags, were sold in one year than in probably the previous twenty years.

Two years after the Queen's visit, Menzies was tempted to reach too far in his affection for Britain. In July 1956, President Nasser of Egypt threatened to nationalise the Suez Canal. As it was important for global commerce, the British and the French resolved to thwart Nasser. Menzies, conscious of the canal's vital role for his nation, consented to go from London to Egypt as the negotiator. His own cabinet was not convinced that he should be an emissary for what seemed to be an Anglo–French version of gunboat diplomacy, nor that he should promote a policy actually opposed by Australia's military ally, the United States. Menzies failed in his mission, Nasser nationalised the canal, England and France retaliated with bombs, and the United Nations threatened to intervene on the side of Egypt. The episode harmed Menzies' name in the eyes of the distant future but most of his fellow Australians were pleased to see him walking the world stage, opposing a potential tyrant who was bent, they thought, on choking the main sea road to Australia.

While Menzies is often depicted as a courtier of Britain, he was, to most people of his own generation, a nationalist, strengthening the nation like nobody before him. In the recollection of Paul Hasluck, his long-time colleague, Menzies never ceased to be himself and never 'lost his own identity as an Australian'. Often the disciple of Britain, he also presided over the first great era of non-British immigration. Inheriting the policy from Labor, he carried it further.

Old ethnic minorities such as the Jews in Melbourne and Sydney, the Germans in the Barossa Valley and on the Darling Downs, the Italians on the tropical sugar-cane fields and Western Ausralian goldfields, and the Afghans in the outback, were now joined by other groups in the suburbs of big cities. Ukrainian Orthodox and Dutch Reformed churches sprang up along with Polish and Czech restaurants, Latvian and Macedonian clubs, Italian and Hungarian newspapers. Immigration, however, was handled with kid gloves whenever the unemployment increased. In 1952, when many trade unionists lost their jobs, the government halved the 160,000 subsidised migrants planned for the coming year.

For a decade or more the largest groups of migrants came from those nations that had been Australia's wartime enemies, Italy and Germany.

They also came, increasingly, from a wartime ally, Greece. Visitors in the mid-1970s noticed especially the way in which Italians and Greeks were making their mark in the big cities, not only in factories and restaurants but also in politics and the professions. Since 1945 about 3.5 million migrants had arrived. Not all stayed, but their effect on the size of the population was astonishing. They had added more to the population since the war than migrants had added in all the previous years extending back to the First Fleet.

Canberra at last grew quickly. When the first Holdens arrived at its petrol bowsers, Canberra was just a baby capital city. Menzies wished it to grow in wisdom and stature: the second of his wishes was achieved. The artificial lake, named Lake Burley Griffin after the thwarted designer of Canberra, gave charm to the straggling low-rise city with its circling streets and avenues of European trees and backdrop of blue ranges. It enticed, at last, many of the departments of the federal government that had long remained in Melbourne. In the 1960s it quickly surpassed Bendigo, Toowoomba and finally Ballarat to become the largest inland city in the continent.

Most Australians, if questioned, would have replied that the nation's symbol was not Canberra but the Snowy Mountains Scheme further to the south. Launched in 1949, in the last gasp of the Chifley government, it was financed by Menzies with the aid of a huge American loan. It called for the excavating of big tunnels that diverted to the inland plains much of the water previously rushing down the Snowy River to the Pacific Ocean. It was a venture in practical politics as well as nation-building, for the hydro-electric stations would help to rescue people in Sydney and Melbourne from firebrand unionists who sometimes disrupted the black-coal mines near Newcastle and Port Kembla.

The Snowy Mountains Scheme marked an era when the engineer was king, when plans for 'national development' fired the people's imagination, when regiments of new migrants could be despatched to the tent and hut towns far from the cities, and when fear of a World War III persisted. Another over-optimistic aim was to harness the Snowy's water and potential electricity to create inland industrial cities, safer from the threat of bombing in time of war. Grand as it was, the scheme was almost a decade too late. Long before it was completed, the world was enjoying a period of cheap oil that pushed black coal aside and also weakened the magic of hydro-electricity. Even the fruit and crops from newly irrigated lands were no longer in such demand. Britain entered the European Community in 1971, virtually closing its own market to many Australian foodstuffs.

5

In retrospect, this was the Indian summer of rural Australia. Prices earned by its foodstuffs were often high, and its wool was sold at freakishly high prices during the Korean War. The larger country towns, nearly all of which stood within 300 kilometres of the coast, breathed optimism. Mackay and Lismore, Horsham and Mt Gambier, Bunbury and Burnie swam in money in the 1950s. Many farming families even made a trip overseas in a P&O or Orient ocean-liner, returning with lantern-slides which they showed to captive friends on a white screen or wall in their living room when dinner was over.

Most observers said, during the first Menzies years, that the halcyon era of Australian mining had passed: minerals had helped to mould the nation but their glittering days were over, it seemed. Mining was important but lived mainly on old discoveries. The main fields – New South Wales' black coal, Broken Hill's silver and lead and zinc, and Kalgoorlie's gold – were discoveries of the previous century. The biggest industrial and mining company in Australia, the Broken Hill

Proprietary, though no longer active at its birthplace in Broken Hill, was the nation's only maker of iron and steel, the largest user of steel, the largest miner of black coal, and the owner of the largest private fleet of ships. BHP was seen as a reminder of the old mining share booms that had vanished, it was thought, for ever.

In the 1950s, to the surprise of many, the rush for minerals resumed. Whereas the continent had long been thought to be totally deficient in many minerals, some of the scarce ones were discovered in this new era of exploration. Bauxite, the raw material of aluminium, was regarded as relatively rare in Australia; but in the 1950s the discoveries in the low ranges within one hour's drive of Perth and near the north-eastern corner of the continent began to convert Australia into the world's largest exporter of bauxite and alumina. The exporting of iron ore had long been banned – stocks must be earmarked for Australia's own blast furnaces – but in the 1960s the world's largest iron-ore ports began to arise in the tropical north-west, to handle the wealth from the rugged Pilbara. Payable oil would never be found in Australia, said some experts, but major fields of oil and gas were found in 1966 by Broken Hill Proprietary and its American partner, Esso, beneath the waters of Bass Strait. The nation was close to self-sufficiency in fossil fuels, just when the oil crisis of 1973–4 dislocated most other nations, compelling their motorists to queue at petrol stations and their powerhouses to ration electricity.

The sheer variety of discoveries was remarkable. On the tropical island of Groote Eylandt in the Northern Territory manganese was found in the 1960s. In dry country in Western Australia, near the empty streets of a former gold town, the nickel of Kambalda was found. Soon Australia was one of the world's major miners of manganese and nickel. In Arnhem Land a large uranium province was being unveiled. Far to the east, in the Bowen Basin of Queensland, massive deposits of black coal were opened for the Japanese market. The sensational run of discoveries was not yet over, and in the 1970s minerals were to replace wool and become the major source of export income.

Why was so much found in areas that had heard the tramp of prospectors for a century or more and been examined and rejected again and again? Those who in 1950 had predicted that the great minerals rush had ended could not foresee the rise of Japan which became the main market for many of the new finds. Japan's appetite for coal, iron ore and alumina spurred the opening of many mineral deposits that had been glimpsed but so far ignored because they had seemed unprofitable. Likewise by the 1960s 'the winds of change' – a phrase recently coined by Harold Macmillan, the first British prime minister to visit Australia – imposed political instability on the newly liberated Third World at a time when Australia was becoming attractive to foreign investors by virtue of its own political stability, its favourable laws on mining leases and taxation, and an improvement in industrial relations. Above all, many of the latest mining fields owed their birth to new geological theories and techniques of exploring. Ingenuity as well as huge sums of money opened up some of the new fields.

Public opinion rather than politicians, who were more realistic, hoped that one day the vast northern half of Australia would be densely populated. But the obstacles were high. Darwin, the main town in the Northern Territory, was smashed by a cyclone at Christmas 1974. The mining field of Mount Isa in north-west Queensland struggled for thirty years to make a profit, though eventually it supported a flourishing town of 25,000 people: the largest town in a vast tract of country. Fortunately sugar-cane flourished on a narrow strip of Queensland coast, and elsewhere the introduction of Brahman genes into the herds of tropical cattle made them more profitable.

In Western Australia a secret American naval communications base with its intricate cobweb of masts and aerials supported another new town at North-West Cape. Further north, the opening of the big Ord

River reservoir in 1972 did not create an irrigated oasis. Crops of cotton had to be sprayed with chemicals as often as forty times a year. In the end that vigorous pest, the cotton bollworm, was the victor. In tropical Australia the capacity of nature to bite those who tried to tame her was formidable. Thus Queensland's giant cane toad, imported from Hawaii in the 1930s to destroy the cane beetle, became a curse more than a cure and eventually found its way across the wide plains to the Northern Territory.

Science was more dexterous in the southern half of Australia. Billions of free-roaming rabbits, a scourge of the countryside since they began to multiply prodigiously near Geelong in the 1860s, were cut down by myxomatosis, a disease released by scientists and spread by mosquitoes. In addition, fertilisers were devised for exhausted lands. With the aid of tiny doses of copper, cobalt and other minerals, barren soils began to blossom. Near the highway from Adelaide to Melbourne a dry stretch known as the Ninety Mile Desert was invigorated by a sprinkling of 'trace elements'. In Western Australia, where wild waves dashed on the coast near Esperance, a vast strip of country came to life when the subterranean clover and other grasses increased nitrogen in the soil.

Even nature smiled on farmers in the south. The seasons turned in their favour. From the late 1880s until the end of World War II, a vast area of south-eastern Australia, covering the hinterland from Rockhampton in Queensland to Port Augusta in South Australia, had suffered from relatively dry seasons; but after 1945, almost by magic, their rainfall increased. The rainy years were rainier than in the past. For the next quarter-century the income of the small farmer, traditionally a battler, improved. Many rural seats that were once likely to vote for Labor or the radical wings of the Country Party now voted for the Menzies coalition. One of Australia's long-serving prime ministers, Malcolm Fraser, first entered parliament in 1955 by winning a rural seat in the favoured pastoral country of western Victoria. The seat, which now seems so true-blue, had been held by Labor in many of the years of rural hardship.

In population, however, rural areas were in decline. Producing more wool and grains and livestock than ever before, they now used more machines and less labour. As the tractor replaced the draught horses, less time and labour were spent in ploughing and harvesting. The motor truck carrying bulk wheat replaced the horse-drawn wagon hauling wheat in heavy bags, each of which had had to be lifted and carried four or five times between the paddock and the wharf and ship. On dairy farms the milking machine replaced the pairs of hands. In the early 1930s, farms employed more people than did factories, but at the end of the Menzies era the factories employed three times as many as farms. Ironically the countryside was losing people because it was so efficient in using machines instead of labour; but in contrast the cities were growing fast, partly because their typical jobs were not so mechanised. They still needed hundreds of thousands of human hands to make shoes and shirts, to make or repair cars and television sets, tap on typewriters and serve in shops and banks.

A hundred and more country towns passed their peak, and their youngsters who left school moved elsewhere to find work. Called 'the drift to the cities', it was a 'drift' full of purpose. To poorer rural people, especially labourers with no stake in the land, the city offered shorter hours, plenty of running water, electric light at home and bright lights elsewhere, and opportunities for their children.

Migrants from Europe preferred to live in a city. Melbourne, favoured by people from continental Europe, grew rapidly in the 1940s, 1950s and 1960s – the first time it had outpaced Sydney since the gold rushes. For a time it seemed possible that by the century's end Melbourne would overtake Sydney in population. Melbourne gained partly because black coal, the old strength of Sydney, was now less important. Moreover Victoria used its own electricity generated cheaply from the massive brown coal of Gippsland. Adelaide, vying with Melbourne as the hub of the motor vehicle industry, also enjoyed a burst of fast growth. It became a haven for new British migrants. Significantly, the Liverpool pop stars, The Beatles, received in Adelaide a rousing welcome which they thought was unparalleled in the world.

Everyone saw The Beatles, in the flesh or in pictures, because television was the wonder of the era. The first television stations were opened just in time to show the Olympic Games staged in Melbourne in November 1956. Frank Packer of Sydney and his Channel 9 won the race to be first on air. At the opening night on the rival ABC television, Menzies and other invited speechmakers appeared in the studio in dinner suits, just as in the early days of radio, and Michael Charlton the cricket broadcaster acted as the compere. He was enjoying a quick smoke and drink at the side when the film broke down. The audience watching from their lounges and sitting rooms – a television was too expensive to be entrusted to a kitchen – had nothing to look at. The studio's cameraman, resolving that the show somehow must go on, turned the camera on the unsuspecting Charlton.

Only Sydney and Melbourne showed television at first. As no landline or satellite linked these cities, the daily films of the Olympic events had to be flown from Melbourne to Sydney for transmitting that evening. The foreign news came by aircraft from overseas and the reels were rushed by van to the television studio. The pleasure gained from the five or six hours of black-and-white viewing aired each day far exceeded the pleasure to be derived from around-the-clock colour television which arrived in the 1970s.

These years experienced swift changes in ways of measuring. One was pioneered in Australia in 1953 when Alan Walsh of the CSIRO discovered how various atoms absorbed energy, thus paving the way for one of the world's great measuring devices for analytical chemistry –

the 'atomic absorption analyser'. In 1966 Australia moved to decimal currency, using dollars and cents in place of pounds, shillings and pence. In 1970 the federal parliament voted to introduce the metric system of weights and measures. Horse-racing was one of the first activities to adopt the change, and broadcasters simply changed yards into metres without missing a breath.

Meanwhile the computer was appearing in nearly every big business, one of its first triumphs being to calculate the weekly pay, a task which formerly occupied a small brigade of clerks. The computer was still big and cumbersome, and massively expensive. In 1970 perhaps a mere 900 computers were operating in the nation.

In the quarter-century from 1945 to 1970, technology more than politics was remoulding the country. Science, more perhaps than now, was hailed as a friend. Pride in the nation's top scientists was high. Between 1960 and 1964, Sir Macfarlane Burnet and Sir John Eccles won Nobel Prizes in medicine, while Alexander Prokhorov a Nobel Prize in physics. Famous in Soviet science for his theoretical work on the precursor of the laser, Prokhorov is virtually unknown in Australia, though he was born in north Queensland in 1916 and attended a small school on the Atherton tableland before emigrating to his ancestral Russia. The high interest in science was mirrored in the public enthusiasm for research in the Antarctic. A headline event was the annual departure of a small ship carrying away Australian scientists who, after crossing the wild seas, would spend a year on that iced continent under the direction of Dr. Phillip Law.

6

The prosperity financed a zeal for education, which jumped back onto the political agenda. The providing of free and compulsory education had been a triumph of the 1870s in the most populous colonies, which briefly became global leaders in educating their children. Then came more than three-quarters of a century in which only slow and cautious steps were made to extend the school life of the typical child. Even in 1945 the merit certificate, awarded to children who had satisfactorily completed the second year of high school, was an adequate prerequisite for many jobs. It was a passport to the police force.

Part of the explanation for this long delay in advancing educational opportunities is that Australia, by world standards, was incredibly prosperous back in the 1870s and 1880s and could afford to spend heavily on schools. Thereafter the prosperity grew more slowly. Australia also suffered because it was in the English cultural tradition. England did not give a strong emphasis to education. In the 1960s its full-time students aged between 16 and 18 formed a low proportion of their age group compared to those in Sweden, Japan and the United States.

There was another reason for Australia's long apathy towards higher education. Its equalitarian attitude was slightly suspicious of education. The Labor Party traditionally did not rank education highly in its reform proposals and the Liberal Party was often more interested in the private schools, which were strong in the secondary sector. The Catholics, knowing the high cost of running their own chain of schools, felt that any advance in the school-leaving age could be a burden. Soon after World War II these attitudes were undermined. Now the high schools multiplied, and the technical schools too. The nation's teachers doubled and then began to double again.

Universities gained from the new respect for education. The belief faded that each big city needed only one university. The seven universities existing in 1945 were to be multiplied by more than five in the next half-century.

Menzies had reigned for seventeen years when in 1966 he decided to resign. If the two years of his wartime prime ministership are added in, his total years as the nation's leader equalled about three-tenths of the history of the Commonwealth of Australia. He presided over swift changes, many of which are no longer in the public's memory. Though intensely British he cemented ties with the United States in defence. When in the early 1960s the United States intervened in Vietnam, he became the first Australian leader to send forces to a war in which Britain was not an ally. Culturally he was neutral towards Asia – a holiday in Bali would never have been his preference – but he was content to watch his country's trade be diverted from the British Isles to Asia. It was during his last years in office that Japan passed Britain as the main buyer of Australian exports.

By the careful selection of judges and by his appointment of Sir Owen Dixon as chief justice he made the High Court of Australia, in his day, a seat of justice possibly 'without parallel in the English-speaking world'. He showered the universities with scholarships: no previous politician did more to boost higher education. Though a Presbyterian, he cemented links with the Catholics controlling the new Democratic Labor Party; and that small party and its votes helped him to stay in office. He broke what was in effect the first commandment of Australian Protestantism: 'Do not permit the public purse to subsidise private schools because such schools are mostly Catholic'. His government began to subsidise primary schools, including Catholic schools. So the commanding victory of Protestants and secularists in the 1870s was overthrown.

In most of the twenty-five years after the fall of Singapore, Australia had been driven partly by the perils of World War II. Leaders, both Labor and Liberal, wished to make their nation more self-reliant. In the event of another war, a strong base of manufacturing and defence industries might enable the nation to fight on, even if isolated from outside help. A larger population would give it military and industrial vigour. Social cohesion, vital in war, would come from a campaign to assimilate new migrants. Full employment would eliminate that nagging social tension which, before the war, was bred by poverty and unemployment. These aims were largely fulfilled by 1970, just when new priorities and aims jumped forward.

• • • • • • • • • •

Black and green
resurrection

Many of the ideas and recipes that had long formed the mental diet
of Australians were again being boiled in a cauldron. The heat came
partly from the Vietnam War. At first that war did not seem likely to
be a social cauldron, stirring and agitating Australian life. It seemed a
remote event, fought in a hidden jungle. Australia entered the jungle
hesitantly, its first armed forces being despatched to Vietnam in 1962 as
'advisers'. R. G. Menzies had seen the war as a way of reaffirming the
importance of the US alliance and of restraining any southerly advance
by communist China. The ambitions of China he exaggerated, the
threat to Australia he probably exaggerated; but these questions were
not easily answered at the time. They were almost the natural response
of a generation which remembered that a quarter of a century earlier
it had failed to recognise early enough the danger arising from Japanese
policies in the same region. Moreover it was less than ten years since
Australia and China had been on opposing sides in the Korean War.

Even the Labor Party which opposed the war shared the fear that in
these perilous times Australia itself could be vulnerable. It saw nearer

Indonesia rather than Indochina as the main source of danger. A. A. Calwell, as leader of the Labor Party, warned in February 1962 that Indonesia could expand aggressively: 'If Indonesia seizes West New Guinea by aggression why should it not look greedily, first perhaps at Timor, then at Papua New Guinea and finally – who is to say? – at Northern Australia'. It was this general air of apprehension that united all political parties: the disagreement was in defining the threat.

The Australian forces sent by ship to Vietnam were steadily increased in the mid-1960s. No longer advisers, they were fighters, with a specific territory to defend and pacify. Many citizens resented their government's new policy of compulsorily recruiting young men for the armed forces – with the aid of a monthly lottery to make the selections. Why, they argued, should conscripted men have to fight, alongside volunteers, in what many viewed as an unjust war? If instead the government had recruited voluntarily, with the aid of high pay, all the 8,000 servicemen deployed in Vietnam in 1968, the war might not have gravely divided the nation. A volunteer army, except in a national crisis, was an Australian tradition.

The anti-war movement became a massive forum for the counter culture. It especially captured the young. The Australians fighting in Vietnam felt the sting of public apathy and derision. Their pain was intensified because their morale was higher, and their military skills more formidable, than the typical American soldier who fought with them in Vietnam. While they were under emotional attack from a section of their own country, they were risking their lives, they believed, in the name of their country. In Vietnam, by the end of 1972, 500 Australians were to die and another 2,400 were to be wounded.

Eventually the nation was divided as fiercely by its role in the Vietnam War as in the latter half of World War I, when the conscription of young men was also the burning question. Most Australians supported the war in Vietnam until it was seen as exacting too high a price for a victory that receded year after year. The ardent opponents of the war were also mistaken. They saw the North Vietnamese as freedom fighters, as morally superior, as exemplars of a simple and worthier way of life than Western capitalism. Those Australians who marched through the streets in their tens of thousands, and pleaded for an end to the war, had no inkling of the ruthless rule that would ultimately be imposed on the South Vietnamese after their defeat. Most wars, at some stage, are characterised by polarised, simplified attitudes within the same nation.

The opposition to the Vietnam War often embodied a rejection of some of the mainstream ideas of Western society. While Vietnam spurred the slogans, many of the new ideas might well have circulated vigorously even if there had been no war. Together these ideas were to alter Australia in many ways.

2

Quietly or noisily there arose a cult of the young. Their favourite music, rock-and-roll, seemed to unify them. Many of their attitudes to the war, to the older generation and to its old-fashioned habits were expressed through music. The contraceptive pill, used from the early 1960s, gave sex a new freedom. Drugs were hailed by pop singers and surreptitiously tested by their audience. Cheaper cars brought a new mobility to the young, and the widespread prosperity and higher pay enabled them to leave home earlier: the previous barriers to a young couple living together, unmarried, was the combination of Christian morality and the harsh fact that they could not afford the rent. The new generation gap was widened by what was depicted as the tyranny of older politicians, staying at home but forcing young men to join the army and possibly even fight in Vietnam.

Nearly every trusted or accepted idea was challenged by this mood of liberation. It was no longer so clear what the majority of people believed in, so fast did the spin-dryer of opinions whirl about. Editors looked twice at indignant letters addressed to them and beginning with the words, 'All right-thinking people'. The right-thinking people were becoming fewer, and in any case they might no longer agree on what was right. In the new uncertainty, there was less censorship of books deemed too erotic or too revolutionary. A bare breast or buttock was now glimpsed on television. Feminists and homosexuals joined the ranks of the liberated. The rising generation tended to shun church: they deserted Sunday Schools in their droves.

Equal rights for women became a popular slogan. In 1969 the Commonwealth Arbitration Court called for the payment, by progressive stages, of equal wages for equal work. More of the married women stayed in the workforce, whereas the old tradition was that women in full-time jobs should retire when they married. In 1966 the Reserve Bank caused a stir by allowing married women on its staff to take leave when they were about to have a baby and to continue to receive their pay. More women won seats in parliament and high posts in the law, business and education. The pace of change was steady more than swift, but by 1990 two premiers were women and a female judge sat on the High Court.

Several of these reforms had floated vaguely in the air for decades, but now the air carried lightning and thunder. Almost unnoticed, the threats and fears which had helped to keep society together were melting. The threat of hell, voiced from some pulpits, was less pervasive and less potent; and many of the young were no longer to be seen in the congregation. The risk of dying prematurely had lessened, except for the young driving their first car. The threat of unemployment had almost vanished, for a time, and the social stigma of being unemployed was weaker. The fear of an unwanted pregnancy was declining, and many new mothers were content to remain unmarried. In 1970 South Australia became the first Australian state to legalise abortion. This surge of ideas invaded all prosperous Western nations and easily penetrated those two Western nations that were seriously engaged in war in Vietnam: the United States and Australia.

Nature returned to favour. Wildernesses, wild rivers, rainforests, expanses of swamp land and windblown peaks became icons, to be preserved at all costs. Even deserts ceased to be so feared. In the high country of Tasmania there was a campaign to save the idyllic Lake Pedder and its charming beach from being drowned by a hydro-electric scheme. In 1972 a small green party fought parliamentary elections in a vain attempt to save the lake. Hydro-electricity was the spiritual father of modern Tasmania, and soon it was to be arrested and convicted. Already the killing of whales in Australian waters was vigorously opposed; only the whaling station at Albany was still at work.

The extreme veneration for nature caught older Australians by surprise. Traditionally nature had been seen as an enemy as well as ally. Droughts, floods, bushfires and gales on the sea lanes pitted themselves against the pioneers and sometimes won. Adam Lindsay Gordon had been intensely popular, partly because his poetry depicted nature as a femme fatale 'with fire and fierce drought on her tresses'. By 1970, raw nature was no longer seen as such a menace. It seemed less menacing to a nation of city-dwellers, many of whom had never seen a venomous snake except on television.

Delight in nature, unmitigated delight, was winning an army of enthusiasts by 1970. The Australian Conservation Foundation, formed five years earlier, united enthusiasts of the left and the right. High in its ranks were not only political radicals but the chief justice Sir Garfield Barwick and the mining leader Sir Maurice Mawby, who had belonged to an earlier, regional green crusade − an amateur band of field-naturalists whose practical ideas revegetated and transformed the dust-swept city of Broken Hill in the late 1930s.

The 'light greens', believing in economic growth as well as in preserving rare species and places of rare beauty, were still in the ascendancy. Later they would become the unconscious captives of the small numbers of dedicated and professional 'dark greens', who opposed all kinds of economic development. The dark greens likened nature to the Garden of Eden. With the declining appeal of communism, many young people who might have once sympathised with it became dark greens. So too whole streets of suburban enthusiasts who earlier had been middle-roaders. Whereas communists traditionally worshipped technology, the dark greens challenged it. Uranium and nuclear technology was one of their targets. In the early 1970s the Northern Territory became one of the world's main potential sources of uranium, after astonishing discoveries were made in what later became the Kakadu National Park. The crusade to ban the mining of uranium was partly successful.

Australia was an ideal forum for those determined to conserve nature. It was not only rich in coal, uranium, lead and other polluting minerals but was also the home of so many unique but vulnerable species of flora and fauna. It also had tentative possession of huge areas of the Antarctic, the only continent which in its icy purity could be saved from human intruders.

Over-population was singled out as one of the world's gravest dangers. Indeed in the early 1970s a global scarcity of food and energy was widely but wrongly predicted for the following decade by many scientists in Europe and North America. The idea that nations should no longer take pride in an expanding population fell on receptive ears in Australia, where the rate of population increase in the past twenty years had, through immigration, been almost the fastest in the industrialised world. Unemployment was growing, and immigration was cut. Moreover, Europe with its declining birth-rates and high prosperity was ceasing to be such a source of eager migrants.

The dark-green message was suspicious of economic growth – the eager goal of the Chifley and Menzies years – and of the avid accumulating of worldly possessions. The arts fitted snugly into this new reaction against materialism. Compared with education, the arts had won little money from state governments and even less from the wealthier Commonwealth government. But their prestige was rising. In 1969 prime minister John Gorton set up the Australia Council, modelled somewhat on the Canada Council, to promote ballet, opera, Aboriginal arts, live theatre, pottery and other crafts which, unlike literature and painting, had rarely received public grants.

On the shores of Sydney Harbour an opera house, designed by Joern Utzon of Denmark, had been under construction for years. The expense soared far beyond all estimates, and Utzon went home, never returning to see his building in all its splendour. Opened in 1973, the Opera House became a fresh and exciting symbol of the fast-growing nation. That Joan Sutherland was the world's great soprano and performed often on this new stage in her own home city enhanced its appeal. In Melbourne and Sydney a higher proportion of the population than in Paris and London now attended opera. John Pringle, the newspaper editor who wrote the observant book *Australian Accent*, thought the Opera House unfurling its sails on the headland was like a noble church in Venice, lapped by a blue bay even more magical than the shores of the Adriatic:

> There it stands, like Santa Maria della Salute on the lagoon in Venice, a perfect symbol linking the city to the sea, welcoming incoming ships with its wide open arches, shining brilliantly in the summer sun or gleaming palely by moonlight, contemporary in feeling yet reminding us of other ages when great buildings were built to the glory of God or the splendour of princes.

The idea was Danish in origin but soon the Opera House was seen as an expression of nationalism and of a growing affection for Australian landscape and the encircling sea. Talented young film-makers shared and promoted the same nationalism. A captivating series of feature-length films, beginning in 1975 with Peter Weir's *Picnic at Hanging Rock*, indirectly celebrated the landscape. The picnic of schoolgirls was in a craggy setting not far from Melbourne, and *The Man from Snowy River* rode his horse in the dramatic mountains south of Canberra. *Breaker Morant* was mainly set in the Boers' South Africa, but the strange rounded hills of Burra, South Australia, were annexed by the cameras, while the film *Gallipoli* commenced with haunting scenes of the nearer outback in Western Australia. Both were primarily stories of wars fought alongside British soldiers far from home, but they trumped up an anti-British feeling that was a vital part of the recharged Australian nationalism. Perhaps the most influential of all Australian films, *Gallipoli* was first screened in 1981. It enthused a new generation of young people about a symbolic event that seemed to be fading from the nation's imagination.

3

Australians were more alert to the region of the globe in which they lived. Mainly pale-skinned peoples of European descent living close to Asia, they seemed a racial and cultural oddity. Already their White Australia Policy – a term disowned officially since 1940 – was being dismantled. It was too offensive to Asians, and it reflected a world that was passing. It had been essential for Australia's survival as a young democracy in that era when the gulf – in religion, culture, language and skills – between a Chinese peasant and an Australian worker was unmanageably wide. Now the cultural gulf was narrower, as many

Asian students realised when they studied in Australia under the Colombo Plan, which was devised in 1950 by Percy Spender, minister for external affairs.

Hundreds of Asian migrants including the Japanese wives of Australian servicemen were quietly allowed to live in Australia, and eventually were granted citizenship. In the 1950s Australia took over from Britain the Indian Ocean outposts of Cocos and Christmas Island, whose inhabitants were mostly of Malay and Chinese descent. After some official dallying they were given the right to settle in Australia. The old dictation test, sometimes applied at ports to unwelcome or ineligible migrants, was abandoned in 1958. In recent years it had rarely been applied.

The White Australia Policy, almost dead, was occasionally defended officially. It was said to have long prevented 'the frictions and tensions which can come from permanent enclaves and a divided nation'. Most leaders of the new Asian nations understood that argument. They themselves had no intention of opening their doors to numerous foreign immigrants, even from neighbouring lands. Indeed Australia had already liberalised its immigration and citizenship laws far more than did those Asian nations which occasionally, with some justification, accused it of bigotry. Meanwhile, some Asian migrants, understandably, felt worried that one day a version of the White Australia Policy might be revived in their new homeland, thereby making them inferior citizens. After 1966, there was faint chance of such a revival.

Australians continued to rule Papua New Guinea, but the colonial era was hastening to an end. In September 1975, it formally became an independent nation. The timing was perhaps too early, but the United Nations said it could never be too early. The parliament in Port Moresby bravely set out to guide and govern one of the most divided of all nations: a land of hundreds of tribes and languages. Subsidies from Australia poured in, some of it trickling inside the pockets of the

251

• • • • • • • • • •

nation's elite. But to listen to a debate in the new parliament house in Port Moresby, and to see the spectators in the gallery leaning forward, utterly absorbed in the spectacle and the arguments, was to realise how quickly an empathy with democracy was growing. Few of the new nations in Africa have been so successful in maintaining a working democracy.

At home the outback Aborigines were no longer forgotten. If nature was now in favour, then they must be in favour too, for their life was close to nature. The astonishing length of time for which they had occupied Australia became known, and that quickened interest in them. In 1956 the archaeologist John Mulvaney conducted an excavation near Mannum in South Australia, in a habitable rock-cave above the twisting Murray River, and with the help of the new method of radio-carbon dating he found that Aborigines had first lived there more than 5,000 years ago. That date was soon outdated. The ashes from a human cremation of more than 20,000 years ago were found further along the Murray–Darling Basin in 1968. The time of first Aboriginal occupation was pushed back to 40,000 years, and even further. A family who flew from Australia to spend a holiday in Italy, declaring that they longed to live amidst ancient history, now had to refine their way of expressing themselves: their homeland also had a long human history.

With many colonies in Africa and Asia becoming their own masters, and with European nations now being lectured on how lamentably they had treated native peoples, Australia had to sit up and take notice. One day in an international court it might well be placed in the witness box or even, as an accused, in the prisoner's dock, though it possessed strong as well as weak arguments on its side.

Most people of part-Aboriginal ancestry more or less belonged to mainstream Australia, enlisting in wartime, working for their living, and voting on election day. In the cities most of these people did not know or didn't care to know whether they had some black ancestry. At the other extreme were full-Aborigines, conscious of and proud of their ancestry. How many 'tribal' or 'bush' or 'full-blood' Aborigines survived was not known with certainty. In 1966 the census tried to count them. The score was 80,207 who were of half-Aboriginal ancestry or more. Of these, maybe 45,000 were totally so. Maybe a few dozen actually lived a version of the same wandering life which their ancestors had followed for thousands of years.

Aborigines now had a stronger bargaining position. Churches which had run mission stations offered to move out. Forceful black folk began to speak up, some voicing grievances that should have long been remedied, and others claiming land: in 1967 the Gurindji people occupied part of Wave Hill pastoral station in the Northern Territory. Equal pay for Aborigines working on pastoral stations was awarded by the Commonwealth Arbitration Commission, a decision which increased the pride but diminished the well-being of Aboriginal stockmen, whose numbers rapidly diminished. Many of the welfare activities done in the name of justice for Aborigines had mixed effects, and in the outback their role in the paid workforce has fallen drastically. The policy of assimilating most Aborigines into mainstream society was replaced by a form of racial separatism, displaying its own defects and merits. Who was Aboriginal was largely left for individuals and groups to decide. One-sixteenth part of Aboriginal blood could be sufficient.

It is widely believed that before 1967, when a federal referendum was passed by a big majority, no Aborigines were allowed to vote. In fact, the great majority already held the right to vote. For many decades the right of Aborigines to cast their vote had differed from state to state, and even differed between federal and state elections. In the southern half of Australia a vote had usually been allowed to a person who was less than half-Aboriginal in ancestry and lived near a town, but few full-Aboriginal people had the vote: in the Northern Territory they did not have voting rights until 1962. It was a proud day when, in 1971, Neville Bonner of Queensland became a federal senator, but many of his Aboriginal kinsfolk continued to resent the fact that they had been second-class citizens for so long, and that frequently their culture had been decried.

4

Every category of people seemed to be riding a big dipper, some falling and others rising. The churches were declining by the 1960s. Each Sunday they had to compete, for the first time, with rival entertainments. Twenty years earlier there were few cars to take families on a Sunday drive, no cinemas and city shops were open, and there was no television to keep them home on Sunday evening. The front doors of hotels were locked throughout Sunday, except to the *bona-fide* travellers, and they were few. Those who stayed at home on Sunday and turned on the radio at 11 am or 7 pm in the hope of hearing alternatives to a church service had to fiddle the knob several times.

A law, usually called the Sabbath Observance Act, banned serious spectator sport on Sunday, while in some farming districts a farmer who ploughed on Sunday was asking for frowns or rebukes in the nearest town, to be followed by divine wrath around harvest time. Then in the late 1960s Sunday was laundered to match the new secular era. The churches suffered: first the Presbyterians and Methodists and other nonconformists whose attendance at church had been high and later the Catholics. By the early 1990s less than one-quarter of the population went to church with some regularity. The decline of the churches was a sweeping social revolution, because they had done more than any other institution, public or private, to civilise Australians.

The decline disturbed priests and pastors. It altered the social life which had centred on churches and their tennis courts and numerous clubs. Traditionally most voters had known the religion, or professed religion, of those running for the highest offices, and they counted it a matter of some significance that Ben Chifley was a Catholic and his wife, so it was whispered, was a Presbyterian. The Labor Party in 1955 had been split by religion. By the end of the century the religion of a premier or prime minister was often noted but not seen as decisive in his quest for votes.

These new attitudes, whether to Aborigines, nature, women or religion, were at first called trendy. Often they carried a touch of rebellion. They marked the dividing range between the era of the Liberal's Bob Menzies, who raised his heavy eyebrows at such attitudes, and the era of Labor's Bob Hawke, who in the 1980s welcomed most of them. The human bridge linking the two eras was Gough Whitlam, who won office in December 1972, thus ending twenty-three years of Liberal rule. Educated mainly in Canberra, the son of a high public servant, he was a lawyer with a sense of the majesty of language and the wit to turn it to his advantage. A commanding figure, he could not ride a wave without trying to command it to halt or accelerate.

In Canberra many of the new attitudes were already being translated into law but Whitlam carried them further. He implemented many of his promised changes before he had even selected a cabinet. In his first days in office he personally took thirteen portfolios or ministries and made decisions in most of them. He promptly took steps to open diplomatic relations with China; he abolished the sales tax on the contraceptive pill; he began to withdraw the very last troops from Vietnam; and released from censorship the film *Portnoy's Complaint*. When he recovered his breath he did more.

Those surfing the new wave of ideas thought that they had found a hero. Years later one of his opponents, Sir James Killen, was generous in summing him up, calling him 'one of the most fascinating and complex political figures in this nation's history'.

• • • • • • • • • •

In the course of three years, Whitlam and his ministers poured money into the arts and abolished fees at universities – a gesture which benefitted the wealthier families rather than the poorer. They set aside vast areas for national parks, and planned to concede land rights to Aborigines in the Northern Territory – the only large territory which Canberra controlled. They tried to transform health services including those for Aborigines: this was the era when money was believed to cure nearly all ills. They devised an honours system, the Order of Australia, which eventually was to replace the knighthoods and other imperial honours. And they sponsored an opinion poll which selected the music but not yet the words of a new national anthem, 'Advance Australia Fair'.

Whitlam thought on the majestic scale. He issued credit on a scale to match. Impatient, he tried to do too much too quickly. His policies seriously weakened Australia's economy at a time when the world economy was temperamental. In the end, the cow which he was so busily milking almost dried up. By then he had lost control of the Senate while he was still supreme in the House of Representatives. The two houses were in deadlock. Each political party had a valid case but that only intensified the sense of outrage felt by the other. Nothing did more to undermine Labor's public standing than a scandal over a public loan, secretly being negotiated in the Middle East through a Pakistan bagman, Mr Tirath Khemlani, whose dealings were concealed from parliament and nearly all other responsible authorities that had a right to know.

In November 1975, to the indignation of dedicated Labor supporters and the relief of their opponents, the governor-general, Sir John Kerr, stepped in. Though he had been Whitlam's own appointee, he dismissed Whitlam. Appointing the Liberal leader Malcolm Fraser as temporary prime minister, Kerr ordered a federal election so that the deadlock could be resolved by the people. Fraser triumphed at the election, and Labor was able to retain only 36 of the total of 127 seats in the lower house.

November 1975 had been a political volcano. The ashes descended for years, darkening the political sky and clouding the way in which Whitlam and Fraser were perceived. It was not recognised that Fraser, combining an unusual mix of radicalism and conservatism, actually accepted some of Whitlam's policies while refining or erasing others. He enabled large areas in the Northern Territory to pass to Aborigines; he welcomed the first Vietnamese migrants; he did not withdraw support for the arts; he initiated the policy of multiculturalism – a word of many meanings – and opened a special ethnic television channel. While he believed in economic development he set aside the beautiful Kakadu in the Northern Territory as a national park, halted mining on exotic Fraser Island, and banned whaling. In foreign policy he was ardently against Soviet communism, an attitude which won him many friends amongst Chinese communists. As one of the forceful leaders of the British Commonwealth, he was a vigorous sponsor of the new nation of Zimbabwe, then in its hopeful phase, and an ardent advocate of reform in South Africa. As expected he tried to curb federal spending.

After Malcolm Fraser won the election of 1975, most commentators expected years of political turmoil. Fraser's personality partly invited it: his unusual path to victory invited it; and the indignation in the Labor Party seemed to assure it. Curiously a strange stability slowly descended on the land. Fraser held office longer than any previous prime minister except Menzies. Fraser's successor, Bob Hawke, in turn served longer than any previous Labor prime minister, so that a period of sixteen successive years knew only two prime ministers. A few years later came John Howard, a Liberal, who was to surpass even Fraser and Hawke in political longevity.

A nation on walkabout

In 1980 the world's political outlook was gloomy. The Soviet Union was fighting in Afghanistan, the Cold War was alive, and soon would emerge the threat of 'Star Wars' between the great powers. Patrick White, the novelist who had recently won a Nobel Prize, spoke for those Australians who carried anti-nuclear banners in the processions held on their secular version of Palm Sunday. He warned that a nuclear war would endanger even those who initially survived it. It would slowly infect 'the less directly involved surface of this globe – as it revolves in space – swathed in its contaminated shroud'. The world's economy was also jittery, with unemployment rising and inflation more dramatic than in almost any year since the end of World War II. Such was the erosion of the value of each coin and banknote that the smallest coins became almost worthless. The last Australian one-cent coins and two-cent coins were to be minted in 1990, and soon they were seen rarely at the cash registers. For the previous six years there was another indicator of the higher prices prevailing: the new 100-dollar note which was twice the value of the highest note previously in circulation.

2

The war in Vietnam had ended, with Saigon quickly falling to the communists in April 1975. The Socialist Republic of Vietnam, formed in 1976, ruled over the whole nation. In the next few years, hundreds of thousands of people fled from Vietnam, and many from Cambodia and Laos too. Most went to Thailand and Malaysia where they crowded into coastal camps.

Just before Saigon fell, several hundred Vietnamese refugees were granted visas to come to Australia. They included the Vietnamese-born wives and children of Australian citizens, thirty-four Catholic nuns and at least 283 war orphans. Australia had a responsibility to accept more of these refugees, but how many? The decision was hard. Whitlam and his party had been against Australia's participation in the war which had thrown up these refugees. He also thought most refugees would be anti-communist and, most likely, would be Liberal voters when they became Australian citizens. Nor were Bob Hawke and most of his trade unions, initially, sympathetic to these refugees. They would compete for scarce jobs at this time of high unemployment. The new Fraser government was more sympathetic. Malcolm Fraser had been minister of the army and then minister for defence during several of the years when Australians were fighting in Vietnam; and he was willing to welcome many of the South Vietnamese who were loyal allies in the war but now faced persecution at home. Even he did not instantly make offers of large-scale help. His government could not ignore public opinion, which was wary. These conflicting attitudes were to be a rehearsal of a similar debate in 2001 when more ships arrived with Asian refugees, on the very eve of a federal election.

The first boat carrying Vietnamese refugees slipped into Darwin, unannounced, in April 1976, after a voyage of 6,000 kilometres. Its few passengers were taken ashore and then flown south to migrant hostels in the capital cities where they were housed and fed – and taught English – at the government's expense. Later that year, in two fishing boats, another 106 Vietnamese reached Darwin. Next year, on the eve of a federal election in which illegal landings might become a major topic, more Vietnamese arrived in Darwin. Six boats arrived on 21 November, and Darwin's mayor wondered whether the quickening flow would become a flood. One week later another fishing vessel, the *Song Be 12*, slipped into the harbour with 160 people including three Vietnamese soldiers. The communist government of Vietnam demanded that the people and the boat – reportedly stolen by these 'pirates' – be sent back to Saigon. Already a total of 5,000 Indochinese refugees had arrived legally, mostly coming by air and holding valid visas issued by Canberra. That was just the beginning.

In 1978 the Vietnam government began to nudge or push Chinese families from Saigon, now known as Ho Chi Minh City. The Chinese, having been the vigorous capitalists in an economy which was becoming socialist, were now out of favour. Moreover the governments of Vietnam and China were at loggerheads, and so the local Chinatowns were penalised for a second reason. So thousands more set out to join the Indochinese refugees already living in camps on the coasts or borders of Thailand and Malaysia. Others fleeing fighting or chaos in Cambodia and Laos added to the pressure. The refugee camps became congested and less hygienic. Feelings of boredom or hopelessness were widespread. Many families had been broken up after adults or children were left behind when the hired fishing vessel had to depart suddenly.

Australia selected more families and individuals from the crowded refugee camps, and flew them to Sydney and Melbourne. By 1982, a total of 70,000 Indochinese refugees had arrived. In the public eye the 2,000 who had arrived in boats seemed typical but they were the exception. By the end of the decade the total inflow of Indochinese refugees had passed 120,000. Of all the countries that accepted these refugees, Australia and Hong Kong were taking the highest share, measured as a proportion of their own population.

The inflow proved to be a turning point in how Australia was peopled. Since World War II, the immigration policy had tried to discourage the forming of ethnic ghettos in the cities. This goal, sometimes ignored, was now quietly abandoned in practice. The new Indochinese migrants kept together. Soon corners of suburbs and lengths of shopping streets were known as 'Little Vietnams'. At the same time the government allowed more European migration, especially family reunions. Traditionally, New Zealanders were allowed to move freely to Australia, and the ailments of their home economy fostered that migration, especially to Sydney: beach-side Bondi became almost a suburb of Auckland. Whereas Australia in the 1970s had experienced a low rate of immigration, the inflow in the late 1980s was perhaps the highest in the developed world.

3

Australia was becoming more an Asian land, in its migration and tourism and inflows of investment. Japan sent the largest number of tourists, and often they stayed in hotels owned by Tokyo. Japan was the largest buyer of Australian exports, and Japanese cars competed with locally made Holdens, Fords and Chryslers on local roads. But the Japanese, unlike other Asians, showed little desire to emigrate.

Towards the end of Britain's cultural reign, Melbourne schoolmaster A. A. Phillips had observed that many Australians tended to display a 'cultural cringe' towards what they once called affectionately 'the old country'. Now the cringe was sometimes directed to Asia rather than to Britain. When the aged Emperor Hirohito died in Tokyo in 1989, the Australian flag was flown at half-mast on public buildings, by order of the Hawke government. The official memory was short. At the end of World War II the Emperor would have been tried as a war criminal if Canberra had had its way.

Cheap air travel had reshaped the act of migration. In the mid-1960s for the first time a majority of migrants came to Australia by air rather than sea, and within ten years those who arrived in a passenger liner were few. Moreover the overwhelming majority of migrants came from nearer lands. Migration had long been subsidised in order to entice Europeans to make the long journey to Australia, but now they had little desire to leave prosperous, peaceful Europe. Their places were taken by Asians who gladly came without subsidy: the airfare from Asia was cheap.

By 1985 more than half the immigrants who arrived and stayed were Asian, many of them refugees. Certain suburbs in Sydney, Melbourne, Brisbane and Perth, both poor and rich, steadily attracted large minorities of Chinese, Indians, Malaysians, Sri Lankans, Filipinos, South Koreans or Indochinese. Twenty years later, Melbourne's phone books revealed that the Vietnamese surname of Nguyen and the Indian name of Singh – with sixty columns of names between them – were fast catching up on the Smiths and Browns. In certain of Sydney's western suburbs, which were havens for Middle Eastern migrants, a new and expensive mosque was a more familiar sight than a new Christian church.

The two waves of post-war migration were not alike. The first had come from European lands and its migrants quickly found work. Public opinion welcomed them in general, for the country needed people in order to defend itself. In contrast the second wave was culturally and racially more diverse, and arrived in an era when unemployment was higher. Unfortunately many of these migrants were directed towards public housing in the declining factory suburbs where unemployment was widespread. Likewise there was no longer a popular ideology in favour of high migration. The green movement was wary of a fast-growing population. Most Aboriginal leaders also opposed fast growth, though their views were rarely reported.

A mixture of generosity and self-interest sponsored this latest inflow of migrants. Political parties vied for the ethnic vote and, under the slogan of family reunion, selected too many unskilled migrants: a high level of unemployment was experienced by some of the new migrants, even after three years in residence. In 1990, the unemployment among recent Indochinese and Lebanese migrants was close to 30 per cent. In contrast new migrants in most ethnic groups, especially those stronger in skills and languages, easily found a job. They saw Australia as a unique land of hope, especially for their children. 'Where else', they said, 'could we find such freedom and such opportunity?'

The latest inflow was championed by an ideology called multi-culturalism. Largely borrowed from Canada, the ideology was sometimes the reverse of the old policy which sought assimilation. Paul Keating rightly hoped that all Australians, irrespective of their birthplace, should now 'feel as though they matter and that they are important'; but one risk was that migrant groups were now positively encouraged to maintain their old homeland loyalties. Indeed the national soccer league had to be reshaped to quell ethnic animosities. Australia now was said, often with some justification, to be an impressive example of unity through diversity and an embryo nation of all the nations – but the penalty is high if the formula should ultimately fail. It will be decades before this fascinating experiment can be safely pronounced as a triumph, a mingled success or the potential creator of a nation of tribes.

With the emergence of Islamic terrorism, the official policy of multiculturalism would have to retreat. In 2008 the goal of unity through diversity began to seem slightly naive after some migrants and even the children of migrants were convicted of secretly planning to set off explosions in public places where, had they succeeded, the death toll of fellow Australians would have been high.

A scurry of events gave flavour to the final two decades of the century. The land that traditionally was so far away was becoming a magnet for foreign tourists. Even the small city of Cairns, nestling between stretches of mangroves on the shore and sugar-cane on the plain, became a major airport as Japanese tourists poured in to see the Great Barrier Reef and the coastal rainforest. A procession of jets flew Japanese and other tourists from the coast to Ayers Rock or Uluru, that impressive natural monument that was formally handed back to Aborigines in 1985. For the first time tourists could drive around the rim of the entire continent on an all-bitumen road, though it was often narrow and liable to flood after tropical rain.

As in every previous decade, major floods and droughts and bushfires came and went: 16 February 1983, a day of fierce bushfires, especially near Melbourne, was known as Ash Wednesday. In the outback new technology arrived to meet long-standing needs. July 1985 was long remembered in the arid opal-mining town of Coober Pedy because a desalination plant began to supply fresh water. In 1987 the Hawke government decided to build six Collins-class submarines, a most ambitious and costly project that was finally completed in the new century. In 1988 in Canberra a new parliament house, more like a fortress or bunker in appearance, was opened by the Queen. In that same year the nation celebrated the 200th anniversary of the landing of the British. To be amongst the several million spectators lining the hilly shores in Sydney on the morning of 26 January 1988, and to see the harbour swamped with sails and the quiet pride on so many faces, was to feel the presence of all those pioneers, now forgotten, whose hard work had built the nucleus of a nation.

This was the decade when heart transplants became common and AIDS caused its first death. In 1987 the first mobile phone appeared.

• • • • • • • • • •

Few other countries in the world took so eagerly to this innovation, and for a time the sudden ring of the pocket phone snapped the silence of concert halls and churches. Long-distance phone calls to the far side of the world, usually so expensive that they were rarely made except at Christmas, became frequent with the aid of satellites high above the earth. Then came in the early 1990s the start of the personal computer craze, which soon ceased to be a luxury. A private message typed in a living room in Hobart reached a house in Kiev or Santiago, in a matter of moments, for a trifling fee.

The internet, like the television before it, was about to challenge the dominance of the newspaper as the source of news. Already the afternoon newspaper was in swift decline. The last of the popular papers, Melbourne's evening *Herald*, was merged in 1990 by its new proprietor, Rupert Murdoch, himself a promoter of the electronic media. Perhaps the best known of the world's media magnates, his first asset had been an Adelaide afternoon paper, the *News*, which gave its name to his News Corporation and its spreading overseas empire of television stations, newspapers, magazines, book publishers, film studios and satellites. Each day his global empire, now centred on the United States, reached hundreds of millions of eyes and ears, compared to the 400 which his grandfather had reached in an earlier but powerful medium: a Presbyterian pulpit in suburban Melbourne.

By 1990, the pattern of life was far removed from that of forty years before. People were living longer and choosing to retire to warmer coastal towns, especially in New South Wales and Queensland. Divorce was common and the single-parent family was almost normal in many suburban streets. So many married women were in paid work, and needing care for their children, that childcare centres supplanted 'eventide' homes in their rate of growth. In many suburbs the typical child no longer walked to school but was driven there; streets that had always been deemed safe were no longer so trusted. Whereas at

265

one time a schoolgirl of twelve did not even own a wristwatch, now she owned a mobile phone. Her grandparents at the same age had probably not eaten one meal in a café or restaurant, not even a birthday dinner, but now roadside restaurants of American ancestry provided hamburgers and chicken pieces for millions of school-age children and their birthdays and treats.

4

The surnames in the news were more polyglot than in the era of such prime ministers as Hughes, Bruce, Lyons and Menzies. In 1990 the head of the largest public company was Estonian by birth, the premier of the largest state was of Hungarian descent, the most celebrated heart surgeon was of Chinese birth, and the best known scientist was of Austrian origin. Parbo, Greiner, Chang and Nossal were just four surnames in the new cosmopolitan sweep of names, but in schools were thousands of other energetic, ambitious students – Chinese, Indian, Korean, Armenian, Chilean, Rumanian – who would one day make their name. At the same time, women belatedly won high offices. Dame Leonie Kramer chaired what is now the Australian Broadcasting Corporation before becoming the first woman to sit on what traditionally were all-male tables, the boards of the major banking and mining companies. In 1990 Dr Carmen Lawrence became premier of Western Australia and Joan Kirner of Victoria. They had made their first careers in education, a huge profession that now vied with trade unions as a recruiting ground for Labor politicians. Meanwhile the first woman was allowed to ride a horse in the Melbourne Cup and the first women graduated as pilots in the Royal Australian Air Force.

In federal politics the long dominance of the Liberals and their rural partner, the Nationals, was ebbing. Since December 1949 this coalition had ruled for all but three of the thirty-three years. In the federal election of 1983, Bob Hawke defeated Malcolm Fraser and inaugurated the longest period of Labor rule in the history of federal politics. The unbelieving son of a Congregational clergyman, Hawke was the gregarious and popular head of the trade union movement. He soon defied the Labor Party's traditions by dismantling fences that had long protected much of the economy. He exposed more factories to world competition. Many owners, not mentally equipped to cope with lower tariffs, padlocked their factory doors and sold their machines. In effect, several hundred thousand jobs were transferred from Australia to factory towns in east Asia.

Paul Keating, when federal treasurer for Bob Hawke, was innovative. He untied the knots of financial regulation and freed the flow of funds in and out of the country. In December 1983 the exchange rate of the Australian dollar, no longer fixed by the government, was allowed to float from day to day. Its value soon slumped. For more than twenty years it was to be worth much less than the American dollar.

Banking was still dominated by four big banks, all locally owned with an impressive web of branches extending to remote towns. The oldest, Westpac, was a child of the convict era, being founded in 1817 as the Bank of New South Wales. The second oldest, the ANZ Bank, was the offspring of the wool boom of the 1830s and the London money pouring into the wool colonies. The National Bank, formed in the first gold rushes, was opened in 1858 with a Melbourne board, soon to be followed by a rival Adelaide board; while the Commonwealth Bank was created by Andrew Fisher's Labor government in time to open its doors in 1912. Each of the four had swallowed rivals during a long life.

The big four and their secure world were exposed to a stampede of new foreign rivals in 1985. In one year, more trading banks set up their offices in Australia than in the preceding hundred. In the star-struck years of the late 1980s, the competition for big business between the new foreign banks and the big four went too far. Foreign capital poured in. A shonky consortium or a reckless entrepreneur was likely to find somewhere the handshake of a friendly banker.

Hawke and Keating exposed capital but not labour to intense competition. Deregulation stopped at the doorstep of the big trade unions. While their membership as a proportion of the total workforce continued to decline, their political influence was at its peak. Their stronghold was the public sector, which was not yet exposed to the new theory that competition was best. In Canberra the public servants multiplied, and that city blossomed, enjoying the highest average income of all Australian cities at the very time when many rural and some urban areas were in economic trouble.

Canberra was insulated partly by its own prosperity, and yet the heads of several of its departments did warn that rising overseas debt was dragging the economy into deep water. Keating, vigorous in his off-the-cuff remarks, finally conceded on 14 May 1986 to John Laws, the king of Sydney radio, that Australia was so burdened with soaring overseas debts that it might become 'a banana republic'. Towards his own warning, Paul Keating later was to prove somewhat hard of hearing.

Meanwhile, new entrepreneurs soared on borrowed money, much of it enticed from New York, Tokyo and London. Such a conspicuous flaunting of wealth, whether in huge mansions or private jets, had not been seen in the nation since the prodigal 1880s. The booming cities of Perth and Brisbane each housed more tycoons than Sydney could display thirty years previously. At first the public rejoiced in the dashing exploits of some of the high-spenders, especially Alan Bond, who, reaching Perth as a young English tradesman, became so rich that he could afford to build the ocean yacht which won the America's Cup from the USA in 1983.

The public was spellbound or vexed by some of the extravagances of the new rich in the brief time that they were very rich. Alan Bond, whose companies ranged from a television network to breweries (at one time he was the world's fifth-largest brewer) bought such toys as the St Moritz Hotel in New York and the most expensive painting in the world, Van Gogh's *Irises*. In December 1989, towards the end of the boom, he sailed into Hobart in one of his glamorous yachts, the blue-and-white *Drumbeat*, only to be told that the drum was summoning him to face his creditors. He faced them reluctantly, and eventually served time in prison. Some of the once-rich entrepreneurs, instead of facing those they had fleeced, fled overseas – to a farmhouse in Majorca, an apartment in Poland or some other hideaway, leaving others to stay at home and salvage what they could from the wreckage.

During the property boom the skylines of cities were altered. The share boom, which largely ended in October 1987, gave way to a mania to build skyscrapers. Property prices went through the roof, and by the start of the new decade the moneylenders were papering over the holes in the ceiling. In 1990–91 Australia was in recession: unemployment reached 11 per cent, interest rates touched 20 per cent and the nation's overseas debts were a burden. The tall cranes almost disappeared from the building sites. In the central business districts of Sydney and Melbourne, one-quarter of the office space was empty. The vacant offices, floor after floor of them, were reminiscent of the empty little skyscrapers deserted during the depression almost 100 years previously.

The boom had fanned corruption in high places. In Western Australia, two former premiers had to face trial. Both went to prison. The boom had fanned recklessness in some of the big banks. The state banks of both Victoria and South Australia had been tempted to lend far beyond their borders. Their losses were sensational. Pyramid, a building society based in Geelong and soon the biggest in Victoria, was a favourite of the small depositors. They were shocked by its sudden collapse. In Sydney the head office of Westpac, the oldest bank in the land, was in a state of alarm. Some observers thought the bank might topple. And yet by the end of the decade the nation was entering a long mining boom and a new era of over-heated prosperity.

· · · · · · · · · ·

18

Symbols in the wind: the Queen and Mr Mabo

In the last quarter of the century, the nation's links and symbols shook in the winds. The British links were weakened by a decline of British migrants. Moreover, trade with Britain slid to a mere 3 per cent of the total after Britain entered the European Community. Tourist and sporting ties between the two countries remained powerful, but other ceremonial and symbolic links were frayed in the 1970s by the new Australian system of honours and the withdrawal of favoured treatment at the passport desk for Australian visitors entering Britain. The Queen formally became the Queen of Australia, and new citizens taking their oath swore allegiance not to the Queen but to Australia.

These changes came gradually. Hawke as prime minister did not press aggressively for the cutting of links with Britain. He enjoyed more personal popularity than perhaps any previous leader and he guarded his popularity by stepping back or even retreating when any of his symbolic proposals met strong opposition. He even pushed for a bill of rights, which was more common in the European than the British political tradition. In effect it increased the power of the High Court at the expense of parliament's own power.

Hawke's own bill of rights proved to be an extraordinary mixture of rights proclaimed – 'no person shall be held in slavery' – and of rights ignored. The right to own private property was not even listed among the thirty-two articles. The Human Rights Commission, in assessing rights and wrongs, was specifically permitted to protect secret informers and poison pens. Some critics called it the 'bill of wrongs'. The High Court, in deciding which specific right should be paramount when two rights were in conflict, was to be handed a crucial power which hitherto belonged to parliament. The House of Representatives passed this revolutionary bill but the Senate hesitated, debating it at more length than any previous bill in the history of the house. In 1986, when the Australian Democrats combined with the Liberals to defeat it, Hawke gave it a quiet burial.

2

Paul Keating, ousting Hawke as Labor's leader in 1991, was ready to pursue Aboriginal land rights with determination. As a result of earlier land laws, vast areas of Australian soil were already held by Aboriginal trusts and groups, and they formed almost a corridor extending right across the continent from the Southern Ocean to the Timor Sea. Much of the soil was poor and parched but in all it covered 15 per cent of the nation's territory. That corridor was soon enlarged. In 1992 a majority of members of the High Court of Australia, in a complicated and eloquent judgment, ruled that the Aborigines were entitled to much more of Australia.

The case had been initiated by Eddie Mabo and by other claimants from the Murray Islands in Torres Strait. The islanders of Torres Strait were primarily Melanesian, and their traditional economy and land system differed sharply from those of the Aborigines. The High Court ruled that Eddie Mabo and his kinsmen were entitled to their land but also affirmed that Aborigines on the Australian continent, which was not then the subject of this litigation, were entitled to lay claim to huge areas of land. In essence what the High Court called 'native title' had not been extinguished by the coming of the British in 1788. Earlier Australian and British judges, no matter how learned, had utterly misunderstood the common law, so the High Court implied.

The Mabo judgment was perhaps the most far-reaching ever delivered by the High Court. It represented a tendency of some judges to see the highest court in the land as a law-making body, as almost a third federal house of parliament. Most members of the court – not all – saw themselves as official interpreters of public opinion, a task which in a democracy is usually entrusted to an elected parliament. They argued that 'the contemporary values of the Australian people' called for a new deal for Aborigines. It was true: a new deal was called for, but it was parliament's task to make and resolve that call. In its majority judgment the court appealed to history, but it is not clear where the seven justices of the court had each found their version of history, for formally they heard no evidence relating to the Aboriginal history of mainland Australia. Many historians were delighted, and many astonished, by the unsubstantiated historical statements which appeared, sometimes in emotive language, in support of the conclusions reached by a majority of judges. Aboriginal leaders who for years had insisted that land was their first priority were entitled to feel elated, for they had conducted a masterly campaign for their rights. On the other hand Aborigines whose traditional lands had been in the capital cities and the adjacent grasslands had to live with their disappointment. They had received virtually nothing from the High Court.

Some prime ministers would have rejected the High Court's judgment. Keating boldly took the chassis built in the High Court and added his own wheels. His Native Title Act, functioning from the first day of 1994, enabled tribunals to decide which public lands should be returned to Aboriginal owners. Such lands were to be held communally and not individually. Land could be sold to the state and federal governments but not to people of another race, and not even to another Aboriginal tribe or clan. A venture in goodwill, the law affirming the existence of native title went a little way towards easing the sense of grievance held by most Aborigines in remote regions. It also spurred confusion, for it was not easy to understand, even with the help of teams of competing lawyers. The rigidly racial basis of the new system of land tenure privately mystified some reformers who had long fought against racial discrimination.

Soon the wheels attached by parliament to the chassis built by the High Court began to wobble or fall off. The High Court continued to act as a third parliament, for it had to interpret or build on the basic principles that it alone had discovered. Moreover, the judges themselves were seriously divided about some of the complicated legal and political issues at stake, as well as the version of Australian history they promulgated.

3

In 1996 the long period of Labor rule, by Hawke and then Keating, was ended at the federal election. John Howard, a Sydney lawyer, led the victorious coalition of Liberals and Nationals. He was to hold office for eleven years and eight months, thus surpassing the term of all previous national leaders except his hero, Sir Robert Menzies. Howard eventually had high success in lowering unemployment and in spurring economic growth. With his treasurer, Peter Costello, he initiated the most ambitious tax reforms since World War II, but his attempt to change the rules of industrial relations did not fully succeed.

Howard was to face more overseas crises, nearly all of which were unpredicted, than any previous peacetime prime minister. He faced the Asian economic 'meltdown', a crisis in Indonesia and then in East Timor, and the rise of Islamic terrorism, in response to which he sent Australian forces to Iraq and Afghanistan.

Aboriginal affairs were another persistent problem. How to ease the grievances of Aborigines, how to improve black–white relations, and how to apportion blame and shame were divisive topics in national politics. The Howard government, when new, had to meet the High Court's new judgment in a case initiated by the Wik Aboriginal peoples of north Queensland. The court, amidst controversy, revised or refined its view of native title. Ownership of half of the area of Australia, mostly land with few industries and few inhabitants, was now in dispute. Soon the courts faced a long backlog of claims, with many areas becoming the target of rival Aboriginal groups. It was hoped, over-optimistically, that the law would lead to a variety of compromises and some satisfaction for all sides in the dispute. Fifteen years after the first Native Title Act, vast areas were still in dispute.

Early in the new millennium, three of every four Aborigines lived not in the outback but in cities or large towns and had little to gain from the Native Title Act. They followed a mainstream Western life. Most were Christian, and few followed their traditional religion. Only one in every eight was able to converse in an Aboriginal language. In contrast those Aborigines who lived in outback and tropical Australia were torn between the desire to cling to their traditions and the eagerness to embrace the trucks, foods, alcohol, sports and entertainment of the outside world. Most were either unemployed or not often at work. Few lived to old age. The young children of these Aborigines living in remote places were also vulnerable. They were prone to infections of ear, eye and chest, attended school irregularly, and at the age of fifteen were less likely to be literate than white children or Aborigines living in cities. They had little chance of finding useful work.

In many of these remote settlements, sexual violence against girls and women was widespread, but the Australian government usually accepted the demand of male Aboriginal leaders that no police should be permanently present. In the end the government felt obliged to intervene in lawless settlements. Here and there, in contrast, were serene Aboriginal oases that banned alcohol or tried other social experiments. In the mid-1990s far to the west of Alice Springs the Nganampa region – with a population of about 3,000 and maybe another 800 regularly passing through – introduced a health service that dramatically cut malnutrition and diseases in young children.

In nearly every region and big city, Aborigines were producing a few strong and highly articulate leaders. Notable in the new generation were Noel Pearson, Marcia Langton and Warren Mundine, who said what previously was almost unsayable: that Aborigines had to accept part of the responsibility for their plight, their social breakdown, and find a way out of it. In mainstream life, other Aborigines made their mark. In some sports, ranging from football to athletics, the Aborigines now reared champions out of all proportion to their numbers. Their paintings were admired in art galleries in New York and Paris. Significantly, thousands of Australian families of mixed ancestry took pleasure, perhaps for the first time, in proclaiming that their Aboriginal ancestry was more important to them than their European. Between 1986 and 2011 those Australians officially calling themselves Aboriginal or Indigenous doubled in number, reaching a total of 548,000 or 2.5 per cent of the population – a new peak. In only one area, however, did they form a politically influential group. In the Northern Territory, Aborigines formed 27 per cent of the total population, and in March 2013 one of their politicians, Adam Giles, became chief minister.

4

Cultural and social attitudes, even more than economic doctrines, separated the main political parties. National identity, and a sense of national pride or guilt, were amongst their main battlegrounds, and there John Howard rejected Labor's policies. He had no time for what was christened 'the black armband view' of Australia's history.

The republic was one of the ideological battlefronts. In 1992, Paul Keating, almost out of the blue, had proposed that Australia should become a republic. During the following months, from prepared speeches and off-the-cuff remarks which he made with colour and pungency, slowly emerged his crucial arguments. He accepted that Australia was virtually an independent nation, and that inside its territory the Queen of Australia, Elizabeth the Second, exercised no real power. But to depose her formally as Queen would emphatically make the nation seem independent in the eyes of the world. Australia, he argued with less plausibility, would never have an intimate and equal relationship with Asia until it ceased to parade British symbols.

The Australian flag, and especially the British flag which occupied one quarter of that flag, was another of his targets – until perhaps he saw the political dangers of attacking the flag. He realised that the present flag, in which the stars of the southern cross are so prominent, conveyed a strong emotional appeal even to many of his Labor colleagues who were republican. Moreover most Australians supported the existing flag.

Like many of the early republican leaders, Keating was of Irish descent and displayed an anti-British virus in some of his remarks, but he spoke essentially as a patriotic Australian. Likewise the defenders of the existing system, while they were proud of the nation's long British connection, spoke essentially as patriotic Australians. Two versions of Australian nationalism thus confronted one another. Curiously, Keating did not place the republic high on his political agenda. It was his hope that Australia would be a republic in time for the opening ceremony of the Olympic Games in Sydney in the year 2000.

Keating lost office after he had planted and watered the seeds of the republic. It was Howard who really promoted the public debate, though he personally did not wish to see a republic. In Canberra in February 1998 a constitutional convention was held, amidst massive publicity. The 152 delegates – ranging from the prime minister and the six state premiers to many Aborigines, one Torres Strait Islander and the delegates directly elected by the people – debated whether Australia should become a republic. On the final day, eighty-nine delegates – a decisive majority – voted in favour of a republic.

The blueprint for the proposed republic was simple. The new president would carry out the ceremonial duties traditionally performed by the governor-general and would also be the umpire if a political crisis like that of 1975 should arise again. Whereas the governor-general had been selected personally by the prime minister, with the formal blessing of the Queen, the new president would be nominated by the prime minister and then endorsed formally by a joint sitting of the House of Representatives and the Senate. In essence all federal politicians would have a vote, with a majority of two-thirds required in order to endorse the appointment. But the formula for removing a president from office was arbitrary. If a president was deemed to misbehave, instant dismissal at the hands of the prime minister was permitted.

The change seemed simple, but first the people themselves had to approve it. The nation could not become a republic until the Commonwealth of Australia's formal constitution was specifically altered; and that in turn required the consent of a majority of all the voters and, in addition, a majority of voters in four of the six states.

The referendum to decide whether Australia would become a republic was to be held in November 1999. Opinion polls – until a month before the day of decision – affirmed that the republicans would win. Most newspapers and members of the media were republicans, though they differed on the exact kind of republic they would like. Most federal politicians were republicans. Even many of the vigorous opponents of the republic were actually republicans who wanted a different kind of republic. The people, they said, must directly elect the president, in the American style. But as Sir Zelman Cowen pointed out, a president of such a republic could, by virtue of his popular election, claim to have a public mandate which even a prime minister might not always be able to claim. Henceforth a dispute between prime minister and president 'could place our parliamentary system in peril'.

On the Saturday of the decision, soon after the polling booths closed in the eastern states but before they closed in Western Australia, the result was clear: the republicans would lose. Opposition to the republic was strong amongst women, and strong in the big outer states though not in the populous south-east corner of the continent. To the dismay of the all-republican Labor Party, the opponents of the republic proved to be surprisingly strong even in those blue-collar suburbs that traditionally voted Labor. Most rural areas were emphatically against the proposed republic; and the vast plains straddling the border of New South Wales and Queensland, and occupying an area much larger than Greece, recorded a 'no' vote of almost 80 per cent. A majority of people in every state voted against the republic: only in Victoria did the republicans come close to victory. And yet by some definitions Australia has been a republic for decades. The refusal of the Queen, even when so requested, to intervene in the political crisis of November 1975 was emphatic proof that the monarch possessed symbolic influence rather than real power. In the words of the poet Les Murray, that episode was the 'final Singapore' of the monarchy in Australian politics. Australia, he added, was now a republic 'lightly disguised as an absentee monarchy'. When will the royal disguise be removed? Soon another Australian leader, invoking the votes of the people, will try again.

5

Howard disagreed with the Labor Party not only on history but also on geography. What was to be Australia's relationship with Asia? Should it be close, intimate and preferential, or should Australia see itself, at least for the next few decades, as a distinctive nation with ties to both West and East?

A popular slogan of the previous thirty years was that Australia is part of Asia. Like most simple slogans it conveyed a slice of truth and a slice of make-believe. While the northerly parts of the nation were close to Asia, most Australians lived in cities or rural regions that were far from Asia. Indeed, Paris and Rome are much closer to Asia than is Canberra, but France and Italy are never said to be part of Asia. Moreover, the areas of Australia that are nearest to Asia are sparsely settled and likely to remain so in the medium future. They have recently been turned, in effect, into a buffer zone, with vast expanses occupied by heritage areas and national parks, and vast territories held exclusively by small groups of Aborigines.

Any military threat to the nation is likely to come from Asia: any civil unrest with regional ramifications is likely to occur in south-east Asia or in the nearer islands of the Pacific. Indonesia had twice expanded in the direction of Australia. In 1963 it peacefully occupied Dutch New Guinea. In 1975 it moved into Portuguese East Timor and, one year later, made it the twenty-sixth province of Indonesia. Not until 1999, however, were the East Timorese permitted to make their own decision about their long-term future. When finally they voted for independence, they suffered violence from Indonesian forces and sympathisers. Howard resolved that Australia should restore order, and Major General Peter Cosgrove led an international force consisting of 4,500 Australians, 1,600 Thais and the armed representatives of twenty other nations. Inevitably the new nation of East Timor, poor and dislocated, had to rely on financial aid from Australia.

Whether Australians like it or not, they live close to the east-Asian sphere of influence. Furthermore, Australia is sparsely populated, whereas China,

India and Indonesia – all in the same region – form three of the four most populous nations in the world. Indonesia is also the largest Muslim nation in the world, though moderate in its religious fervour. When in the 1990s small groups of militant Muslims began to denounce the United States as the symbol of evil and decadence, Indonesia was bound to feel the effects of this widening rift. After the Islamic radicals attacked New York and Washington on 11 September 2001, Australia became a military ally of the United States and thereby a possible target for Islamic terrorists.

In the Indonesian resort of Bali, the main tourists since the 1970s had been Australians, especially those wearing jeans and sandals. The journey to Bali was not long; there was no jet lag. After hippies and surfers opened the route to Bali, they were followed by 'swinging singles' who celebrated with beer and spirits and wine, and by quiet families. Bali became an intensely popular resort: only New Zealand was more popular with Australians. Bali also gained popularity because the falling value of the Australian dollar in the 1980s weakened the pull of Britain and the United States as destinations for travellers.

A militant Muslim group which was tempted to attack Australia as a symbol of Western decadence did not have to travel south. In Bali the nightclubs and the hotel swimming pools, the restaurants and street stalls and beaches were swarming with young Australian tourists. On the evening of 12 October 2002, two deadly explosions hit an area crowded with revelling tourists. Of the 202 people who died, eighty-eight were Australians.

No other national tragedy unfolding on foreign soil in a time of peace so stirred the typical Australian. The prime minister, John Howard, had to express publicly his people's strong emotion and even revulsion, while maintaining ties with the Indonesian government in Jakarta. Within a few years, memorials to the Australian victims were set up not only in Bali but also in Melbourne, Perth, Canberra and the coastal centres of Coogee and Ulladulla in New South Wales. Despite the tragedy, Bali regained its appeal as an idyllic resort. While some observers predicted that Australian tourists would never go back to Bali, they soon returned in their thousands.

In commerce, as in tourism, Australia was drawing closer to Asia. By the 1960s Japan was Australia's main trading partner, and in turn it was to be challenged by China. By 2010, more than half of Australia's trade, both in value and in volume, was with Asia, and China now filled the role which the British Isles and Western Europe had long filled.

Many of the new skyscrapers of Shanghai were built of steel made from Australian raw materials; the electricity in tens of millions of Chinese and Japanese apartments was generated from Australian coal and natural gas; and one in every three aircraft flying across the China Sea and the Indian subcontinent – and indeed the Atlantic – was likely to be constructed of aluminum smelted from Australian alumina. For their part most Australians used a wide range of electronic equipment and hardware, and wore clothes and footwear, made in China. The final prosperous years of the long Australian economic boom that ended dramatically in the spring of 2008 owed more to China, and its demand for Australian minerals, than to any other factor. Australia survived the global financial crisis, thanks to China.

Meanwhile, more and more Chinese were coming to Australia as students and others came to work or invest or retire. In suburban Sydney the electorate represented by one of the nation's two longest serving leaders, John Howard, was especially favoured by incoming Chinese, but they did not vote for him at the 2007 federal election, in which he lost power. Significantly his successor as prime minister, Kevin Rudd, knew China more intimately than he knew the British Isles. The foreign language known to early prime ministers such as Barton and Deakin and to later prime ministers such as Menzies and Whitlam had been Latin, or occasionally French or classical Greek; but Mr Rudd preferred Mandarin.

In recent decades the attitude of the typical Australian towards China has mellowed. The strange traditional mixture of suspicion, intolerance and goodwill had been replaced, at times, by over-tolerance. Thus, China's persecution of religious and political minorities aroused less concern in Canberra than did the far milder restrictions imposed peacefully by the Fiji Government on its Indian citizens.

Australia's links with China continued to multiply. In each year, scores of schools paid visits to schools in China. In every major Chinese city were dozens of Australian business offices. In Australia in 2011 a total of 600,000 residents spoke, at home, a Chinese language. During several months of the following year, for the first time in the history of Australian tourism, Chinese visitors outnumbered those from the British Isles. Chinese migrants even outnumbered British migrants.

In Canberra in 2012 there was confident chanting that this was the 'Asian Century', and an official report, 'Australia in the Asian Century', declared that our future lies primarily in that continent and that we now possess the good fortune to be close to what will become the world's great commercial honey pot. That our relative proximity to China and India and Nearer Asia might be a source of grave danger as well as deep satisfaction was barely considered in the massive report. Instead, Australia's war against Japan in 1941–45 and its post-war military activities in Malaysia, Korea, Vietnam and Afghanistan were summed up but camouflaged in the sentence, 'Our nation also has the strength that comes from a long history of engagement with countries in Asia.'

Not since the early 1940s, when the Japanese peril was urgent, were Australian citizens so conscious that their country might be approaching another crossroads. In that time of the peril, the United States quickly replaced Britain as Australia's main military ally; but seventy years later, it seemed possible that the United States might not only cease to be so powerful but might cease, by mutual consent, to be Australia's strongest and friendliest ally. In the coming decades Australia's interests and sympathies in military and diplomatic affairs might oscillate between the United States and China, or move more towards neutrality, or even embrace India, which in 2060 could be the world's most populous country and occupy one of the highest places on the ladder of economic power.

· · · · · · · · · ·

19

The vast open spaces

For a century and a half the nation had ridden on the sheep's back, but now the sheep was limping. Wool was losing its glamour under pressure from synthetic fibres. Moreover the advent of central heating in homes and offices lessened the need in winter to wear warm, woollen clothes. In the 1970s, wool ceased to lead the nation's exports. The Soviet soldiers wore wool during the stern winters they usually experienced, but soon the Soviet army ceased to be so massive and so it bought less wool. Almost as a last resort, wool was advertised and marketed in fashionable quarters of the world as a special product and promoted like soap and perfume. The ingenuity of the promoters could not lift the price of wool. In turn, a run of dry seasons frustrated many Australian wool-growers, and in 2008 the nation's population of sheep was its lowest in some ninety years.

Most of the stately mansions in the countryside, and the mansion-like shearing sheds, had been financed from the wool cheques. The owners of those pastoral estates were hailed as wool kings and in the year 1890 would have provided perhaps ten of Australia's twenty richest families. Today not one wool king has a place in that list. In each wool district the shearing season crowned the year and drew a procession of thousands of shearers on foot, bicycle or in horse-drawn vehicles – and every bush pub along the way rejoiced in their arrival – but by the 1980s the work for Australian shearers was declining, and they were rarely depicted in colour magazines or on television as the typical outdoor Australian.

2

New rural industries arose and a few old ones revived. It was hoped that grapevines – at one time planted more for the production of dried fruits – might sustain a large export of wine. Even in 1984 the area of vines planted for sultanas and other dried fruits in Australia was still almost as large as the combined area planted with the four main wine grapes – shiraz, muscat, rhine riesling and grenache. The vineyards multiplied in the next quarter-century, even in Tasmania and coastal Victoria and Margaret River (WA), regions where a grapevine had been noticed only on trellises along the back verandah. By the year 2005, wine was not yet a major export-earner, but on millions of foreign dinner tables, in places as far apart as Hong Kong and Sweden, an Australian bottle of wine was opened at least once a week.

Dairy farming was transformed by the trend to bigger farms and by machines that might milk 1,000 cows on farms where once there were only forty. The herds of beef cattle increased, some cattle stations being amongst the biggest in the world. Sugar was still grown in the narrow, fertile plains of the warmer stretches of the Pacific coast, making Australia the fourth largest of the world's sugar exporters. The sale of live sheep and cattle grew, especially to Islamic countries. The nation, when drought did not reign, was also one of the world's five or six big wheat exporters. Cotton, of scant importance in 1945, so flourished that half a century later Australia was behind only the United States and Uzbekistan as an exporter.

Most rural industries suffered somewhat because they had to compete on the world markets against produce heavily subsidised by Europe and the United States. Some Australian politicians, along with those from Canada, Pakistan, Indonesia and other rural exporters, believed that diplomacy could topple these trade barriers, and that the politicians and bureaucrats of Brussels and Washington would be converted to free trade. A religious-like conversion to free trade was almost witnessed at an international conference in Cairns in 1986, but the fervour died during the homeward flight of most of the delegates to their offices in the northern hemisphere. Twenty years later the Cairns Group gathered again in the north Queensland city, and had little to rejoice in.

Many mineral discoveries, large and small, were made in the last quarter of the twentieth century. Some were made in abandoned mines and on the edge of ghost towns. The world's largest deposit of diamonds was found in the north-west, and Australian diamonds soon appeared on thousands of fingers or served as the cutting edge of thousands of diamond drills that explored for minerals. Not far from the Argyle diamond deposit was found, beneath tropical seas, the huge gas deposits and oil reservoirs of the North-West Shelf. In the 1980s its natural gas was pumped to Perth and the alumina refineries of the south – along a pipeline that made the celebrated water pipeline, opened at Kalgoorlie in 1903, seem a toy – while additional volumes of gas were frozen and shipped regularly to east Asia. In 1987 a surge in the price of gold induced Australian mines to pass all previous peaks of output, even dwarfing the output of the richest year of the 1850s. Australian bauxite and alumina were even more important to the world; and yet at the end of World War II, the continent was believed to hold no worthwhile deposit of bauxite. In addition, coal and iron ore, copper, silver, lead, zinc, nickel, mineral sands, manganese and other minerals were mined vigorously. Of the world's sea traffic in iron ore and coal, the largest share now originated in Australia and came from ports that had not been on the map – or were insignificant – some forty years ago.

Uranium was another surprise. In 1975 one of the world's most remarkable mineral deposits was ingeniously found far below the arid surface at Olympic Dam in South Australia. There was no convincing sign of any uranium and copper near the surface of the ground. The area was isolated and parched, and one of the nearest points on the map was a vast expanse of salt and cracked mud, optimistically called Lake Torrens. At Olympic Dam, deep exploration revealed the outline of a huge mineral deposit, the likes of which had not been seen elsewhere in the world. It held perhaps 40 per cent of the world's known reserves of uranium oxide. As if this wealth was not sufficient it was also, by the early 2000s, the fourth largest deposit of copper in the world and perhaps the fifth largest of gold. It seemed likely that this gigantic Olympic Dam mine would yield, in the course of its long life, more real wealth than all the mining fields of the continent had produced throughout the nineteenth century.

Australia became one of the three most prolific mining countries. It was also the head office of the world's biggest mining company, BHP Billiton, which had been launched after the discovery of silver and lead at Broken Hill in 1883. The world's third largest mining company, Rio Tinto, also had its origins in Broken Hill as well as in a celebrated copper mine in Spain. Minerals now provided half of Australia's income from exports. And the rebuilding of China, and its new steelworks and powerhouses and skyscrapers, was boosting the prices paid for coal, iron ore and several other minerals shipped from Australian ports.

Only a tiny fraction of Australians have set eyes on the heartlands of the latest mining boom, which lie far from big cities. At Kalgoorlie is a public lookout from which tourists see and hear the blasting of the gold-bearing rock in what they call the 'super pit', a vast quarry cut in the bright-yellow and brown rock, and widened or deepened every hour of the year. In 1900, on what is now the very top of the quarry, had stood miners' townships and main streets and churches and schools, with steam engines surrounded by tall stacks of firewood, and shafts down which thousands of miners went to work. The site of these towns has been devoured by this huge quarry.

Likewise, few Australians have an opportunity to watch the huge ships being escorted by tugs along the dredged channel into the isolated harbour of Port Hedland, Western Australia, where they load iron ore bound for Asian ports. Forty years previously this was a shallow inlet amongst the mangrove trees; and the arrival of any small steamship was a pleasing event that enticed residents to the town pier in order to watch. In 2005, this became the first port in Australia to move 100 million tons of cargo in a year. Seven years later, the tally reached 250 million tons, a world record for bulk cargoes. A typical ship now entering the port is twice as long as the playing arena of the Sydney Cricket Ground. The iron ore loaded into these massive ships has come by long railway from the ridges and dark gorges of the distant interior – a terrain vividly painted by one of the country's finest artists, Fred Williams.

Nearly 2,000 kilometres to the east of Port Hedland are the huge copper and lead-zinc deposits of Mt Isa, discovered in 1923 by a passing horseman. They too contradict the belief held by many intellectuals in Australian cities that mining is a simple activity and almost unworthy of a nation which sees itself as sophisticated. The temperature of the deeper parts of these mines would almost be too hot to allow human activity if it weren't for the enormous volume of chilled air pumped down. The cool draught is dispatched by the biggest air-cooling machinery in the southern hemisphere. In the words of one employee, it is the equivalent of sending underground 'about 9,000 tons of party-ice a day'. From the towering chimney of the nearby smelters a cloud of sulfur dioxide flows with the prevailing winds to the distant coast and beyond. A small part of the clouds falls on uninhabited ridges within one hour's stroll of the smelters. There, the ecologists report, the insects are fewer and the reptiles not so diverse.

3

From this mining boom, Queensland and Western Australia gained the most. Since the early 1960s, each grew at a much faster pace than old states in the south-east corner. Such dynamic leaders as Sir Charles Court in Perth and Sir Joh Bjelke-Petersen in Brisbane gave high priority to fostering economic growth in these two states. They also attracted population because of their warm climate. In Australia and the West the rising preference for a warm climate was aided by the cheap refrigerator, the air-conditioner, the decline of labouring work beneath the hot sun, and the declining impact of malaria, dysentery and other tropical diseases. The year is not far away when Queensland will pass Victoria in population, and that will be a momentous event. For more than a century and a half Victoria and New South Wales had taken turns to be the leader, and now another rival is in sight.

Space and endless horizons retained a special corner in Australians' imaginations. As Robin Boyd, the architect and critic, observed in 1968, 'Australia gives generously certain physical blessings, such as sun, sugar, sport and space in an increasingly crowded world'. With the blessing of vast spaces, and the minerals they enclose, the two big outer states, Queensland and Western Australia, have been growing at a faster percentage than the old heartland of Australia near the Hume Highway. Today, Queensland and Western Australia, if added together, almost equal New South Wales in population. Already they now hold more than one-quarter of the nation's population and it is possible that by the end of this century they will hold nearly half the population of Australia.

Between 1945 and 2008 the nation's population leapt from seven to twenty-one million. It grew at a faster pace in the second half than the first half of the twentieth century. Of the new migrants, most settled in cities. By the early 2000s, five cities each held more than one million people, Sydney leading with over four million, followed by Melbourne,

Brisbane, Perth and Adelaide. While Melbourne was more the home of the first European wave of post-war migrants, Sydney was the home of the second, or Asian and Middle-Eastern wave.

The later migrants, unlike the earlier European migrants, rarely reached the small country towns and the outback. There, most of the middle-size towns and nearly all the small crossroad townships were in decline. The towns which once saw hundreds of athletic men arriving on foot or bicycles for the annual shearing and watched the heavy horse-wagons carrying away the wool were often suffering the most. Wheat towns joined the wool towns in decline. Today even the inland towns which pour out mineral wealth are mostly small and lack even a shopping centre deserving of the name. Their employees arrive by plane, work long hours for high wages for a few weeks, and then fly back to Perth, Townsville, Rockhampton or other coastal towns to spend a week or two with friends and family.

Australia is increasingly the story of a few large cities, but a thousand half-forgotten townships still view themselves as the emotional heart of the nation. Many began to decline after the 1950s; others had long been in decline. They lost inhabitants mainly because their industries were becoming highly mechanised and simply did not need much labour. Machines had replaced human hands and muscles in mining, shearing, harvesting, road-mending and a dozen other tasks.

4

The trend is mirrored in a fast-vanishing town in western Queensland called Isisford. Founded in 1874, it stands on the banks of the Barcoo River, which flows through the dry grasslands – when it holds enough water to flow. Isisford at first catered for the sheep-owners and their employees living as far as 500 kilometres away; and when they wished to attend a dance or a horse-race, borrow money from a bank or go to church, they followed dusty roads to this little town and its wide earthen streets and line of wooden verandahs. In the fifteen years after World War II, when wool prices were high, the town especially flourished. It had a resident doctor, a hospital that treated outpatients, a branch of the Bank of New South Wales, two churches and rather more hotels, and a new convent school as well as a government school. On Saturday night the open-air picture theatre was crowded: television was the toy of the cities for a quarter-century before it reached the outback.

A long regional drought in the 1960s ended the boom. After the price of wool fell, the sheep were increasingly replaced by cattle, which needed less supervision. As most of the local families now owned a car or truck they could sometimes drive north to glittering Longreach and spend, in that big town, money that they once spent in Isisford. Slowly the population fell, year by year. The Catholic priest became a Sunday visitor rather than a resident. The convent's school closed in 1970, by which time the town had twenty-three vacant houses. Hotels declined from three to two, and their bedrooms were rarely occupied. The doctor shut his rooms, the butcher and baker and grocer walked away, and the old post office was closed. The police station was manned by one constable instead of two. A town that once possessed three rival racing clubs – with their own committees and race meetings, each enticing spectators to the town – now ran only one meeting a year.

The town's last stronghold was the shire council with its own office and road-making equipment. By an edict issued from faraway Brisbane, the local shire was 'merged' with Longreach: in effect it was abolished. In 2008, when Isisford produced a book about its past, the fading town was scarcely noticed by most of those tourists who passed through in their campervans on their long-planned winter jaunt around Australia. But the few remaining citizens who remembered its heyday, when 500 people lived there, felt that something unique was vanishing. Recalling life in Isisford, one resident tried to define its unique quality. 'We were content with what we had', she said proudly. What is more, 'I think that we all had a wonderful time enjoying what we had.' The same fond obituary was spoken in similar dying towns.

5

In each region the climate remained unpredictable. Drought was a regular ordeal. Henry Lawson, walking across the plains clouded with red dust, described drought as 'the red marauder'. Around the year 2000, the red marauder began to hover again.

Its psychological impact was heightened by an unexpected trend called global warming or 'climate change'. The phrase is rather ambiguous in Australia, a country which has experienced drastic changes of climate even in the two centuries since the first British settlement. In the populous south-east quarter of the continent – roughly extending from Brisbane around to Adelaide – the years from about 1850 to 1890 were favourable. In the following half-century the dry years were numerous and droughts were long. As wool was then the dominant export and as a significant proportion of the nation's breadwinners were farmers, the whole economy was battered more than it is today by dry years.

Then the skies changed again. For at least thirty years after World War II, the rainfall became greater. Droughts intervened but were shorter. Moreover, many of the leading politicians had experienced when young the harshest droughts and were determined to dam water. They sponsored scientific but frustrating experiments in rain-making and cloud-seeding in the 1950s. They built a mosaic of dams and water diversions extending from the Ord River in the nation's north-west to the Murray and Snowy rivers in the south-east. Even the big cities enlarged their reservoirs at a faster pace than their population multiplied. The inevitable soon occurred. Water from full dams was sold by the government authorities at very cheap prices, and much of it was thoughtlessly wasted in city and country. Furthermore, two new crops – rice and cotton – annually absorbed enormous sheets of water in the Murray–Darling Basin.

Meanwhile, a whole generation, reared mainly in the cities, became complacent about water. The frenetic era of dam-building, lasting for more than half a century, came to an end. Even in Tasmania, a display case of hydro-electric schemes, the large dam planned for the Gordon and Franklin rivers was abandoned as a result of sustained protests. Across the nation hardly one major dam was to be commenced in the years 1980 to 2010. The green movement, politically strong and alert, opposed new dams because they robbed the living rivers and creeks, and their billabongs and swamps. It was almost as if the nation had forgotten how tough and soul-destroying was a very long drought.

Now another such drought slowly descended. It was experienced with dismay in places as far apart as the Darling Downs near Brisbane, the Darling Ranges near Perth, and even amongst the old red gums lining the banks of the River Darling. During the years 2001 to 2009, cities that had been prodigal with water were forced to become careful and then frugal. The watering of lawns and the washing of cars was banned or restricted in cities as different climatically as Melbourne and Brisbane. In the grain lands of the south, most of the small farm dams were low or empty, and harvest after harvest was below the average. Maybe half of the nation's rural districts – and their large towns and small crossroad townships – were suffering.

A summit was convened in Canberra in November 2006 to assess this crisis; and a high official announced that the drought in the Murray–Darling Basin was the kind of monstrous drought to be experienced only once in a thousand years. An assertion that was impossible to validate, it was widely believed. Most experts on climate, however, could not feel sure whether this new drought was as harmful as the Federation drought of a century earlier. After all, the two driest years, since nation-wide records of rainfall have been available, were not in the twenty-first century but in 1902 and 1905.

The drought went on and on. Perhaps more dams should be built? The onset of global warming led many climate scientists to announce that such reservoirs would be pointless. They lamented that in future years not enough rain would fall to fill them. The scholar who became the government's foremost climate adviser was eloquent in prophesying a permanent shortage of fresh water in city and country. Perhaps the more moderate scientists should have spoken up and dowsed his fears. Most fell silent.

Novel sources of water were sought for the fast-multiplying population in most of the capital cities, and in 2006 the nation's first desalination works were opened by the ocean at Kwinana near Perth, to be followed by half a dozen other works built as far away as the Gold Coast, on the Pacific Ocean. Melbourne, now growing at a faster pace than Sydney, built the largest such works at massive cost. The treated water, when needed, would be very expensive. Even when not needed, it had to be paid for: such was the harsh economics of desalination.

As the drought extended, the eucalypt forests in south-eastern Australia became highly flammable, as if just one match could set them alight. In February 2009, close to Melbourne, bushfires killed 173 people, most of whom died on an intensely hot day christened 'Black Saturday'. Many of the victims, young and old, lived in houses built close to dry forests; and if they tried to escape the oncoming fire they found the bush roads already blocked by burning trees.

The extremely hot February of 2009 and the tragic bushfires were widely but not universally attributed to the onset of global warming. Such blazes and possibly such heat, however, were not unique in Victoria. The bushfires of Black Saturday were certainly not as extensive as those of 6 February 1851, when so much of Victoria was burned that the dense cloud of smoke and the hot northerly winds brought an afternoon of darkness to coastal towns in Tasmania.

• • • • • • • • • •

At last the long drought broke. In eastern Australia in 2010, nearly all districts received more than their annual average rain fall. Next year was almost a deluge. Indeed, those two successive years formed one of the wettest times since 1900 when the nation-wide system of rainfall records commenced. Terrible floods were experienced in numerous rivers along the Pacific coast of Queensland and the north coast of New South Wales. Coal mines in the Bowen Basin were flooded.

In January 2011, a sudden flood on the Brisbane River threatened to devastate the low-lying suburbs of Australia's third largest city. The damage was compounded because in a reservoir upstream the inflowing fresh water – allowed to rise dangerously high – suddenly had to be released. The roaring tumble of water heightened the existing flood that was already overflowing the riverbanks within cooee of the new skyscrapers of Brisbane city. The century-old poem by Dorothea Mackellar once again became one of the best known in Australia, for she had written about this sunburned land of climatic contrasts, of long droughts and sudden flooding rains.

By the last half of 2012 nearly all the main reservoirs in the eastern half of Australia were overflowing or almost full. In city streets and botanical gardens and parks, tall old European trees that seemed likely to die came to life again. In the safer farming country, the small natural lakes that had been dry for years were again speckled with waterbirds. From Adelaide and even Sydney a small aircraft carried crowds of tourists to look down on the mighty Lake Eyre briefly brimming with water, a sight rarely seen, and pelicans standing on sandy country that was normally desert. On the other hand, the south-west corner of the continent missed this wetter period. The wheatfields in Western Australia and the booming city of Perth remained dry.

The skies changed again. Those who had scoffed at the weather forecasters were surprised to see the rain clouds almost disappear. To many districts in Queensland, the dry period returned and at the time of writing is still reigning. In Victoria, in that handsome pastoral terrain originally called by the Latin name Australia Felix, or 'Australia the Happy', the five months ending in April 2013 were the driest ever recorded on old pastoral properties. In those same months, much of tropical Australia missed its normal wet season. Still, it was far too early to talk of the start of a new drought. Soon the tropical section of the Pacific coast was visited again by floods, and even Sydneysiders complained of too much rain.

These unexpected climatic somersaults, and the failure of the more gloomy of the weather predictions, made many voters wary of the scientists' claims to know all about climate. Indeed, inside Australia there was more public scepticism towards long-term climate prediction than possibly in any other major agricultural country. The scepticism was especially strong among farmers and pastoralists, geologists and the mining industry, and Liberal and National voters. In contrast, belief that the climate was changing and that the causes were man-made was strongest among scientists, teachers, journalists and generally among Labor and Green voters.

In the nation year by year, public opinion fluctuated about the extent of climate change and whether the governments should take urgent steps to reduce the emissions of carbon dioxide. Indeed the federal election in 2007 was fought partly on this topic, the victor Kevin Rudd calling it the greatest moral challenge of the era. Again the election in 2010 was fought partly on this topic, this time with the victor, Julia Gillard, promising not to impose a tax on carbon dioxide. In short, Labor had changed its policy. Yet another turnabout followed. Labor, in order to win the support of the small Greens Party, had to jettison that most recent promise and instead to impose a tax on Australia's coal-burning power stations, aluminium smelters and other heavy emitters of carbon dioxide. The so-called 'carbon tax' became law in July 2012. One of the highest such taxes in the world, and far above any imposed in Europe and the Americas, it gave delight to all those who believed that Australia should lead the world in declaring war on most of the fossil fuels. Less enthusiastic were those households and industries whose electricity bills soared.

Now the carbon tax was viewed by most Australians as more of a threat to their standard of living than as a way to combat global warming. At the federal election of 2013 the Liberals' leader, Tony Abbott, promised to repeal the tax, and his campaign was victorious.

Climate is a tantalising and complicated topic. Whether it will reshape the nation's economic future during the lifetime of children now beginning school is a question only a brave prophet can attempt to answer.

· · · · · · · · ·

20

Sails and anchors

What makes the history of Australia so distinctive? Two factors or influences – distance and climate – strongly shaped it during the last two centuries, and even shaped the earlier Aboriginal history as well as the short European history. Sometimes acting like sails and sometimes like anchors, these factors both promoted and retarded changes.

2

Changes of climate moulded the human history of Australia. A momentous event was a prehistoric phase of global warming, which was accompanied by a great rising of the seas. The incoming waves affected most inhabitants of this land, whether they lived on the coast or far inland. Another period of global warming that has only recently arrived is mild compared to that earlier episode. Even if the gloomiest predictions for this latest warm episode prove to be correct, it will still be dwarfed by the long period of warming that was experienced long ago by Aborigines.

• • • • • • • • • •

In the space of less than 10,000 years, the physical shape as well as the climate of this land was altered by the slow-rising seas. Tasmania and its people were finally cut off from the mainland. Australia was permanently severed from New Guinea. The rising seas gave the final shape to the present Torres Strait Islands, the inhabitants of which are relative latecomers.

At the same time, the climate changed. The cold tundra and sparse vegetation of western Tasmania gave way to rainforest. In the south-east quarter of the continent the inland rivers, summer after summer, ceased to be replenished by the melting of vast areas of mountain ice and snow. The daily temperatures of Uluru and the centre of the continent became hotter, and the vast northern reaches of the continent became tropical. The marvellous Great Barrier Reef, which some scientists predict will be endangered in the coming century by warming seas, was itself the result of these warming waters and the new coastline formed by that momentous period of climate change.

This virtual separation from the outside world exerted a long-term influence on the Aborigines. Human contacts between Australia and the Indonesian archipelago became rare: so far as is known, there was no contact with New Zealand. In essence the Aborigines were largely cut off from peoples of the outside world, at the very time when that world was being transformed by the domestication of plants and animals. The very concept of gardening and the hoarding of food reached the highlands of New Guinea thousands of years ago and even penetrated the Torres Strait Islands; but so far as is known it did not reach Australia until the coming of the British.

The way of life of New Guinea was transformed by this economic revolution, but the Aborigines' way of life was not touched. Hence in 1788 when the incoming British confronted this old way of life on the shores of Sydney Harbour, the puzzlement was acute. Neither people could comprehend the other. Their deeply held values and preferences were separated by a chasm. This is a crucial fact in our history and remains so, though there is a reluctance to acknowledge it. Even today the chasm between the viewpoints and attitudes of mainstream Australians and urban Aborigines on the one hand and the more remote Aborigines on the other hand is great.

Climate change and the great rising of the seas exerted another powerful effect. The Aborigines, during their continuing isolation from the outside world, had clung to a distinctive way of life which, almost everywhere else, was overthrown. Alas, they possessed no immunity to the new diseases that, across the seas, became part of human existence during the world's first era of farming and herd-keeping. Many of those new diseases stemmed from close contact, for the first time, between human beings and domesticated animals such as cows, sheep, goats and chickens. The diseases arrived in Australia with the British settlers in 1788 or soon after. They raced ahead of the first Europeans who ventured inland. They decimated the Aboriginal population so quickly that for a time it seemed that all might be wiped out. In turn the British occupation of the favoured parts of the whole continent was accelerated by the fast decline in the local population.

Even after the British began to settle this land, climatic variations remained powerful. Thus the Federation drought was a turning point in Australian history, desiccating a vast sweep of country.

3

Distance from the leading nations of the world has moulded Australia's history. Aborigines, as we have seen, remained largely isolated from the outside world after the rising of the seas. Therefore their way of life changed slowly. Likewise, British Australia, in the nineteenth century, was isolated by the wide oceans and the slow sea routes from the British Isles. Australia was far away from the main source of its institutions, migrants, capital, new inventions and ideas, and from the main market for its exports. In the nineteenth century it could export to Britain only those commodities such as whale oil, wool and gold, where the profit was big enough to cover the high shipping costs. Australia, being far away, rarely competed with North America in enticing migrants from Britain, Ireland and continental Europe. Australia's long-time scarcity of women was indirectly the result of distance from Europe. The prospect of a long and costly voyage determined which kinds of individuals and families decided to emigrate.

The military crisis faced by Australia in the summer of 1941–42 was shaped by distance. The swift advance of the Japanese armed forces, the collapse of the British naval base at Singapore, and the swelling fears that Australia itself might be invaded were shaped by the fact that Australia's traditional defender – the British navy – was far, far away. In contrast the Japanese attackers were, at the start of the Pacific War, relatively close.

Australia is one of the three or four oldest, continuous democracies in the world, and the long-term success of democracy here was aided by the fact that the nation has never been invaded. This is true of the other long-standing, continuous democracies in the world. These few long-standing democracies are nearly all protected from dangerous enemies by obstacles – by wide sea or by high mountains. If Australia lay near the mighty hubs of political power, it would have incurred a higher risk of being invaded during at least one of the world wars. Yet again, distance and isolation have helped to shape what is distinctive about Australia's history.

In the decades since World War II, east and south Asia have risen in importance but the power of distant Europe has declined. Therefore Australia's links with closer Asia, especially in trade and migration and tourism have multiplied. Increasingly, Australia is influenced by these new dynamic nations: they are close as well as dynamic.

Some observers proclaim that distance is dead. The web, email and the satellite picture that leap across the globe have, reportedly, killed distance. Today, ideas and messages, images and pictures, travel with the speed of lightning. And yet earlier generations of distinguished observers had also proclaimed that distance was dead. In 1885 the celebrated English historian, J. A. Froude, announced in his best-selling book *Oceana* that a Briton could now reach Australia as quickly as his grandmother could reach New York half a century previously. 'Steam and telegraph,' he wrote, 'have made an end of distance.' Distance, however, is relative: it lies in the mind as well as on the map. True, the world has shrunk, and the flight from Paris to Sydney takes only a day and a night. But in this hectic, hurrying century, a journey of twenty-four hours seems like an eternity, and is a strong deterrent to long-distance travel in the minds of would-be tourists.

Certainly in the transportation of cargoes, distance is not dead. Those firms that ship bulk commodities such as coal and bauxite know that it is much cheaper to send cargo to a port that lies 4,000 rather than 8,000 kilometres away. The cargoes on which so much of the nation's economic life depends are transported slowly and expensively by sea. The huge cargo ships carrying coal or iron ore from Australian ports are more than a thousand times larger than Captain Cook's *Endeavour*, herself a converted coal ship, but they cannot exceed thirty sea miles an hour even when they are racing against the clock.

Distance from the world's main markets is still a burden. Some economists have calculated that Australia would have a higher standard of living if it were situated somewhere in the northern hemisphere, and not too far from the United States and Europe, or not too far from Japan and China.

4

The continent has been shaped by new technology, even in Aboriginal times. European immigrants were avid to apply the latest inventions in order to cope with difficult terrain, climate and long distances. They were quick to try new modes of transport, whether the Boston clipper, English railway, the steamship and container ship, aircraft, car and truck, and pipeline. They were alert to the benefits of the telegraph, telephone, long-distance radio, television and email. They were quick to import and adapt ancient means of transport, including the camel, which was suited to the dry interior. The locally grown foods that most Australians eat today are partly the result of ingenuity, based on plants and animals imported here and then bred or adapted to meet local conditions.

Australians have gained much from the ingenuity of other nations, and it has gained something from its own. One stream of Australian inventions arose from attempts to solve universal human problems. Many of the solutions were medical, including Howard Florey's discovery of penicillin, Norman Gregg's discovery of how rubella or German measles harms pregnant women, and Graeme Clark's creation of the bionic ear. Another stream of inventions was inspired by obstacles that were primarily Australian. In the nineteenth century many of the early farmers had to plough difficult ground and grow crops in soils, climates and vegetation zones not encountered in Europe. They had to harvest the crops quickly and cheaply, because rural labour was often scarce and expensive. To meet such rural needs there arose the Ridley stripper and the stump-jump plough in South Australia, H. V. McKay's harvester and Trewhella's jack in Victoria, and the belated use of fertiliser and 'trace elements' to enrich soils that were deficient in phosphate and other minerals. Australia, it is said, is the world's great museum of soil deficiencies, and indeed the nation now grows most of its wheat on soils that are naturally deficient in phosphate.

The most notable Australian discovery was the flotation process, inspired by an acute metallurgical problem emerging at Broken Hill in about 1900. The problem initially was how to treat the complex ores that were rich in zinc, but defied the existing American and European processes. Broken Hill employees and managers – with the aid of Melbourne brewers – were ingenious in overcoming this difficulty. Versions of this flotation process are now used to produce enormous quantities of a variety of minerals in places as far apart as Siberia and the Andes. What the flotation process has added to the standard of living of the world's peoples is almost beyond calculation.

The relations between nature and people are a continuing theme of Australia's history; and technology lies near the core of that theme. The Aborigines and their simple technology sometimes were conquerors and sometimes destroyers of nature. Various species of animals became extinct during the early years before British settlement or were soon reduced to a small, vulnerable population after the first British settlers landed. More change was inflicted on nature in 200 years by Europeans than in probably 50,000 years of Aboriginal occupation. Irrigated plains were stricken with salinity, vast forests were felled, thousands of gullies were eroded, and the tilled or overgrazed land was blown away as dust clouds. Rabbits, foxes, cats, cane toads, and even the Aborigines' own dingo, introduced from other lands to enhance daily life or solve rural problems, preyed on native animals and birds. European carp ravaged native fishes in inland rivers. Numerous native plants, insects and animals were wiped out by the coming of introduced species, by the building of reservoirs and roads, and by the expansion of the coastal cities and the clearing of land for farming and grazing.

The advantage of these costly changes was that a continent, once so unyielding, now provided food and shelter for tens of millions of people in the world. Australia is more productive, more important to the world, than its own population would suggest. It feeds more people in other lands than in its own. In a bumper year Australia feeds not only its own people but the equivalent of more than eighty million people living in nations as far apart as Egypt and China. Australia also supplies hundreds of millions of overseas people with all the coal, iron, other minerals and fibres that they need. One of its achievements in the last 200 years is to multiply enormously, for the benefit of much of the world, the annual produce of a difficult continent. So we return full circle to that insoluble dilemma: how do we weigh the loss suffered since 1788 by a host of Aborigines alongside the gains made by perhaps one hundred times as many other human beings in Australia and lands across the seas?

5

Ancient and modern Australia was shaped by the outback. That vast area covering more than half of the continent was the product of a dry climate and of the long distances separating the outback from the main Australian cities and harbours. Even if the outback had been wet and fertile it would have suffered from isolation. Always sparsely inhabited, the outback possesses not even one town large enough to be designated a city by European criteria. It possesses not one landlocked, inland state – not one Colorado, Nevada or Manitoba. Its vast plains were not crossed by an east–west railway until 1917 and by a north–south railway until the twenty-first century. On the other hand the plains and the climate, ideal for aviation, were the birthplace of the best known Australian airline, Qantas.

While Britain and Ireland were cramped, Australia held space almost without limit. The word outback signified that sense of space. It must have been used in conversations before finally appearing in print, but on 17 April 1869 it was first employed in the rural newspaper, the *Wagga Wagga Advertiser*. Welcome rains had fallen further inland, prompting the reporter to predict, 'Grass will be abundant out back'.

'Outback' began life as two words but eventually became one. A versatile word, it spread like a dust storm. Soon every Australian understood vaguely or precisely its meaning, though the exact meaning depended on where they lived. Thus when a traveller reached a homestead in arid country some 600 kilometres from the sea he might inform his hosts that it was wonderful at last to be in the 'outback'. But he might promptly be corrected and told that that the real outback was not here but further out, further back. As Henry Lawson wrote in 1901: 'Out-Back is always west of the Bushman, no matter how far out he be.' To those living in Western Australia, however, the outback is more to the east.

Often the outback is viewed as the real and distinctive part of the land. It is the home of legends: the inland explorers Sturt and Stuart and Forrest; Paddy Hannan carrying his waterbag when he discovered the gold of Kalgoorlie; and John Flynn's flying doctors who tend the sick in more than half of the continent. The outback was the home of the billabong where, in that national song, the jolly swagman of 'Waltzing Matilda' met his end. It was the setting for influential books, including Mrs Aeneas Gunn's *We of the Never Never*, and for popular films such as *A Town Like Alice*. It was the home of much of the ancient Aboriginal art, and also the Papunya painters who in the 1970s inaugurated that new school of Aboriginal art.

Long after the British arrived, a place of asylum for tens of thousands of Aborigines was the outback. There the essence of the old Aboriginal way of living, thinking and dreaming tended to survive the longest. There, even today, are nearly all the small settlements and outstations where Aborigines try to control their own collective destiny and preserve some of the traditions of which they are proud. This area is also the main home of the big mines, and even the miners find the geographical obstacles are acute.

The twenty-three million Australians are concentrated in two long and narrow coastal corridors. In contrast the outback is thinly peopled. Being so vast, dry and isolated, the outback largely explains why the nation as a whole is sparsely inhabited. Measured by people to the hectare, Australia is more deserted than all the African nations except Western Sahara, Namibia and Mauritania. In the entire Americas and Asia, only the three nations of French Guiana, Greenland and Mongolia are peopled more thinly. If the outback constituted a separate nation, it might well rank as the most deserted of all the world's nations. That simple statistic is a measure of how much the duo of distance and drought still shape the continent.

A short chronicle of Australian history

50000 BC	The first Aborigines have already arrived
16000 BC	Seas begin to rise again
8000 BC	Tasmania cut off from Australian continent
6000 BC	Torres Strait is formed
2000 BC	Arrival of dingo
1486	Portuguese reach Cape of Good Hope: Asia unlocked
1600	Indonesian fishermen regularly visit north Australian coast
1606	Spanish ship passes through Torres Strait
1697	Dutch find Swan River
1770	Captain Cook finds eastern Australia and Great Barrier Reef
1788	British fleet reaches Sydney. Norfolk Island settled
1803	British settle in Tasmania
1815	Road built across Blue Mountains to inland plains
1817	The name Australia, replacing New Holland, catches on
1820	Governor Macquarie offers farmland to Aborigines
1824	Brisbane and Moreton Bay founded
1825	Tasmania (Van Diemen's Land) becomes independent of New South Wales
1829	Perth is born

• • • • • • • • • •

1835   Melbourne is born

1836   Adelaide is born

1838   At least 200 Aborigines massacred at Myall Creek (NSW)

1842   Rich copper found at Kapunda (SA)

1847   Anaesthetic first used by Australian dentists

1850   Britain grants main Australian colonies a wide measure of self-government, including right to erect tariff walls

1851   Rush for gold in New South Wales and Victoria. Victoria (Port Phillip District) separates from New South Wales

1853   Last convict ship reaches Tasmania

1854   Eureka Stockade at Ballarat stormed by soldiers

1856   South Australia and Victoria pioneer secret ballot at elections

1858   Australian Rules football played in Melbourne's parklands

1859   Queensland becomes independent colony

1861   Death of Victorian explorers Burke and Wills. Horses run in inaugural Melbourne Cup

1866   Victoria becomes protectionist; New South Wales remains a free-trader

1868   The last convict arrives in Western Australia

1870   Last British garrison leaves eastern Australia; the British fleet remains

1872   Telegraph line links London and Adelaide via Darwin

1873   Victoria initiates free, secular and compulsory schooling

1877   Australia's population passes 2 million

1878   Bushranger Ned Kelly robs his first bank

1879   First national park proclaimed, near Sydney

1883   Steam train links Melbourne with Sydney

1885   Broken Hill Proprietary Co. formed to mine silver-lead

1886   Birth of dynamic union, the Amalgamated Shearers' Union

1890   Western Australia granted self-government

1891   Australia's sheep exceed 100 million but numbers soon halved by drought

1893   Financial panic, with many banks closing doors. Discovery of Kalgoorlie, Australia's biggest goldfield

1894   South Australia grants the vote to women

1895   Song 'Waltzing Matilda' is composed

A short chronicle of Australian history

• • • • • • • • • •

1899	Australian troops sail for South Africa and Boer War
1900	New South Wales inaugurates pensions for old colonists
1901	Six states federate, forming Commonwealth of Australia. Debate on federal bill to curb Asian immigration
1904	Federal law compels the arbitrating of industrial disputes
1906	Australia governs British New Guinea (Papua)
1908	Queenslander finds first oilfield in Middle East
1911	Northern Territory transferred from South Australia to the Commonwealth
1914	World War I declared: Australians capture German New Guinea
1915	ANZAC soldiers land on Gallipoli. BHP opens steelworks in Newcastle
1919	Australia has prominent voice at Paris Peace Conference
1921	Edith Cowan is first female politician in Australia. Labor Party adopts socialist platform. QANTAS airline launched in outback Queensland
1923	Hughes ousted as prime minister (1915–23). Country Party wins five of 11 portfolios in Bruce government (1923–29)
1924	Law for compulsory voting in federal elections
1927	Canberra replaces Melbourne as federal capital city
1930	Telephone service between Australia and England
1932	Sydney Harbour Bridge is opened. Worst year of the Depression with unemployment over 30 per cent
1933	Western Australians vote to secede from Commonwealth
1936	Australia formally takes control of half of Antarctica
1938	Hardwood converted to paper at Burnie mills (Tas.)
1939	Manufacture of military aircraft at Port Melbourne
1942	Darwin bombed; Battle of Coral Sea
1945	End of World War II (1939–45). An Australian judge presides at trial of Japanese war criminals. Commonwealth pays unemployment and sickness benefits
1946	A.A. Calwell launches mass European migration scheme
1948	Most wage-earners gain 40-hour week. First mass-produced Australian car, the Holden
1949	In federal election, Chifley (1945–49) loses to Menzies

1950   Indonesia becomes independent nation. Australia joins in Korean War (1950–53)

1954   Elizabeth II is first reigning sovereign to visit Australia

1955   Labor Party splits over communism

1956   Melbourne stages the Olympic Games. Television reaches big Australian cities

1959   First major power station opened in Snowy Mountains

1961   Iron-ore boom begins in Pilbara (WA)

1963   Qantas orders three 707 jets; RAAF orders supersonic bombers

1964   New South Wales government employees receive four weeks annual leave. Federal aid to certain Catholic colleges

1965   Australian battalion lands in Vietnam

1966   Menzies retires as prime minister (1939–41, 1949–66) Payable oil found beneath Bass Strait. Japan passes Britain as Australia's main export market

1968   Tasmanians vote for a gambling casino in Hobart

1969   Arbitration Court accepts principle of equal pay for women. The Poseidon boom in nickel shares

1970   Street marches and 'moratorium' against Vietnam War. A record 170 million sheep, but wool losing its export dominance

1972   Whitlam leads first federal Labor government for 33 years. Australia gives diplomatic recognition to China

1973   Opening of Sydney Opera House

1974   Cyclone flattens much of Darwin

1975   Papua New Guinea ceases to be an Australian territory. Colour television arrives. Constitutional crisis ends in defeat of Whitlam by Fraser. Discovery of huge mineral deposit at Olympic Dam (SA)

1976   Aborigines granted increasing part of Northern Territory. Mining banned on Fraser Island (Qld)

1979   Kakadu National Park proclaimed

1980   'Multicultural television' in Sydney and Melbourne

1982   As leading cargo port, Sydney and Botany Bay now surpassed by Dampier (WA), Port Hedland (WA) and Newcastle

1983   Australia and New Zealand begin to create common market. In federal election, Fraser loses to Hawke. Australian yacht wins America's Cup

1984   Foreign banks enter Australia in new era of financial deregulation

1985   Ayers Rock (Uluru) formally handed to Aborigines

1986   Senate blocks the Bill of Rights. Aboriginal population leaps 42 per cent in five years

1988   Grand parliament house opened in Canberra

1990   End of the boom; 'eighties entrepreneurs' begin to topple

1991   Keating replaces Hawke in Labor coup

1992   Recession–depression, with unemployment above 10 per cent

1994   Native Title Act opens vast lands to Aboriginal claimants in the outback

1996   John Howard wins federal election, ending Labor's 13 years in power

1998   Northern Territory rejects plan to become the seventh state

1999   Voters reject formula to make Australia a republic. Australia leads military contingent of many nations in East Timor

2000   Olympic Games held in Sydney

2002   In Bali, 88 Australians die in a terrorist attack

2003   Australian forces, already fighting in Afghanistan, join in US attack on Iraq

2006   Canberra 'summit' to discuss long drought in Murray–Darling Basin, the nation's main food bowl

2007   Labor's Kevin Rudd, defeating John Howard in federal election, proclaims climate change as the great 'moral challenge'

2008   The globe is hit by financial crisis, but Australia's mining boom – based on exports to China and East Asia – continues. Western Australia dominates the nation's exports. Perth's population grows by 25 per cent in the decade to 2011

2009   In February, Victoria suffers from deadliest bushfires so far recorded in Australia – 173 are killed

2010   The long drought in east Australia is ended by heavy rains and floods, but drought persists in south-west Australia. The late

• • • • • • • • • •

Mary MacKillop, founder of the Josephite Sisters, becomes the first Australian to be proclaimed a saint. Labor's Kevin Rudd is ousted by Julia Gillard, who becomes the nation's first female prime minister

2011   Australian universities increasingly compete with North America and Europe for foreign students, thus making education a vital source of export income

2012   Chinese and Indians head recent surge of immigrants to Sydney and Melbourne

2013   Australia's population, a mere 7 million in 1945, more than trebles to 23 million. The long mining boom begins to falter but iron ore, coal and other minerals still dominate export revenue. The Liberals under Tony Abbott decisively win the federal election

· · · · · · · · · ·

Further reading

The books on this short list have been selected either because they are important interpretations and sources of Australian history, because they are widely debated or because they had an influence on parts of my book. Alas, many other important books are not listed here, through shortage of space.

Aboriginal history

Berndt, R. M. & Berndt, C. H. with Stanton, John. *A World That Was: The Yaraldi of the Murray River and the Lakes, South Australia*, Melbourne University Press, 1993.

Blainey, Geoffrey. *Triumph of the Nomads*, Macmillan, 1975.

Flood, Josephine. *The Original Australians*, Allen & Unwin, 2006.

Gammage, Bill. *The Biggest Estate on Earth*, Allen & Unwin, 2011.

Mulvaney, D. J. *Encounters in Place: Outsiders and Aboriginal Australians 1606–1985*, University of Queensland Press, 1989.

Strehlow, T. G. H., *Songs of Central Australia*, Angus & Robertson, 1971.

Windschuttle, Keith. *The Fabrication of Aboriginal History*, Macleay Press, 2002, vol. 1.

Australian history after 1788

Breward, Ian. *A History of the Churches in Australasia*, Oxford University Press, 2001.

Carlyon, Les. *Gallipoli*, Pan Macmillan, 2001.

Cozzolino, Mimmo. *Symbols of Australia*, Penguin Books, 1980.

Crowley, Frank. *Modern Australia in Documents*, Wren, 1973, 2 vols.

Forrest, Peter and Sheila. *On the Banks of the Barcoo*, Isisford Shire Council, 2008.

Goldsworthy, David & Edwards, Peter (eds). *Facing North: A Century of Australian Engagement with Asia*, Melbourne University Press, 2001, 2003, 2 vols.

Gordon, Harry. *An Eyewitness History of Australia*, Rigby, 1976.

Hirst, John B. *The Strange Birth of Colonial Democracy: New South Wales 1848–1884*, Allen & Unwin, 1988.

Hughes, Robert. *The Fatal Shore*, Collins, 1987.

Lake, Marilyn & Reynolds, Henry. *Drawing the Global Colour Line*, Cambridge University Press, 2008.

Massy, Charles. *The Australian Merino*, Viking O'Neil, 1990.

McMinn, W. G. *A Constitutional History of Australia*, Oxford University Press, 1979.

Faulkner, John & Macintyre, Stuart, *True Believers: The Story of the Federal Parliamentary Labor Party*. Allen & Unwin, 2001.

Pringle, J. D. *Australian Accent*, Chatto & Windus, 1965.

Robinson, Portia. *The Hatch and Brood of Time: A Study of the First Generation of Native-born White Australians 1788–1828*, Oxford University Press, 1985, vol. 1.

Roe, Michael. *Quest for Authority in Eastern Australia 1835–1851*, Melbourne University Press, 1965.

Schreuder, Deryck M., & Ward, Stuart. *Australia's Empire*, Oxford University Press, 2008.

White, Colin. *Mastering Risk*, Oxford University Press, 1992.

Yarwood, A.T. *Asian Migration to Australia*, Melbourne, 1964.

Yule, Peter, & Woolner, Derek. *The Collins Class Submarine Story*. Cambridge University Press, 2008.

Long histories of Australia

Atkinson, Alan, *The Europeans in Australia: A History*, Oxford University Press, 1997, 2004, 2 vols.

Australians: A Historical Library, Fairfax, Syme and Weldon, 1987, 11 volumes.

Bolton, Geoffrey (ed.). *The Oxford History of Australia*, Oxford University Press, 1986–2001, 5 vols.

Cathcart, Michael (ed.). *Manning Clark's History of Australia*, Melbourne University Press, 1993. (This is a skilled abridgement of Clark's six volumes published from 1962 to 1987.)

Some standard reference works

Australian Dictionary of Biography, Melbourne University Press, 1966–. The seventeenth volume was published in 2007.

Barker, Anthony, *What Happened When: A Chronology of Australia 1788–1990*, Allen & Unwin, 1992.

Davison, Graeme, John Hirst & Stuart Macintyre. *The Oxford Companion to Australian History*, Oxford University Press. 1998.

Historical Records of Australia, Commonwealth Parliament, 1914. Its 33 volumes published important documents from the 1780s to about 1850.

Murray-Smith, Stephen (ed.). *The Dictionary of Australian Quotations*, Mandarin, 1992.

Ransom, W. S. (ed.). *The Australian National Dictionary*, Oxford University Press, 1988. This volume explains the origins and changing meanings of Australian words.

Sawer, Geoffrey. *Australian Federal Politics and Law*, Melbourne University Press, 1956, 1963, 2 vols.

Souter, Gavin. *Acts of Parliament*, Melbourne University Press, 1988. This volume is a history of the federal parliament.

Year Book Australia, Australian Bureau of Statistics, published annually.

People and Place, Centre for Population and Urban Research, Monash University, 1993–2011.

Individual lives

Ayres, Philip. *Malcolm Fraser*, William Heinemann, 1987.

Blainey, Ann. *I am Melba: A Biography*, Black Inc., 2008.

Day, David. *John Curtin: A Life*, HarperCollins, 2006.

Frost, Alan. *Arthur Phillip 1738–1814*, Oxford University Press, 1987.

Howard, John, *Lazarus Rising*, HarperCollins, 2010.

Martin, A.W. *Robert Menzies: A Life*, Melbourne University Press, 2 vols, 1993, 1999.

Roderick, Colin. *Henry Lawson: A Life*, Angus & Robertson, 1991.

Whitlam, Gough. *The Whitlam Government 1972–75*, Viking, 1985.

Index

Abaroo 32

Aborigines 47, 119, 196, 252–3, 256,
    275–6
  alcohol 49, 121, 276
  arrival in Australia 3–6
  art 276, 303
  assimilation 120
  attitudes to 45, 51, 119
  civic rights 48–9, 86
  clashes with settlers 45–9, 51–2
  cricket team 125
  culture and tradition 10–12, 49, 52,
    120, 252–4, 303–4
  diseases, European 32, 49, 297
  domestication of plants and animals
    296
  Europeans, arrival of 23–4, 31–2, 48–9,
    296–7
  extinction, potential 49–50
  fire, use of 8
  food 9–10
  immunity, lack of 297
  isolation of 296
  land rights 272–4, 275
  languages 12–15, 49, 275
  medicine 11–12, 212
  mixed parentage 119
  Nganampa people 276
  native title 52
  population numbers 15–16, 253,
    275–6
  pre-colonial lifestyle 7–9, 15–16
  religion 12

  reserves 47–8, 121, 256
  ritual 10–12, 49, 52
  rock art 7
  sheep farming, impact of 45, 51
  shelters 8
  tools and technology 10–11, 301
  vote, right to 48–9, 86, 253–4
  warfare 11
  World War II 212

Adelaide 54–6, 57, 82, 96, 101, 191, 238,
    289
agriculture, birth of 20–1
aid, international 118–19, 251–2, 281
AIDS 264
alcohol, sale of 158, 187
Alexander, Samuel 104
Alice Springs 192, 208
America's Cup 268
anaesthetics 62
animals (First Fleet) 88–9
Ansell, Eric 190
Antarctic 192, 193
anti-war movement 244–5, 258
Anzac Day 176
Anzacs 179–80
architecture
  post-war houses 190
  Queensland 100–1
  skyscrapers 269
Arnhem Land
  mineral deposits 234
art 95, 115–16, 131–2, 201–2, 220, 249,
    257

Aboriginal 7, 303
  Heidelberg School 96, 116, 196, 201
artistic talent 201
Ash Wednesday 264
Ashmead-Bartlett, Ellis 175
Asia
  immigration *see* immigration
  links with 44, 189, 241, 250–1, 255,
    261, 280–1, 299
astronomy 83
athletics 128–9
Austin, Herbert 160
Australia, naming 37–8
Australia Council 249
Australia House 194
Australian Broadcasting Commission 201
Australian Broadcasting Corporation 201
Australian character 105, 109–10, 130–1,
    300
  war, impact of 179–80
Australian Conservation Foundation 247
Australian Country Party *see* National
    Party
Australian dream 157
Australian Natives Association 117
Australian Workers Union 107
aviation 161, 192, 213, 220, 300, 303
  airforce 203, 205, 206, 211
Baker, Sidney J. 221
Bali bombing 281–2
Ballarat 80, 92, 96, 148, 232
  gold rush 74–6
banks 172–3, 267–8
  1890s financial crisis 133–4, 146, 157
  1930s depression 197
  1980s boom and bust 269–70
Banks, Joseph 14
Barton, Edmund 150, 169, 283
Barwick, Sir Garfield 247
Bass Strait oil and gas 234
Beaufort (Fiery Creek) 77
The Beatles 238
Bendigo 80, 96, 232
Bennett, George 111
bill of rights 271–2
birth-rate 189–90, 248

Bjelke-Petersen, Sir Joh 289
'Bodyline' cricket 188
Boer War 173
Bond, Alan 268–9
Bonner, Neville 254
Botany Bay 27, 28–9, 56–7
Bourke, Sir Richard 63
Bowen Basin 234
boxing 129
Boyd, Arthur 201
Boyd, Martin 201
Boyd, Robin 289
Bradfield, Sir John Job 194
Bradman, Donald 188, 220
Brady, E. J.
  Australia Unlimited 192
Brahe, May 187
Bridges, Harry 214
Brisbane 53, 96, 289–90
Britain 169
  defence allies 144, 173–4, 204–7, 213,
    298
  European Community, entering 233
  immigration *see* immigration
  ties to 169–71, 174, 188–9, 214, 230,
    261, 271, 277–8
  trade with 274
Broken Hill 55, 93, 96, 108, 184, 234,
    247, 287, 301
Broken Hill Proprietary (BHP) 165, 179,
    205, 219, 234, 287
Bruce, Stanley Melbourne 192, 200, 266
bullocks 88, 95, 161
Burke and Wills 82–3
Burley Griffin, Walter 196
Burne-Jones, Edward 162
Burnet, Sir Macfarlane 239
bushfires 264
Cairns 101, 264
Calcutta 34
Calwell, Arthur 224, 244
camels 82, 83, 154
Canadian Revolution 62
Canberra 149, 195–7, 202, 232, 255, 268
cane toad 236, 301
capitalism 106, 109, 198, 249

cars 160–1, 190–1, 209, 214, 245
  Australian-made 226–7
cartoonists 221
Cartwright, Reverend Robert 47
Casey, R. G. 215
Catholics 63, 103, 107, 169, 177, 190,
    219, 240, 254–5
  politics, in 147, 199, 230, 241, 255
cattle 23, 41, 88, 102, 163, 235, 285, 291
Centaur 211
Champion of the Seas 80
Charlton, Michael 238
Chifley, Ben 200, 217, 221–4, 227, 228–9,
    232, 249, 255
childcare 265
children
  'currency' children 35–6, 38
  mortality 190
  post-war birth-rate 189–90
China 223, 255, 260
  communism 216, 229, 243
  ties with 281–2, 287
Chinese immigrants 60, 109, 118, 151–2
  gold rush 79
  restrictions on 151
Christmas 113–14
Churchill, Winston 213
'citizens of the world' 118
civic rights 84–5
  Aboriginals 48–9, 253–4
  compulsory voting 200
  settlers 61–2, 84
  women 138, 139, 158
Clark, Graeme 300
Clarke, Marcus 113–14
  For the Term of His Natural Life 67–8
Clarke, Reverend W. B. 64
climate 99–100, 112–14, 130
climate change 6, 7, 17–20, 292–4, 295–7
coal 45, 90–1, 161, 162, 205, 227, 232,
    233–4, 237, 248, 286–7, 299
Cobb & Co coaches 80, 95
Coghlan, Timothy 96, 189
Cold War 258
Collingwood football club 115
Colombo Plan 251

colonisation, European 56
Commonwealth Bank of Australia 156,
    173, 267
communism 184, 198, 227, 229, 248
Communist Party 184, 229–30
computers 239, 265
conscription 177–8, 198, 212, 244
constitution 146–9
contraceptives 189–90, 245
convicts 28, 33–5, 64–8, 171
  Aborigines, relations with 32
  food shortages 30
  free migrants and 64–5
  mortality rates 33
Cook, Captain James 14, 27, 48, 56, 299
Cook, Sir Joseph 169, 181
Cooktown 101
Coopers Creek 82, 83
Coral Sea, Battle of the 210
Corrigan, Tommy 127
Cosgrove, Major General Peter 281
Costello, Peter 275
Court, Sir Charles 289
Cowan, Edith 188
Cowen, Sir Zelman 279
cricket 125, 126, 188, 220
CSIRO 202, 238
Cunningham, Allan 81
Cunningham, Peter
  Two Years in New South Wales 36
Curr, Edward 50
Curtin, John 200, 203, 206, 212–13, 222
cyclone 235
D'Arcy, William Knox 162–3
Dale, Reverend Dr R. W. 105, 109
Danish immigrants 100
Darwin 82, 101, 208
  bombing 207–8
  cyclone 235
Darwin, Sir Charles 50
Davis, Arthur Hoey 164–5
  On Our Selection 165
Dawson, Andrew 141
de Surville, Jean 56
Deakin, Alfred 99, 150, 169, 283
Dedman, J. J. 222

defence 143–5, 146, 173, 243–4, 280, 298
  conscription 177–8
  military training 173
  munitions 213–14, 264
  spending money on 203, 223
democracy 85–7, 298
Democratic Labor Party (DLP) 230, 241
Dennis, C. J. 165
depression
  1890s 134–6, 157
  1930s 197–9
deregulation 268
dingoes 19–20, 40, 301
disease 32, 35, 49, 97, 190, 297
dismissal of Whitlam government 256–7
distance 295, 297–300
divorce 187, 219, 265
Dixon, Reverend James 63
Dixon, Sir Owen 241
dogs 89
dole 224
Donaldson, Jack 128
drought 134–6, 157, 166, 219, 264, 291,
  292–3, 297
drugs 245
Dry, Richard 85
Drysdale, Russell 201
Duntroon 173
Durack, Fanny 129
dust storms 135
Dutch colonisation 56, 215
Dutch explorers 25–6
East Timor 280–1
Eccles, Sir John 239
education 102–4, 140, 150, 156, 200, 202,
  220, 239–40, 276
  international students 282
Edwards, Major-General J. B. 144–5
egalitarianism 141–2, 171, 246
employment 105–6, 109, 135, 185, 242
  children 104–5
  depression 135
  factories and workshops 165–6, 179,
    225–7
  hours of work 106–7, 130, 140, 156,
    184–6, 197

labour subsidies 154
minimum wage 139, 156, 158, 197
offshore 267
post-war immigration and 225–6
unemployment 97, 184, 197, 231, 246,
  248, 258, 269
wages 186, 190, 197, 246, 253
wartime 178, 209
Endeavour 299
environmental issues 247–8, 257
Esso 234
ethnic rivalry 263
Eureka Stockade 75–6
Evatt, Dr Herbert V. 200, 223
explorers 81–2, 137, 193
exports 44–5, 163–4, 170, 172, 189, 197,
  285–6, 298–300, 302
  Australian-made products 226
  free-trade 286
  gold 80, 164
  mining 234–5, 286–9
  wheat 54, 98, 135, 163
  wool 39–41, 80, 164, 178–9, 189, 233,
    235, 284–6
Eyre, Edward 81
farming 47, 97–8, 185, 219
  birth of 20–1
  cotton 236, 285, 293
  irrigation 99, 236, 292–3
  political protection 199
  small farmers 164–5
  technology 54, 98, 108, 300–1
fast food 266
Federation 145–50
Fern Tree Gully 115
film industry 250, 303
First Fleet 29, 56–7, 67, 111
  Aborigines, relations with 31–2
  animals 23, 39
Fisher, Andrew 140, 150, 169, 267
fishing, Aborigines 9–10
Flack, Edwin 128
flag 155–6, 277
Flinders, Matthew 37
flora and fauna 301–2
  domestication 20–1, 300

imported 114
naming 14
pre-colonial 6
preservation of 247–8
Florey, Howard 300
flotation process 166, 301
Flying Pieman 122
Flynn, Errol 201, 214
football
Aussie Rules 115, 118, 125–6
rugby 126
soccer 125, 263
Ford, Henry 160
Forrest, John 137–9, 303
France
colonies 56–7
explorers 25, 32, 56–7
World War II 204, 211
Frase, Simon 147
Fraser, Malcolm 236, 256–7, 259, 267
Free Traders 150
Fremantle 137, 138
Froude, J. A. 299
Fusionists 199
Gallipoli 175–7, 180, 204, 206
gambling 123–4
Garden, Jock 184
gas 83, 90, 185, 218
natural 162, 234, 286
Geelong football club 125, 126
George, Henry 139, 140
Germany 170
immigrants from 60, 100, 201, 231–2
military rise of 173
World War I 174–82
World War II 204–14
Ghan 192
Gibson, Elsie 176
Giles, Ernest 113
Gipps, Sir George 42
global warming 292
gold 53, 65, 133, 163, 178, 198, 286–7
gold rushes 71–81, 99, 102, 122
goldfields, life on 77–8
Gordon, Adam Lindsay 115, 124, 247
Gorton, John 249

government 84–5
business and 158, 267–8
dismissal of Whitlam 256–7
early self-government 62, 75–6, 84–7, 137
Federal and State, powers of 148, 150, 158, 194–5
independence 182
parliaments 84, 86
States *see by name of State*
wartime rules and regulations 218–19
Grainger, Percy 201
Greek immigrants 153, 189, 232
Gregg, Norman 300
Gregory, Augustus 81
Grey, Captain George 46
Groote Eylandt 234
Gunn, Aeneas 303
Gurindjii people 253
Haggard, Robert 156
hanging 220
Hargraves, Edward 71–2
Harnett, L. J. 226
Harrison, James 90
Hasluck, Paul 231
Hawke, Bob 255, 257, 259, 262, 264, 267–8, 271–2
Hawkesbury rail bridge 93
Hayter, Henry 104–5
Heidelberg School 96, 196, 201
Heysen, Hans 201
High Court 273–4
Hitler, Adolf 203, 214, 217
HMAS *Sydney* 173, 174–5, 211
Hobart 36, 53, 57
Holden, Edward 160
homosexuality 220
horse-racing 123–4, 127, 239
horses, working 88–9, 161, 190–1
Howard, John 257, 274–5, 278, 280, 282, 294
Howe, Jacky 107, 131
Howitt, William 65
Hughes, Robert
The Fatal Shore 68

Hughes, W. M. 'Billy' 140, 177, 181, 188, 204, 266
Hume, Fergus
  The Mystery of a Hansom Cab 89
Hume and Hovell 81
humour 221
hydro-electricity 232–3, 247, 293
immigration 97, 118, 138, 152–3, 166, 171–2, 250–1
  depression, during the 135–6
  free migrants 57–61, 99
  gold rush 72, 79
  mortality rates 61
  post-WWI 189, 262
  post-WWII 224–6, 231–2, 262
  refugees *see* refugees
  restricting 151
  strangeness of Australia 111–13
  test 151, 251
Indian immigrants 152
Indonesia 19, 22, 215–16, 243–4, 280–1
  Aborigines, migration of 4
  early contact with Australia 22–3
  Muslim population 281
  World War II 207, 210
industrial disputes 107–8, 156, 178, 184, 205, 227
industrial revolution 24, 40
internet 265
Irish
  convicts 34
  immigrants 59, 100, 118, 177, 199
  miners 75
iron ore 234–5, 286–8, 299
irrigation 99, 236, 292–3
Isisford 290–2
Islam 215–16, 263, 275
isolation 297, 298, 302–3
isolationism 118, 198, 203
Italy
  immigrants 153, 189, 231–2
  World War II 204, 205
Japan 189
  export market, as 235, 241, 282
  immigrants 151, 152
  military rise of 173, 182, 205

post-war treatment of 223–4, 229
  tourism 261, 264
  World War II 204–14, 298
Jewish immigrants 118, 201, 225, 231
Johnson, Jack 129
Johnson, Lyndon B. 215
Johnson, Richard 63
Kalgoorlie 55, 96, 128, 137–9, 198, 233, 286, 287–8, 303
Kapunda 54
Keating, Paul 207, 263, 267–8, 272–4, 277–8
Kelly, Ned 98
Kendall, Henry 115
Kerr, Sir John 256
Khemlani, Tirath 256
Killen, Sir James 255
King, Reverend R. L. 64
Kipling, Rudyard 171
Kirkland, Katharine 42–3
Kirner, Joan 266
Kokoda Trail 210
Korean War 229, 243
Kormoran 211
Kramer, Dame Leonie 266
Labor Party 200, 240, 256–7, 267
  Communist Party and 230
  depression (1930s) 198
  establishment 139–41, 150, 156
  post-war 221–2, 243–4
  splits 230, 255
  World War I 177–8
  World War II 203, 206, 212–13
Lake Burley Griffin 232
Lake Condah 8
Lalor, Peter 75
land rights, Aboriginal 272–4, 275
Lang, Jack 198
Langton, Marcia 276
languages, Aboriginal 12–15
Latham, John 200
Launceston 53, 63
Law, Dr Phillip 239
Lawrence, Dr Carmen 266
Lawson, Henry 95, 117, 171, 292, 303
Laycock, Elias 126

League of Nations 182
Leichhardt, Ludwig 81
Lewis, Essington 205, 212
Lhotsky, John 111
Liberal Party 199, 205, 240, 255
    early years 150, 156, 228–9
    post-war 222, 266–7
Lightning 80
Lindsay, Lionel 201
Lindsay, Norman 201
Lyons, Enid 104
Lyons, Joseph 199, 203, 205, 266
Lyster, F. J. 166
Mabo, Eddie 272–3
Mabo decision 272–4
Macarthur, Elizabeth 28–9, 39, 44
MacArthur, General Douglas 208, 213, 223
Macarthur, John 39
Macassans 22
McCombie, Thomas 91
McCormack, John 187
McCubbin, Fred 116
Mackay 101
McKay, H. V. 98, 301
Mackellar, Dorothea 117
Macmahon Ball, William 223
Macmillan, Harold 235
Maconochie, Captain 65
Macpherson, Christina 95, 124–5
Macquarie, Lachlan 37, 47–8
Madigan, Dr C. T. 193
Mahon, Hugh 188
Maltese immigrants 189
Mammoth Cave 6
manners 171
Mannix, Archbishop Daniel 177
marriage 187, 219–20, 246
Marsden, Reverend Samuel 39
Marshall, Archibald 159
Martineau, John 87
Marvellous 196
massacres 45–6
Mawby, Sir Maurice 247
Mawson, Sir Douglas 193
measles 35, 49

medicine 62, 94, 213, 300
    Aboriginal 11–12, 212
Melanesian immigrants 100, 153
Melba, Dame Nellie 187
Melbourne 53, 57, 80, 96–7, 130, 149, 195, 209, 213, 225, 237–8, 289
Melbourne Cup 123–4, 266
Melbourne football club 125, 126
Menzies, Robert G. 200, 205–6, 228–33, 238, 240–1, 243, 249, 255, 257, 266, 274, 283
merino 39, 40, 44
metric system 239
Michell, A. G. M 166
Midway, Battle of 210
Milne Bay 210
minerals 26, 54
mining 54–5, 233–5, 286–9
    alumina 234, 235, 282, 286
    bauxite 234, 286, 299
    coal *see* coal
    copper 54–5, 181, 286, 287, 288
    diamonds 286
    flotation processes 301
    gas *see* gas
    gold *see* gold
    iron ore 234–5, 286–8, 299
    lead-zinc 287
    licences 74–5
    manganese 234, 286
    nickel 234, 286
    silver 93, 96, 233, 286
    steam power 89–90
    technology 108, 264, 301
    uranium 234, 248, 287
missionaries 47, 63, 121
    Australian 119
Mitchell, Major Thomas 81
Monash, Sir John 179, 180
money 109, 133, 197, 267
    Commonwealth loans 194
    currency 156, 239, 258
    1890s financial crisis 133–4, 146, 157
    1980s boom and bust 268–70
    World War II, during 209
Montgomery, Bishop H. H. 171

Morrow, James 98
motor bikes 191
Mount Isa 235, 288
Mount Morgan 162–3
multiculturalism 257, 262–3, 266
Mulvaney, John 252
municipal councils 62
Murdoch, Rupert 265
Murdoch, Sir Keith 201
Murray-Darling Basin 293
Murray, Gilbert 104
Murray, Sir Hubert 155
Murray, Les 279
music 170, 201, 245
Myall Creek 46
national parks 115–16
National Party 199, 229, 236, 266
nationalism 117–18, 141–2, 172–3, 231,
    250, 277–8
native title 273–4, 275
Native Title Act 274
nature, delight in 247–8
'New Australians' 225
New Guinea 17, 18, 154–5, 193, 244,
    251–2, 280, 296
  Aborigines, migration of 4
  agricultural revolution 21
  World War I 174, 181
  World War II 207, 210, 217
New South Wales 36, 37, 68, 98, 149
  defence 143
  education 103
  politics 140
  railways 93–4
New Zealand 27, 47, 56, 108, 115, 261,
    281
  Commonwealth of Australia discussions
      145, 147
  defence 143
  voting rights 139
Newcastle 45, 96, 161, 165, 179, 226, 232
Newland, Simpson 119–20
newspapers 90, 221, 265
Nganampa people, 276
nicknames 221
Noble, John 44

Nolan, Sidney 201
Norfolk Island
  convicts 30–1, 66–7
  flax 28
Norris, Dr Kingsley 186
Northern Territory 55, 101, 134, 192,
    234, 248, 256, 257
nuclear testing 229
nurses 196
  wartime 176, 180, 218, 219
oil 161, 163, 233, 234, 286
Olympic Dam 287
Olympic Games 128, 238, 278
Ord River reservoir 235–6
Order of Australia 256
'outback' 302–3
Oxley, John 81
Pacific Island immigrants 100, 153
Packer, Frank 238
paddle steamers 55, 80, 90
Page, Dr Earle 199
Pankhurst-Walsh, Adele 184
Papunya painters 303
Parkes, Sir Henry 145, 147
parliaments 84, 86
Paterson, 'Banjo' 95, 117, 124–5
patriotism 277
Payne, Herbert 200
peace movement 203
Pearl Harbor, attack on 206
Pearson, Noel 276
pensions 156, 197, 217, 224
Perry, Bishop Charles 113
Perth 53, 136, 138–9, 191, 234, 290
petroleum 160–1, 209, 218, 234
Philip, Captain Arthur 29
  Aborigines, relations with 31–2, 48
Philippines
  World War II 204, 207, 208
poetry 95, 115, 117, 124
Polding, John 63
politics 139–42, 198–200, 277
  government see government
  industry and 199–200
  post-war 221–4

pollution 226
population 105, 193, 224, 289–90, 304
  Aboriginal 276
  capital cities 96–7, 102, 149, 237–8, 289–90
  early nineteenth century 35–6
  free migrants 57–8
  gold rush 79–80, 81
  inland towns 290
  over-population 248
  pre-colonial Aborigines 15–16
  Queensland 101, 289
  rural, declining 237, 290–1
Port Hedland 288
Port Moresby 155, 210, 251–2
Portuguese explorers 25–6
postal services 91, 101, 122, 158
Postle, Arthur 128
poverty 97
Prince of Wales 206
Pringle, John 249
prisoners of war 206, 220, 223
Prokhorov, Alexander 239
protectionism 146, 158
QANTAS 192, 303
Queen Elizabeth, visit of 230
Queensland 53, 79, 93, 134
  Commonwealth of Australia, as part of 147, 149
  government 101
  mining 234, 289
  population 101
  weather 99–100
Quick, Jack 146–7
Quin, Edward 134–5
rabbits 89, 202, 236, 301
railways 80, 91–5, 115, 136, 150, 158, 163–4, 191–2, 302
rationing 209–10, 218, 227
recession 269
refugees 201, 224–5, 257, 259–61
Reid, George 150, 194
religion 55, 63–4, 114, 169, 186
  Aboriginal 12
  declining 246, 254–5
  missionaries 48

republican debate 277–80
  referendum 279–80
Repulse 206
Rhodes Scholars 200
Rice 293
Richardson, Henry Handel 201
Rio Tinto 287
Rivett, Sir David 220
Roberts, Tom 96, 116, 131–2
Robinson, George 9
Rockhampton 100
rowing and sculling 126–7, 131
Rubenstein, Helena 214
Rudd, Kevin 283, 294
Russell Falls 115
sailing 126
St Vincent 66
Salvado, Bishop 13
scientific advances *see also* technology
  medicine 62, 94, 213, 264–5, 300
Scottish immigrants 100, 118
Scullin, James 200
seals 44
Searle, Henry 127
seas, rising 17–20, 296, 297
sewerage 97, 190
Shearer, John 160
shearing 107, 131, 285–6
sheep 39–45, 51, 64, 83, 90, 135, 164, 284, 291
shepherds 41–2
Simpson, Alfred 193
Simpson Desert 193
Singapore, fall of 204, 206, 207, 208, 298
Sloan, Alfred P. 227
smallpox 32, 49, 60
smoking 187
Snowy Mountains Scheme 232–3
socialism 198–9, 227
South Australia 98, 220
  defence 143
  education 102
  railways 93
  religion 55
  taxation 139
Southern Cross 75, 155

Soviet Union 159, 180, 198, 214, 257, 258
Spence, William Guthrie 106–7
Spender, Percy 251
sport 122, 130–2, 186, 188, 220, 254,
        271, 276
    athletics 128–9
    boxing 129
    cricket 125, 126, 188, 220
    cycling 128
    football *see* football
    heroes 127
    rowing and sculling 126–7, 131
    sailing 126
    swimming 129
    tennis 128, 129
squatters 42, 74
Statute of Westminster 182
Stawell 90
steam power 88–91, 108, 160, 161, 165,
        299, 300–1
steamships 80, 91, 101
steelworks 165, 179, 184, 234
Stephens, Brunton 145
strangeness 111–12
Streeton, Arthur 116, 201
Stuart, Jon McDouall 81–2, 303
Sturt, Charles 81, 89, 303
Suez Canal 91, 230
sugar plantations 100, 154, 164, 285
'susso' 197
Sutherland, Joan 249
Sydney 57, 96–7, 130, 149, 195, 209,
        237–8, 290
Sydney Cove 53
    establishment 29
    food shortages 30
Sydney Harbour Bridge 194
Sydney Opera House 249–50
Syme, David 90
tariffs 158
Tasmania 6, 42, 56, 62, 63, 64, 134, 220,
        247, 293
    Aborigines 9, 10
    convicts 65, 66–7
    defence 143
    education 103–4

    national parks 115
    pre-colonial 4–5, 18, 19
    settlement 36–7
Tattersall's Sweep 124
taxation 139, 158–9, 194, 275
    interstate 143, 146, 150
    wartime 212–13
Taylor, Professor Griffith 192–3
Tebbutt, John 83
technology 62–3, 91, 108, 160–1, 165–6,
        238–9, 264, 300
    Aboriginal 10–11
    farming 54, 98, 108, 236, 300–1
    household 185–6
    post-war 226–7
    steam power 88–9, 108, 160
telegraph line 80, 82, 108, 137, 300
telephones 185, 300
    mobile 264–5
television 238, 300
tennis 128, 129
Terra Australis 37
territorial acquisition 193
terrorism 275, 281–2
Theodore, Ted 198
Thomson, Herbert 160
Thunder, Andrew 77
Timor 4, 25–6, 207, 244, 280–1
Townsville 101
trade with Britain 271
trade unions 184, 198–9, 268
    establishment 105–7, 140–1, 147, 156–7
    post-WWII 222, 231
    World War I, during 172, 177
transportation 33–5, 64–8
travel and tourism 159, 220, 233, 261–2,
        264, 271, 281–2, 299
Trenwith, William 147
trepang 22, 45
Trickett, Edmund 126
Tucker, Albert 201
Ullathorne, Reverend W. B. 65
United Nations Organisation 223, 231
United States of America 56, 86, 96, 141,
        191
    immigration 58, 60, 79

independence from Britain 28
ties to 214–15, 231, 241, 243
welfare 159
World War I 180
World War II 208–9, 213, 214
universities 104, 170, 200, 202, 218, 240
uranium 234, 248, 287
urbanisation 96–7
Utzon, Joern 249
vegetation
pre-colonial 6, 18–19
Victoria 98, 139
depression and drought 135–6, 146
gold rush *see* gold
railways 93
Vietnam War 241, 243–4, 247, 255, 259
volcanoes 7
vote, right to 84–6
Aboriginals 48–9, 86
Wakefield, Edward Gibbon 54
Walsh, Alan 238
Walsh, Tom 184
'Waltzing Matilda' 95, 124–5, 303
war 166–82, 203–19
memorials 183, 223
Washington Treaty 181
water
artesian 99, 162
drought *see* drought
weather *see* climate
Webb, Sir William 223
weddings 186–7, 219–20
Wedge, J. H. 46
Weir, Peter 250
welfare 59, 156, 158–9, 183–4, 224, 253
West, Reverend John 64
Western Australia 67, 93, 101, 134, 136,
235, 289

education 102, 138
gold rush 79, 137–8, 178
government 86, 136, 149
secession movement 198
Western Front 177, 180
whaling 37, 247, 257
wheat 54, 98, 135, 163, 290
White, Patrick 258
White Australia Policy 152–3, 154,
250–1
Whitlam, Gough 255–7, 259, 283
Wik decision 275
Williams, Fred 288
Williamson, Frank 115
wind power 161
wine 164, 285
Wirraway aircraft 205, 206
Wolseley, F. Y. 90
women 213
convicts 35
equal rights 246–7, 265–6
farming 185
free migrants 59
marriage 187, 219–20, 246
politics 187–8, 266
sport, and 129
voting rights 138, 139, 158, 187–8
Women's Christian Temperance Union
158
Women's Peace Army 184
woodchopping 131
wool 39–41, 80, 108, 133, 164, 178–9,
189, 199, 233, 235, 284–6, 291
World War I 169, 174–82
World War II 203–14, 217–18, 298
Yarra Park 125
Yokahama Specie Bank 189
Zig Zag railway (Lithgow) 92